序　言

　　學習出版公司已經出版兩本針對最新國中會考英文聽力測驗的書:「國中會考英語聽力測驗①」和「國中會考英語聽力測驗②」。已經有許多國中採用來加強九年級學生的聽力,內容豐富,練習充足,深獲好評。

　　當初「國中會考英語聽力測驗①②」針對即將面臨國中會考的九年級生而設計,故內容較難。許多國中英文老師反應,為了能讓七、八年級的學生,提早適應未來的英文聽力,希望能有一本程度較容易的英文聽力練習本,作為橋樑,同時可以提升學生的英文聽力,也能增加學生對英文聽力的信心和興趣。

　　因此,學習出版公司因應許多老師的要求和同學的意見,出版了最新的「國中會考英語聽力入門」。題型依照教育部公布之範例,分成三部分:辨識句意、基本問答、言談理解。每回共20題,共18回,360題。讓七、八年級同學可以一回只要寫 20 題聽力,不容易疲乏。但同時為了要能讓同學持續練習聽力,故本書設計了 18 回,如此同學便能有充足的練習,以增進英文聽力。

　　做完了「國中會考英語聽力入門」,若還行有餘力,想要繼續練習英文聽力,可以使用「國中會考英語聽力測驗①②」,難度較高,更有挑戰,可以學到更多。

　　本書在編審及校對的每一階段,均力求完善,但恐有疏漏之處,誠盼各界先進不吝批評指正。

編者　謹識

TEST 1

第一部分：辨識句意（第1-3題，共3題）

作答說明：第1-3題每題有三張圖片，請依據所聽到的內容，選出
　　　　　符合描述的圖片，每題播放兩次。

示例題：你會看到

(A) 　　　(B) 　　　(C)

然後你會聽到……（播音）。依據所播放的內容，正確答案應該
選A，請將答案卡該題「Ⓐ」的地方塗黑、塗滿，即：● Ⓑ Ⓒ

1. (A) 　　　(B) 　　　(C)

2. (A)　　　　　　(B)　　　　　　(C)

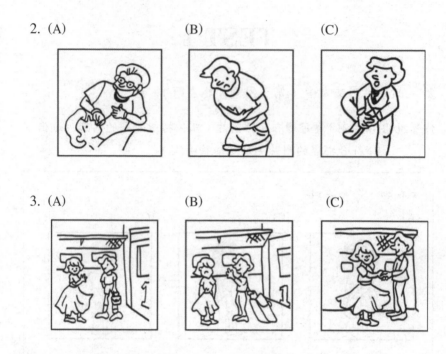

3. (A)　　　　　　(B)　　　　　　(C)

第二部分：基本問答（第 4-10 題，共 7 題）

作答說明：第 4-10 題每題均有三個選項，請依據所聽到的內容，選出一個最適合的回應，每題播放兩次。

示例題：你會看到

(A) She is talking to the teacher.

(B) She is a student in my class.

(C) She is wearing a beautiful dress.

然後你會聽到……（播音）。依據所播放的內容，正確答案應該選 B，請將答案卡該題「Ⓑ」的地方塗黑、塗滿，即：Ⓐ ● Ⓒ

4. (A) It's three hundred and forty dollars.
   (B) It's a safe one.
   (C) Let's go by car.

5. (A) Happy birthday.
   (B) I can make a lantern well.
   (C) Why not?

6. (A) It's a piece of cake.
   (B) Thank you.
   (C) I am a wet blanket.

7. (A) So she has a sweet tooth.
   (B) I think you should just mind your own business.
   (C) My brother doesn't, either.

8. (A) About 150 grams.
   (B) About NT$250.
   (C) About half an hour.

9. (A) She has been here twice.
   (B) She is not my daughter.
   (C) She has gone to Ilan to visit her aunt.

10. (A) That's for sure. It has the world's largest collection of Chinese art.
    (B) That might be boring. Count me in.
    (C) That's why it became less known to people around the world.

第三部分：言談理解（第 11-20 題，共 10 題）

作答說明：第 11-20 題每題均有三個選項，請依據所聽到的內容，
　　　　　選出一個最適合的答案，每題播放兩次。

示例題：你會看到

(A) 9:50.　　(B) 10:00.　　(C) 10:10.

然後你會聽到……（播音）。依據所播放的內容，正確答案應該
選 B，請將答案卡該題「Ⓑ」的地方塗黑、塗滿，即：Ⓐ ● Ⓒ

---

11. (A) It's September.
    (B) It's summer.
    (C) It's winter.

12. (A) One.
    (B) Two.
    (C) Three.

13. (A) Because it's having a summer sale.
    (B) Because it's newly opened.
    (C) Because it's Christmas Day.

14. (A) Salt.
    (B) Oil.
    (C) Oliver.

15. (A) Korea.
    (B) Kenting.
    (C) Hualien.

16. (A) Thomas did.
    (B) Tina did.
    (C) Everyone did a good job.

17. (A) Jeff is preparing a project for Tuesday.
    (B) Manager Chang and Manager Wang are co-workers.
    (C) Jeff doesn't know Manager Chang.

18. (A) How to sweep the tombs.
    (B) How to worship their ancestors.
    (C) The man is explaining the meaning of the Tomb Sweeping Day to the woman.

19. (A) NT$400.
    (B) NT$800.
    (C) NT$1,000.

20. (A) They are talking about their dreams.
    (B) They plan to spend the summer vacation together.
    (C) They are sharing their plans for summer with each other.

TEST 1 詳解

第一部分：辨識句意（第 1-3 題，共 3 題）

1. (**B**) (A)   (B)   (C)

The shorts go well with your shoes. 短褲和你的鞋子很搭。

* shorts〔ʃɔrts〕*n. pl.* 短褲   ***go with*** 和⋯相配

2. (**A**) (A)   (B)   (C)

Hank had a toothache and had two teeth pulled out yesterday. 漢克昨天牙痛而且去拔了兩顆牙。

* toothache〔'tuθ,ek〕*n.* 牙痛
  teeth〔tiθ〕*n. pl.* 牙齒【單數為 tooth】   ***pull out*** 拔出

3. (**B**) (A)   (B)   (C)

Allen waved to Jenny when he got on the train.

艾倫上火車時向珍妮揮手。

* wave〔wev〕*v.* 揮手　　***get on*** 上（車）
train〔tren〕*n.* 火車

第二部分：基本問答（第 4-10 題，共 7 題）

4. (**A**) How much is the helmet? 安全帽多少錢？

   (A) It's three hundred and forty dollars. <u>340 元。</u>

   (B) It's a safe one. 這一個很安全。

   (C) Let's go by car. 我們坐車去吧。

   * helmet〔'hɛlmɪt〕*n.* 安全帽　　safe〔sef〕*adj.* 安全的
   Let's + V. 我們一起～吧　　***by car*** 坐車

5. (**C**) Do you want to go to a lantern riddle party?

   你想要去猜燈謎晚會嗎？

   (A) Happy birthday. 生日快樂。

   (B) I can make a lantern well. 我可以做出很棒的燈籠。

   (C) Why not? <u>為什麼不？好啊。</u>

   * lantern〔'læntɚn〕*n.* 燈籠　　riddle〔'rɪdl̩〕*n.* 謎語
   lantern riddle 燈謎【元宵節舉辦的猜謎活動】
   party〔'partɪ〕*n.* 集會；晚會　　***Why not?*** 為什麼不；好的。

6. (**A**) Did you do well on the final exam? 你期末考考得好嗎？

   (A) It was a piece of cake. <u>那很簡單。</u>

   (B) Thank you. 謝謝你。

   (C) I am a wet blanket. 我很掃興。

   * ***do well*** 考得好　　***final exam*** 期末考
   a piece of cake 簡單的；容易的（= *easy*）
   wet〔wɛt〕*adj.* 濕的　　blanket〔'blæŋkɪt〕*n.* 毛毯
   wet blanket 掃興的人或物

7. (**A**) My sister loves to eat snacks such as candy, cakes, chocolate and pudding.
   我妹妹喜歡吃零食，像是糖果、蛋糕、巧克力和布丁。

   (A) So she has a sweet tooth. 那她很喜歡吃甜食。

   (B) I think you should just mind your own business.
   我想你不該多管閒事。

   (C) My brother doesn't, either. 我弟弟也不喜歡。

   * snack〔snæk〕*n.* 點心；零食　*such as* 像是
   candy〔'kændı〕*n.* 糖果　　cake〔kek〕*n.* 蛋糕
   chocolate〔'tʃɔklıt〕*n.* 巧克力
   pudding〔'pudıŋ〕*n.* 布丁　*have a sweet tooth* 愛吃甜食
   mind one's own business 管好自己的事；不多管閒事
   either〔'iðə〕*adv.* 也（不）

8. (**C**) How long did it take you to finish the report?
   完成這份報告花了你多少時間？

   (A) About 150 grams. 大概 150 公克。

   (B) About NT$250. 大概新台幣 250 元。

   (C) About half an hour. 大約半小時。

   * take〔tek〕*v.* 花（某人）（時間）　　finish〔'fınıʃ〕*v.* 完成
   report〔rı'port〕*n.* 報告　　gram〔græm〕*n.* 公克
   NT$ 新台幣（= *New Taiwan Dollar*）

9. (**C**) Where is your daughter? 你的女兒在哪裡？

   (A) She has been here twice. 她來過這裡兩次。

   (B) She is not my daughter. 她不是我女兒。

   (C) She has gone to Ilan to visit her aunt.
   她去宜蘭看她的阿姨。

   * daughter〔'dɔtə〕*n.* 女兒　　twice〔twaıs〕*adv.* 兩次
   visit〔'vızıt〕*v.* 拜訪；探望

10. (**A**) It's said that a tour in Taiwan wouldn't be complete without a visit to the National Palace Museum.

據說來台灣遊覽，一定要去參觀故宮，不然就不圓滿了。

(A) That's for sure. It has the world's largest collection of Chinese art.

當然。故宮收藏了全世界最多的中國藝術品。

(B) That might be boring. Count me in.

那可能很無聊。我也要去。

(C) That's why it became less known to people around the world.

那就是為何它在全世界較少人知道的原因。

* ***It's said that*** 據說…   tour〔tʊr〕*n.* 旅行；遊覽

not ~ without … 沒有…就不會 ~

complete〔kəm'plit〕*adj.* 完整的；圓滿的

visit〔'vɪzɪt〕*n.* 參觀   ***the National Palace Museum*** 故宮

for sure 肯定的；當然的

collection〔kə'lɛkʃən〕*n.* 收集；收藏

Chinese〔tʃaɪ'niz〕*adj.* 中國的   art〔ɑrt〕*n.* 藝術作品

boring〔'bɔrɪŋ〕*adj.* 無聊的   ***count sb. in*** 把某人算進去

be known to *sb.* 為某人所知   ***around the world*** 在全世界

第三部分：言談理解（第 11-20 題，共 10 題）

11. (**C**) W : I'm going to South Africa on business. It's hot there, right?

女：我即將要去南非出差。那裡很熱，是吧？

M : Not at all. It's hot in Taiwan now, but it is cold there.

男：一點也不。台灣現在很熱，但是那裡很冷。

W : I see. Heavy clothes are necessary.

女：我知道了。厚重的衣服是必要的。

M : You're right. You also need to bring some formal clothes.

男：妳說的對。妳也需要帶一些正式的衣服。

W : Sure, it's better to enter nice restaurants and theaters in a dress.

女：當然，進好的餐廳和戲院，穿正式的服裝比較好。

M : You had better make a packing list.

男：妳最好列一張打包清單。

Question : What season is it in South Africa?

南非現在是什麼季節？

(A) It's September. 現在是九月。

(B) It's summer. 現在是夏天。

(C) It's winter. 現在是冬天。

* **South Africa** 南非　　**on business** 出差
  Not at all. 一點也不。　　**I see.** 我了解了；我知道了。
  heavy〔'hɛvɪ〕*adj.* 厚重的　　clothes〔kloz〕*n. pl.* 衣服
  necessary〔'nɛsə‚sɛrɪ〕*adj.* 必要的
  You are right. 你說的對。　　formal〔'fɔrml〕*adj.* 正式的
  sure〔ʃur〕*adv.* 當然　　restaurant〔'rɛstərənt〕*n.* 餐廳
  theater〔'θiətə〕*n.* 戲院　　dress〔drɛs〕*n.* 正式服裝；洋裝
  had better V. 最好～　　pack〔pæk〕*v.* 打包
  packing list 打包清單　　season〔'sizn̩〕*n.* 季節

12. (**B**) W : John. Are you free on Sunday evening?

女：約翰，你星期天晚上有空嗎？

M : No. I need to go to the cram school. What's up?

男：沒空，我需要去上補習班，有什麼事？

W : Jolin asked us to go to a concert with her. Can you go on that day?

女：裘琳要我們跟她去聽演唱會。你那天可以去嗎？

M：What date is it then?

男：那天是幾月幾號？

W：It's April first.

女：四月一號。

M：What a pity! But you can go with Jolin.

男：真可惜！但是可以和裴琳一起去。

Question：How many people will go to the concert?

　　　　有幾個人會去看演唱會？

(A) One. 一個。

(B) Two. <u>兩個。</u>

(C) Three. 三個。

* free〔fri〕*adj.* 有空的　　**cram school** 補習班

　What's up? 有什麼事？　　concert〔'kɑnsɝt〕*n.* 演唱會

　date〔det〕*n.* 日期　　**What a pity!** 真可惜！

13.(**B**)　W：Mike, you look great in that tie! It looks

　　　　　 fashionable on you. How much was it?

　　　　女：麥可，你戴那條領帶真好看！戴在你身上真時尚。那多少錢？

　　　　　M：Only 680 dollars.

　　　　男：只要 680 元。

　　　　　W：Cool. Where did you get it?

　　　　女：好酷唷。你在哪裡買的？

　　　　　M：At Sun-Moon Department Store. It's having an

　　　　　　 opening sale this month.

　　　　男：在日月百貨公司。這個月有開幕大拍賣。

　　　　　W：Does the department store have anything else on

　　　　　　 sale? I want to buy a watch for my son's birthday.

　　　　女：這百貨公司有其他特價的東西嗎？我想要買一支手錶給我

　　　　　　的兒子當生日禮物。

M : Yes, it does. Look, you'll get a better price if you
　　buy two at a time.

男：是，有的。妳看，如果妳一次買兩支，會有更好的價格。

Question : Why does the department store have a sale?
　　　　　爲何百貨公司舉行大拍賣？

(A) Because it's having a summer sale.
　　因爲它正在舉行夏季大拍賣。

(B) Because it's newly opened.　因爲它新開幕。

(C) Because it's Christmas Day.　因爲是聖誕節。

* look〔luk〕v. 看起來　　tie〔taɪ〕n. 領帶
  fashionable〔'fæʃənəbḷ〕adj. 流行的；時尚的
  get〔gɛt〕v. 買　　*department store* 百貨公司
  opening sale 開幕大拍賣　　*on sale* 特價的
  watch〔watʃ〕n. 手錶　　price〔praɪs〕n. 價格
  at a time 一次　　*newly opened* 新開幕的
  Christmas Day 聖誕節

14. (**B**) W : Willy, you've been to Meinong, and you've even
　　　　　　　seen someone making paper umbrellas, right?

女：威利，你去過美濃，而且你甚至看過人做紙傘，是吧？

M : Yes. It was an unforgetful experience. Do you have
　　any idea how people there keep paper umbrellas from
　　getting wet?

男：是的，這是個難忘的經驗。你知道那裡的人們如何讓紙傘不
　　會弄濕嗎？

W : Not really.

女：不太清楚。

M : They put oil on the umbrellas. The process is difficult.

男：他們把油塗在雨傘上，這過程很困難。

W : So, paper umbrellas are not easy to make.

女：所以說，紙傘不容易做。

M : Right. Fewer and fewer people know how to make good paper umbrellas.

男：是的，越來越少人知道如何做出好的紙傘。

Question : What keeps paper umbrellas from getting wet?

什麼讓紙傘不會弄濕？

(A) Salt. 鹽。

(B) Oil. 油。

(C) Oliver. 奧利佛。

* **have been to** 去過～   **paper umbrella** 紙傘
unforgettable〔ˌʌnfə'gɛtəbḷ〕*adj.* 難忘的
experience〔ɪk'spɪrɪəns〕*n.* 經驗
keep…from ～ 使…不會～   get〔gɛt〕*v.* 變成；變得
wet〔wɛt〕*adj.* 濕的   **not really** 不完全是
oil〔ɔɪl〕*n.* 油   process〔'prɑsɛs〕*n.* 過程
difficult〔'dɪfəˌkʌlt〕*adj.* 困難的
fewer and fewer 越來越少的   salt〔sɔlt〕*n.* 鹽

15. (**A**) W : Good evening, sir. May I help you?

女：先生，晚安。需要我的幫忙嗎？

M : Yes, please. I'd like to take a trip.

男：是的，請妳幫我。我想要去旅遊。

W : What do you have in mind?

女：你有什麼想法呢？

M : Do you know a relaxing place for a vacation?

男：妳知道有什麼可以度假放鬆的地方嗎？

W : What about Puli? It's beautiful and clean.

女：埔里如何？那裡美麗又乾淨。

M : No, thanks. I've been there twice. I am speaking of foreign countries.

男：不，謝謝。我已經去過那裡兩次了，我說的是去國外。

Question : Where would the man like to go?

男士會想要去哪裡？

(A) Korea. 韓國。

(B) Kenting. 墾丁。

(C) Hualien. 花蓮。

* ***would like to V***. 想要～　　　***have…in mind*** 有…的想法

relaxing〔rɪ'læksɪŋ〕*adj.* 令人放鬆的

place〔ples〕*n.* 地方；地點

vacation〔ve'keʃən〕*n.* 休假；度假

What about…? …如何？　　　beautiful〔'bjutəfəl〕*adj.* 美麗的

clean〔klin〕*adj.* 乾淨的　　***speak of*** 談到

foreign〔'fɔrɪn〕*adj.* 外國的　　Korea〔ko'riə〕*n.* 韓國

16. (**C**) W : Well done, Thomas.

女：做得好，湯瑪士。

M : Thank you, Tina. You also played the violin very well.

男：謝謝妳，蒂娜。妳小提琴也拉得很好。

W : It's exciting that we won the contest.

女：這真是太令人興奮了，我們贏得了比賽。

M : Yes. We could win the medal because of everyone's help.

男：是的，我們可以贏得獎牌，是因為每個人的幫助。

W : Sure. It was not anyone's work alone.

女：當然，這不是任何一個人就可以完成的。

M : Let's go celebrate it.

男：我們去慶祝一下吧。

Question : Who did the best in the contest?

　　　　　誰在比賽中表現最好？

(A) Thomas did. 湯瑪士。

(B) Tina did. 蒂娜。

(C) Everyone did a good job. 每個人都表現得很好。

* **well done** 做得好　　violin〔ˌvaɪə'lɪn〕n. 小提琴

exciting〔ɪk'saɪtɪŋ〕adj. 令人興奮的

won〔wʌn〕v. 贏；贏得【win 的過去式】

contest〔'kɑntɛst〕n. 比賽　　medal〔'mɛdl〕n. 獎牌

because of 因為　　help〔hɛlp〕n. 幫助

work〔wɝk〕n. 工作；努力

alone〔ə'lon〕adj. 只有；僅【放在名詞後面】

Let's + V. 我們～吧。　　**go V.** 去～（= go to V. = go and V.）

celebrate〔'sɛlə,bret〕v. 慶祝

do a good job 表現得好；做得好

17. (**C**) W : Jeff! Where are you going?

女：傑夫！你要去哪裡？

M : I'm going downstairs to see Manager Chang about the project this Tuesday. What happened?

男：我要下樓去找張經理問關於這個週二的企畫。發生什麼事了嗎？

W : Nothing. I am on the way to see Manager Wang.

女：沒事。我正要去見王經理。

M : She is downstairs, too.

男：她也在樓下。

W : Right. I have to talk about something with her.

女：沒錯，我必須跟她談點事情。

M : So, let's walk faster in case they leave.

男：那麼，我們走快一點，以防他們離開了。

Question : Which is wrong about the dialogue?

關於這對話，何者是錯的？

(A) Jeff is preparing a project for Tuesday.

傑夫正在準備週二的企畫。

(B) Manager Chang and Manager Wang are co-workers.

張經理和王經理是同事。

(C) Jeff doesn't know Manager Chang.

傑夫不認識張經理。

* downstairs〔'daʊn'stɛrz〕*adv.* 往樓下；在樓下
  manager〔'mænɪdʒɚ〕*n.* 經理
  project〔'prɑdʒɛkt〕*n.* 計畫；企畫
  happen〔'hæpən〕*v.* 發生　***on the way*** 在往…的路上
  in case 以防　leave〔liv〕*v.* 離開
  dialogue〔'daɪə,lɔg〕*n.* 對話　prepare〔prɪ'pɛr〕*v.* 準備
  co-worker〔'ko'wɝkɚ〕*n.* 同事

18. (**C**) W : What do you usually do on the Tomb Sweeping Day?
　　　　　　　Sweep the tombs?

女：你清明節通常都做些什麼事情？掃墓嗎？

　　M : Yes. Tomb Sweeping Day is a very important
　　　　festival for people in Taiwan.

男：是的。清明節對台灣人來說是很重要的節日。

　　W : Why? I don't get it.

女：為什麼？我不懂。

　　M : Actually, we Taiwanese worship our ancestors by
　　　　offering sacrifices to them and sweeping the tombs of
　　　　our ancestors to show our respect for them.

男：事實上，我們台灣人藉由送上祭品來祭祀祖先，並且掃墓來
　　表示對先人的敬意。

W：Wow! So that's the way you show your close connection with your ancestors, isn't it?

女：哇！那就是你們表現你們和祖先有密切連結的方式，不是嗎？

M：Correct! What a tradition it is, isn't it?

男：完全正確！這是個很好的傳統，不是嗎？

Question：What are the two people talking about?

這兩個人在討論什麼？

(A) How to sweep the tombs. 如何掃墓。

(B) How to worship their ancestors. 如何祭祀祖先。

(C) The man is explaining the meaning of the Tomb Sweeping Day to the woman.

<u>男士在跟女士解釋清明節的意義。</u>

* tomb〔tum〕*n.* 墳墓   sweep〔swip〕*v.* 清掃

Tomb Sweeping Day 掃墓節；清明節

festival〔'fɛstəvl̩〕*n.* 節日   get〔gɛt〕*v.* 了解；明白

actually〔'æktʃʊəlɪ〕*adv.* 實際上

Taiwanese〔,taɪwɑ'niz〕*n.* 台灣人   worship〔'wɜʃəp〕*v.* 祭拜

ancestor〔'ænsɛstə〕*n.* 祖先   offer〔'ɔfə〕*v.* 提供；供奉

sacrifice〔'sækrə,faɪs〕*n.* 祭品   show〔ʃo〕*v.* 表現

respect〔rɪ'spɛkt〕*n.* 尊敬   close〔klos〕*adj.* 親密的

connection〔kə'nɛkʃən〕*n.* 連結；關係

correct〔kə'rɛkt〕*adj.* 正確的   tradition〔trə'dɪʃən〕*n.* 傳統

explain〔ɪk'splen〕*v.* 解釋；說明   meaning〔'minɪŋ〕*n.* 意義

19. (**B**) W：Good morning, what can I do for you?

女：早安，我可以替您做些什麼？

M：How much is the beef?

男：牛肉多少錢？

W：You mean the U.S. beef?

女：您是指美國牛肉嗎？

M：Yes.

男：是的。

W：It's 200 dollars a pound.

女：一磅 200 元。

M：I'll take 4 pounds.

男：我要四磅。

W：OK, here you are.

女：好的，這是您要的東西。

Question：How much should the man pay?

　　　　男士應該付多少錢？

(A) NT$400. 台幣 400 元。

(B) NT$800. 台幣 800 元。

(C) NT$1,000. 台幣 1,000 元。

* beef〔bif〕*n.* 牛肉　　pound〔paʊnd〕*n.* 磅【0.454 公斤】
  take〔tek〕*v.* 買　***Here you are.*** 你要的東西在這；拿去吧。
  pay〔pe〕*v.* 付（錢）

20. (**C**) M：How do you plan to spend your summer vacation?

男：妳暑假計畫如何度過？

W：My family and I will go to the Disneyland in Japan.
　　How about you?

女：我的家人和我要去日本的迪士尼樂園。你呢？

M：Wow, that's great.　I have always dreamed of
　　going to Disneyland someday.　Good for you.　As
　　for me, we will go to Kenting in southern Taiwan to
　　enjoy the sun and the beach and go horseback riding.

男：哇！好棒喔。我一直夢想著有一天要去迪士尼樂園。真是太
　　好了。至於我，我們要去南台灣的墾丁，去享受陽光和海灘，
　　並且去騎馬。

W : That sounds cool, too

女：那聽起來也很酷。

M : Yeah. I hope we both have a great time in summer.
　　See you next semester.

男：對呀。我希望我們夏天都能玩得開心。下學期見。

Question : What are the two persons talking about?
　　　　　這兩個人在討論什麼？

(A) They are talking about their dreams.
　　他們在討論他們的夢想。

(B) They plan to spend the summer vacation together.
　　他們計畫一起去度過暑假。

(C) They are sharing their plans for summer with each
　　other. 他們在分享彼此夏季的計畫。

* plan〔plæn〕v. 計畫；打算　　spend〔spɛnd〕v. 度過
summer vacation 暑假　　family〔'fæməlɪ〕n. 家人
Disneyland〔'dɪznɪ,lænd〕n. 迪士尼樂園
Japan〔dʒə'pæn〕n. 日本
wow〔waʊ〕interj.（表示驚訝、喜悅等）哇
dream of 夢想　　someday〔'sʌm,de〕adv. 將來有一天
Good for you. 做得好。　　**as for** 至於
southern〔'sʌðən〕adj. 南部的
enjoy〔ɪn'dʒɔɪ〕v. 享受　　**the sun** 陽光
beach〔bitʃ〕n. 海灘　　**horseback riding** 騎馬
sound〔saʊnd〕v. 聽起來　　cool〔kul〕adj. 很酷的
yeah〔jɛ〕interj. 是的（= yes）
have a good time 玩得愉快　　semester〔sə'mɛstə〕n. 學期
dream〔drim〕n. 夢想　　share〔ʃɛr〕v. 分享
each other 彼此

TEST 2

第一部分：辨識句意（第 1-3 題，共 3 題）

作答說明： 第 1-3 題每題有三張圖片，請依據所聽到的內容，選出
符合描述的圖片，每題播放兩次。

示例題：你會看到

(A)   (B)   (C)

然後你會聽到……（播音）。依據所播放的內容，正確答案應該
選 A，請將答案卡該題「Ⓐ」的地方塗黑、塗滿，即：● Ⓑ Ⓒ

---

1. (A)   (B)   (C)

2. (A)　　　　　　　(B)　　　　　　　(C)

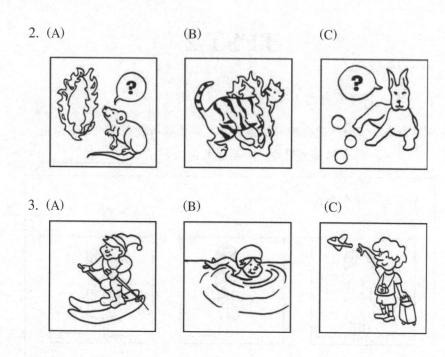

3. (A)　　　　　　　(B)　　　　　　　(C)

第二部分：基本問答（第 4-10 題，共 7 題）

作答說明：第 4-10 題每題均有三個選項，請依據所聽到的內容，選
　　　　　出一個最適合的回應，每題播放兩次。

示例題：你會看到

(A) She is talking to the teacher.
(B) She is a student in my class.
(C) She is wearing a beautiful dress.

然後你會聽到……（播音）。依據所播放的內容，正確答案應該
選 B，請將答案卡該題「Ⓑ」的地方塗黑、塗滿，即：Ⓐ ● Ⓒ

4. (A) There is no question about it.
   (B) But I don't like honey at all. It's too sweet.
   (C) I think Kenting is my first choice.

5. (A) Excuse me.
   (B) No, thanks.
   (C) You are welcome.

6. (A) Yes, I am.
   (B) I like Ruby, too.
   (C) This is Ruby.

7. (A) For a cake.
   (B) In an hour.
   (C) Yes, a burger, please.

8. (A) Oh! No. That's terrible. Did they call the police?
   (B) So did they find anything in the house?
   (C) They must have spent a huge sum of money to repair it.

9. (A) My brothers do.
   (B) My sisters will.
   (C) My sisters and brothers are.

10. (A) She is an astronaut.
    (B) She is going to a party tonight.
    (C) She is washing the clothes.

第三部分：言談理解（第 11-20 題，共 10 題）

作答說明：第 11-20 題每題均有三個選項，請依據所聽到的內容，
選出一個最適合的答案，每題播放兩次。

示例題：你會看到

(A) 9:50.　　(B) 10:00.　　(C) 10:10.

然後你會聽到……（播音）。依據所播放的內容，正確答案應該
選 B，請將答案卡該題「Ⓑ」的地方塗黑、塗滿，即：Ⓐ ● Ⓒ

---

11. (A) On foot.
    (B) On a bike.
    (C) On a scooter.

12. (A) To help her.
    (B) To buy her a cake for Mother's Day.
    (C) To join a party.

13. (A) The woman likes yellow.
    (B) The man thinks the pants are too expensive.
    (C) The man will buy the shirt.

14. (A) David will.
    (B) Sam will.
    (C) The mother will.

15. (A) A wallet.
    (B) A credit card.
    (C) A bill.

16. (A) Yes, he will.
    (B) No, he won't.
    (C) We don't know.

17. (A) Dark and damp.
    (B) Bright and airy.
    (C) Plain and unfurnished.

18. (A) The man and the woman dicussed how to earn some money.
    (B) The man failed to pay with his credit card and ended up paying in cash.
    (C) The woman taught the man how to use his credit card.

19. (A) She prefers the supermarket to the concert.
    (B) She prefers to go to the concert rather than the market.
    (C) She prefers traditional markets to supermarkets.

20. (A) She is angry about a picture.
    (B) She is afraid to talk.
    (C) He dated someone else before.

TEST 2 詳解

第一部分：辨識句意（第1-3題，共3題）

1. (**B**) (A)　　　　　　(B)　　　　　　(C)

Grandpa and grandma are having dinner with chopsticks.

祖父和祖母正在用筷子吃晚餐。

* grandpa〔'grænpɑ〕 *n.* 祖父；外祖父
grandma〔'grænmɑ〕 *n.* 祖母；奶奶
have〔hæv〕 *v.* 吃
chopsticks〔'tʃɑp,stɪks〕 *n. pl.* 筷子

2. (**A**) (A)　　　　　　(B)　　　　　　(C)

The rat can't do any tricks. He can't join the talent contest.

這老鼠不會表演任何特技，牠無法參加才藝比賽。

* rat〔ræt〕 *n.* 老鼠　　trick〔trɪk〕 *n.* 把戲；特技
join〔dʒɔɪn〕 *v.* 參加　　talent〔'tælənt〕 *n.* 才藝
contest〔'kɑntɛst〕 *n.* 比賽

3. (**A**) (A)  (B) 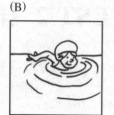 (C)

I go skiing with my classmates every winter.

我每年冬天和我的同班同學去滑雪。

* ski〔ski〕*v.* 滑雪　***go skiing*** 去滑雪
  classmate〔'klæs,met〕*n.* 同班同學

第二部分：基本問答（第 4-10 題，共 7 題）

4. (**C**) Where do you want to spend your honeymoon?

你想要在哪裡度蜜月？

(A) There is no question about it. 這是毫無疑問的。

(B) But I don't like honey at all. It's too sweet.

但是我完全不喜歡蜂蜜，太甜了。

(C) I think Kenting is my first choice.

我覺得墾丁是我的首選。

* honeymoon〔'hʌnɪ,mun〕*n.* 蜜月旅行
  there is no question about… …是毫無疑問的
  honey〔'hʌnɪ〕*n.* 蜂蜜　***not…at all*** 一點也不…
  sweet〔swit〕*adj.* 甜的　choice〔tʃɔɪs〕*n.* 選擇

5. (**B**) How about some coffee? 喝些咖啡如何？

(A) Excuse me. 對不起。

(B) No, thanks. 不，謝謝。

(C) You are welcome. 不客氣。

* ***How about…?*** …如何？　coffee〔'kɔfɪ〕*n.* 咖啡
  Excuse me. 對不起。

6. (**C**) Hello. Is Ruby Chen there? 哈囉，陳露比在嗎？

    (A) Yes, I am. 是的，我是。【應改成：Speaking. 或

        This is she speaking. 表「我就是。」】

    (B) I like Ruby, too. 我也喜歡露比。

    (C) This is Ruby. <u>我就是。</u>

    * ***This is****…*. 我是…。【用於講電話】

7. (**C**) May I take your order now? 可以幫您點菜了嗎？

    (A) For a cake. 爲了一塊蛋糕。

    (B) In an hour. 再過一小時。

    (C) Yes, a burger, please. <u>是的，請給我一個漢堡。</u>

    * ***take*** *one's* ***order*** 幫某人點菜

      cake〔kek〕*n.* 蛋糕   burger〔'bɝgɚ〕*n.* 漢堡

8. (**A**) I heard that Mr. Jones's house was broken into last night.

    我聽說瓊斯先生的房子昨晚被闖了。

    (A) Oh! No. That's terrible. Did they call the police?

        <u>喔！不。那眞糟糕，他們有報警嗎？</u>

    (B) So did they find anything in the house?

        那他們有在房子裡找到任何東西嗎？

    (C) They must have spent a huge sum of money to

        repair it.

        他們當時一定花了很多錢去整修房子。

    * ***break into*** 闖入   terrible〔'tɛrəbḷ〕*adj.* 糟糕的

      call the police 報警   ***must have*** *+ p.p.* 當時一定

      huge〔hjudʒ〕*adj.* 巨大的

      a huge sum of 大量的【接不可數名詞】

      repair〔rɪ'pɛr〕*v.* 修理

9. (**C**) Who is at the theater with Uncle Peter?

誰和彼得叔叔一起去看電影？

(A) My brothers do. 我弟弟。【須將 do 改成 are。】

(B) My sisters will. 我妹妹。【須將 will 改成 are。】

(C) My sisters and brothers are.

<u>我的妹妹跟弟弟。</u>

* theater〔ˈθiətɚ〕*n.* 電影院；戲院

10. (**B**) Why is Mom dressing up?

為何媽媽要盛裝打扮？

(A) She is an astronaut. 她是一位太空人。

(B) She is going to a party tonight.

<u>她今晚要去派對。</u>

(C) She is washing the clothes. 她在洗衣服。

* ***dress up*** 盛裝打扮　　astronaut〔ˈæstrəˌnɔt〕*n.* 太空人

party〔ˈpɑrtɪ〕*n.* 派對　　***wash the clothes*** 洗衣服

第三部分：言談理解（第 11-20 題，共 10 題）

11. (**A**) W：Jason, you are sure to be interested in this flyer.

女：傑森，你一定會對這張傳單有興趣。

M：What's it about?

男：是關於什麼？

W：It says there's a flea market at Fourth Park this weekend.

女：它寫說這週末在第四公園有跳蚤市場。

M："Flea market?" It sounds interesting.

男：「跳蚤市場」？聽起來很有趣。

W : We can go for a walk together and maybe we can find something we need.

女：我們可以一起去走走，或許我們可以找到我們需要的東西。

M : Great. Let's go on Saturday morning.

男：太棒了。週六早上一起去吧。

Question : How will they get to Fourth Park this weekend? 他們這個週末要如何去第四公園？

(A) On foot. 步行。

(B) On a bike. 騎腳踏車。

(C) On a scooter. 騎機車。

* **be sure to V.** 必定　　**be interested in** 對…感興趣
  flyer ('flaɪɚ) *n.* 傳單　　**flea market** 跳蚤市場
  weekend ('wik'ɛnd) *n.* 週末
  sound (saʊnd) *v.* 聽起來
  interesting ('ɪntrɪstɪŋ) *adj.* 有趣的
  go for a walk 去散步　　maybe ('mebɪ) *adv.* 或許
  get to 去；到達　　**on foot** 步行
  bike (baɪk) *n.* 腳踏車
  scooter ('skutɚ) *n.* 機車；輕型摩托車

12. (**A**) W : Kevin, I'm going to make a cake for Mother's Day. Can you come and give me a hand?

女：凱文，我打算做一個母親節蛋糕。你可以來幫我一個忙嗎？

M : I'd love to. What time?

男：我很樂意。什麼時候？

W : What about 3:00 p.m. this afternoon?

女：今天下午三點如何？

M : That's too bad. I am not free then. Can you do it
tomorrow?

男：那真遺憾。我那時沒空。妳可以明天做嗎？

W : Sure, same time.

女：當然，同樣時間。

M : It's a deal.

男：一言為定。

Question：What does the woman ask the man to do?

女士要求男士做什麼？

(A) To help her. 幫助她。

(B) To buy her a cake for Mother's Day.

幫她買一個母親節蛋糕。

(C) To join a party. 參加派對。

* *Mother's Day* 母親節　　*give sb. a hand* 幫助某人
would love to V. 願意～　　*What about…?* …如何？
That's too bad. 真遺憾。
free〔fri〕*adj.* 空閒的　　*It's a deal.* 一言為定。
ask〔æsk〕*v.* 要求　　help〔hɛlp〕*v.* 幫助
join〔dʒɔɪn〕*v.* 參加　　party〔'partɪ〕*n.* 派對

13. (**A**) M : What do you think of the pants, honey?

男：妳覺得這褲子如何，親愛的？

W : Great. The color looks good on you.

女：很棒。那顏色很適合你。

M : Don't you think the color looks too young for me?

男：妳不覺得這顏色對我來說看起來太年輕了嗎？

W : Not at all. Yellow means energy. I like it.

女：完全不會。黃色代表活力。我喜歡。

M：OK. I'll take it.

男：好的。我買這件。

Question：Which is true? 何者為真？

(A) The woman likes yellow. 女士喜歡黃色。

(B) The man thinks the pants are too expensive.

男士覺得褲子太貴。

(C) The man will buy the shirt.

男士會買那件襯衫。

* ***What do you think of…?*** 你覺得…如何？
  pants〔pænts〕*n. pl.* 褲子
  honey〔'hʌnɪ〕*n.*（暱稱）親愛的
  color〔'kʌlɚ〕*n.* 顏色　***look good on** sb.* 適合某人
  Not at all. 一點也不；完全不會。
  mean〔min〕*v.* 意指；表示
  energy〔'ɛnɚdʒɪ〕*n.* 精力；活力
  take〔min〕*v.* 買　　expensive〔ɪk'spɛnsɪv〕*adj.* 昂貴的
  shirt〔ʃɜt〕*n.* 襯衫

14. (**A**) W：David, have you mopped the floor yet?

女：大衛，你拖地了嗎？

M：No, I haven't, Mom. Sam is running around in the living room.

男：不，還沒，媽。山姆在客廳到處跑。

W：I see. Tell your little brother to finish his homework at his desk before I get home.

女：我知道了。告訴你弟弟在我回家前要坐在書桌前完成功課。

M：OK. Then I can finish mopping the floor, too.

男：好的。那我就也可以把地拖完了。

W : Good boy.

女：乖孩子。

Question : Who will mop the floor? 誰會拖地？

(A) David will. 大衛。

(B) Sam will. 山姆。

(C) The mother will. 媽媽。

* **mop the floor** 拖地　　yet〔jɛt〕*adv.*（用於疑問句）已經
  run around 四處跑　　**living room** 客廳
  I see. 我知道了。　　homework〔'hom,wɝk〕*n.* 功課
  desk〔dɛsk〕*n.* 書桌

15. (**C**)　W : Look, there's 500 dollars on the ground.

女：你看，地上有 500 元。

M : Wow, today is your day. You got a fortune for nothing.

男：哇！妳今天真幸運，妳不勞而獲。

W : It's not my money. I can't take it.

女：這不是我的錢，我不能拿。

M : Then what should we do?

男：那麼我們應該怎麼做？

W : We can take it to the police station.

女：我們可以拿去警察局。

M : You are really an honest person.

男：妳真是一個誠實的人。

Question : What did they pick up? 他們撿到什麼？

(A) A wallet. 一個皮夾。

(B) A credit card. 一張信用卡。

(C) A bill. 一張紙鈔。

* ground〔graʊnd〕*n.* 地面
  one's day 某人得意的日子
  fortune〔'fɔrtʃən〕*n.* 大筆錢
  for nothing 毫無理由；白白地（= *for no reason*）
  police station 警察局　　honest〔'ɑnɪst〕*adj.* 誠實的
  pick up 撿起　　wallet〔'wɑlɪt〕*n.* 皮夾
  credit card 信用卡　　bill〔bɪl〕*n.* 紙鈔

16.（**C**）W：Dad, may I have ten dollars?

女：爸爸，可以給我 10 元嗎？

M：Why do you need money?

男：妳為什麼需要錢？

W：I have a plan to save money.

女：我有一個存錢的計畫。

M：What for?

男：為什麼？

W：I want to buy a new iPad.

女：我想要買一台新的 iPad。

M：What happened to your old one?

男：妳舊的那台怎麼了？

Question：Will the father give the girl money to buy a
　　　　　 new iPad?

父親會給女兒錢買一台新的 iPad 嗎？

(A) Yes, he will. 是的，他會。

(B) No, he won't. 不，他不會。

(C) We don't know. 我們不知道。

* plan〔plæn〕*n.* 計畫　　save〔sev〕*v.* 存
  What for? 為什麼？（= *Why?*）
  iPad iPad 平板電腦

17. (**B**)　W：Eric, I need to rent an apartment. Do you know of any available apartments?

女：艾瑞克，我需要租一間公寓。你知道有什麼可以租的公寓嗎？

M：Not really. What kind of apartment are you interested in?

男：不太清楚。妳對哪種公寓有興趣？

W：I'd like one with big windows.

女：我想要有大窗戶的。

M：Have you checked the Net?

男：妳有在網路上查過了嗎？

W：Not yet.

女：還沒。

M：Maybe you can give it a try.

男：或許妳可以試試看。

Question：What may the woman's ideal apartment look like?

女士理想的公寓可能是怎樣的？

(A) Dark and damp.　又暗又潮濕。

(B) Bright and airy.　<u>明亮又通風。</u>

(C) Plain and unfurnished.

簡單而且沒有家具。

* rent〔rɛnt〕*v.* 租　　apartment〔ə'pɑrtmənt〕*n.* 公寓
know of 知道；聽說　　available〔ə'veləbḷ〕*adj.* 可獲得的
Not really. 不太清楚。　　***be interested in*** 對…感興趣
window〔'wɪndo〕*n.* 窗戶　　check〔tʃɛk〕*v.* 查看
the Net 網路　　***give it a try*** 試試看
dark〔dɑrk〕*adj.* 陰暗的　　damp〔dæmp〕*adj.* 潮濕的

bright〔braɪt〕*adj.* 明亮的；有光線的
airy〔ˈɛrɪ〕*adj.* 通風的
plain〔plen〕*adj.* 簡單的；樸素的
unfurnished〔ʌnˈfɝnɪʃt〕*adj.* 沒有家具的

18. (**B**) W：OK! The total will be NT\$ 2,400. Will that be cash or charge?

女：好的！總共是新台幣 2,400 元。付現還是刷卡？

M：I'll pay with a credit card. Here you go.

男：我要用信用卡付款，卡片在這。

W：Thank you. Please wait for a second….

女：謝謝您。請稍等…

(A few seconds later.)

（幾秒鐘後。）

W：I'm sorry, but your MasterCard has been declined.

女：很抱歉，您的萬事達卡無法刷卡成功。

M：What? How could that be? Could you please try it again?

男：什麼？那怎麼可能？可以請妳再試一次嗎？

W：I've already swiped it a couple of times. Would you mind paying in cash?

女：我已經刷了好幾次了。您介意付現金嗎？

M：Sure, no problem. Did you say how much it is?

男：當然，沒問題。妳剛剛說多少錢？

Question：What is the conversation about?

這對話是關於什麼？

(A) The man and the woman discussed how to earn some money.

男士和女士討論要如何賺一些錢。

(B) The man failed to pay with his credit card and ended up paying in cash.

男士無法用信用卡付款，最後用現金付款。

(C) The woman taught the man how to use his credit card.

女士教男子如何使用信用卡。

* total〔'totl〕*n.* 總額　　cash〔kæʃ〕*n.* 現金
charge〔tʃɑrdʒ〕*n.* 賒帳；刷卡
credit card 信用卡　　***Here you go.*** 拿去吧。
wait〔wet〕*v.* 等待　　***for a second*** 一會兒；片刻
later〔'letɚ〕*adv.* 之後　　***MasterCard*** 萬事達卡
decline〔dɪ'klaɪn〕*v.* 拒絕　　swipe〔swaɪp〕*v.* 刷（卡）
a couple of 一些；幾個　　time〔taɪm〕*n.* 次
mind〔maɪnd〕*v.* 介意　　***in cash*** 用現金
conversation〔͵kɑnvɚ'seʃən〕*n.* 對話
discuss〔dɪ'skʌs〕*v.* 討論
earn〔ɝn〕*v.* 賺　　***fail to V.*** 無法～
end up + V-ing 最後…

19. (**C**) W：Will you come with me to the market, son?

女：兒子，你要跟我一起去市場嗎？

M：Well, I am afraid not, Mom. Nina and I are going to a concert today. Besides, I like supermarkets better than traditional markets. They're brighter.

男：嗯，恐怕不能，媽。妮娜和我今天要去演唱會。另外，比起傳統市場，我比較喜歡超級市場，比較明亮。

W：That's true, but I like the interaction among people in traditional markets better.

女：的確是，但是我比較喜歡傳統市場裡人與人的互動。

Question : What does the woman prefer?

女士比較喜歡什麼？

(A) She prefers the supermarket to the concert.

她喜歡超級市場勝過演唱會。

(B) She prefers to go to the concert rather than the market. 她比較想去演唱會，不想去市場。

(C) She prefers traditional markets to supermarkets.

她喜歡傳統市場勝過超級市場。

* market〔'markɪt〕*n.* 市場
well〔wɛl〕*interj.* （說話停頓）嗯
I am afraid not. 恐怕不能。
concert〔'kɑnsɜt〕*n.* 演唱會
besides〔bɪ'saɪdz〕*adv.* 此外
supermarket〔'supɚ,markɪt〕*n.* 超級市場
traditional〔trə'dɪʃənl〕*adj.* 傳統的
bright〔braɪt〕*adj.* 明亮的　　*That's true.* 的確是。
interaction〔,ɪntɚ'ækʃən〕*n.* 互動
prefer〔prɪ'fɜ〕*v.* 比較喜歡；偏好
prefer A *to* B 喜歡 A 勝於 B　　*rather than* 而非

20. (**A**) M : Why don't you say something? You haven't said a word for three days.

男：妳為何不說話？妳已經三天都沒說話了。

W : I have nothing to say to you.

女：我跟你沒話好說。

M : OK. I'm really sorry I lied to you about the photo, but I keep the photo of Linda only because she was my classmate, not because I dated her before. Could you forget about it?

男：好的，我眞的很抱歉，照片的事情我對妳說謊，但是我保
　　留琳達的照片，只因爲她是我的同班同學，不是因爲我之
　　前和她約會。妳可以忘了這件事嗎？

W：No way. I am done with you.

女：不行。我跟你玩完了。

Question：Why won't the woman talk to the man?

　　　　　女士爲何不和男士說話　？

(A) She is angry about a picture.

　　她對照片的事感到生氣。

(B) She is afraid to talk.　她不敢講話。

(C) He dated someone else before.

　　他以前和其他人約會過。

* word〔wɜd〕*n.* 言語；話
　photo〔'foto〕*n.* 照片
　not because ~ but because …　不是因爲～而是因爲…
　date〔det〕*v.* 和…約會
　forget about　別再想；忘了
　No way. 不行。　　*be done with*　和…結束關係
　be angry about　對…感到生氣
　picture〔'pɪktʃɚ〕*n.* 照片

TEST 3

第一部分：辨識句意（第1-3題，共3題）

作答說明： 第1-3題每題有三張圖片，請依據所聽到的內容，選出
符合描述的圖片，每題播放兩次。

示例題：你會看到

(A)　　　　　　(B)　　　　　　(C)

然後你會聽到……（播音）。依據所播放的內容，正確答案應該
選A，請將答案卡該題「Ⓐ」的地方塗黑、塗滿，即：● Ⓑ Ⓒ

1. (A)　　　　　　(B)　　　　　　(C)

2. (A)　　　　　　(B)　　　　　　(C)

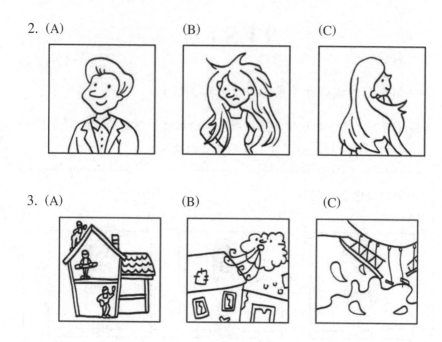

3. (A)　　　　　　(B)　　　　　　(C)

第二部分：基本問答（第 4-10 題，共 7 題）

作答說明： 第 4-10 題每題均有三個選項，請依據所聽到的內容，選出一個最適合的回應，每題播放兩次。

示例題：你會看到

(A) She is talking to the teacher.

(B) She is a student in my class.

(C) She is wearing a beautiful dress.

然後你會聽到⋯⋯（播音）。依據所播放的內容，正確答案應該選 B，請將答案卡該題「Ⓑ」的地方塗黑、塗滿，即：Ⓐ ● Ⓒ

---

4. (A) Yes, he always does.
   (B) Yes, he bought a
       new cellphone.
   (C) No, he just gave me a
       new cellphone yesterday.

5. (A) Yes, she went there by
       plane.
   (B) Yes, she took a train
       there.
   (C) No, she fed the horse
       there.

6. (A) You can come to see
       me off if you like.
   (B) Don't worry. I will ask
       the information desk
       for help.
   (C) Happy birthday.

7. (A) It's June 8th.
   (B) It's Tuesday.
   (C) It's ten past three.

8. (A) Why are you hungry?
   (B) Sure.
   (C) How did it happen?

9. (A) No, I don't think so.
   (B) Thanks, I don't like
       either of them.
   (C) Right. You can say
       that again.

10. (A) I will congratulate
        her on her marriage.
    (B) I don't think it is a
        good sign for her.
    (C) That's her birthday.

第三部分：言談理解（第 11-20 題，共 10 題）

作答說明： 第 11-20 題每題均有三個選項，請依據所聽到的內容，
          選出一個最適合的答案，每題播放兩次。

示例題：你會看到

(A) 9:50.　　(B) 10:00.　　(C) 10:10.

然後你會聽到……（播音）。依據所播放的內容，正確答案應該
選 B，請將答案卡該題「Ⓑ」的地方塗黑、塗滿，即：Ⓐ ● Ⓒ

---

11. (A) For further studies.
    (B) On vacation.
    (C) On business.

12. (A) The noise will stop
       in half hour.
    (B) Derek is practicing
       dancing on the first
       floor.
    (C) Derek is practicing
       dancing at night.

13. (A) About 10 minutes.
    (B) About 20 minutes.
    (C) We don't know.

14. (A) At a café.
    (B) At a bank.
    (C) At a school.

15. (A) She had an accident.
    (B) She had the flu.
    (C) She missed an
       interview.

16. (A) No, she won't.
    (B) No, she doesn't.
    (C) Yes, she likes.

17. (A) Either the man or the
       woman.
    (B) Neither the man nor
       the woman.
    (C) Both the man and the
       woman.

18. (A) Tom missed the
       morning classes.
    (B) Tom never went to
       school late before.
    (C) Tom didn't feel well
       this morning.

19. (A) To open the door by
       themselves.
    (B) To find a place to hide
       their keys.
    (C) To ask a locksmith for
       help.

20. (A) He can't agree with
       what the woman said.
    (B) He can't figure out
       what the woman was
       talking about.
    (C) He totally agrees with
       the woman.

TEST 3 詳解

第一部分：辨識句意（第 1-3 題，共 3 題）

1. (**C**) (A)   (B)   (C)

My cousin is too heavy, so he exercises a lot to lose weight.

我堂弟太重了，所以他做很多運動來減肥。

* cousin〔ˈkʌzn̩〕*n.* 堂（表）兄弟姊妹
  exercise〔ˈɛksɚ͵saɪz〕*v.* 運動　　*a lot*　很多
  lose weight　減重

2. (**C**) (A)   (B)   (C)

Linda always keeps her long hair clean and tidy.

琳達總是讓她的長髮保持乾淨又整潔。

* keep〔kip〕*v.* 使保持
  clean〔klin〕*adj.* 乾淨的
  tidy〔ˈtaɪdɪ〕*adj.* 整齊的；整潔的

3. (**B**) (A)   (B)   (C)

  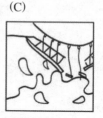

The house was knocked down by the typhoon.

房子被颱風吹倒了。

* ***knock down*** 拆掉；拆毀　　typhoon〔taɪˈfun〕*n.* 颱風

第二部分：基本問答（第 4-10 題，共 7 題）

4. (**A**) Does your father use a cellphone to deal with everyday business?　你爸爸用手機來處理每天的生意嗎？

    (A) Yes, he always does. <u>是的，他總是這麼做。</u>

    (B) Yes, he bought a new cellphone.

        是的，他買了一台新手機。

    (C) No, he just gave me a new cellphone yesterday.

        不，他昨天剛給我一台新手機。

* use〔juz〕*v.* 使用　　cellphone〔ˈsɛl,fon〕*n.* 手機
  deal with 處理　　business〔ˈbɪznɪs〕*n.* 生意
  bought〔bɔt〕*v.* 買【buy 的過去式】

5. (**A**) Did your daughter fly to Tokyo yesterday?

    你女兒昨天飛去東京了嗎？

    (A) Yes, she went there by plane. <u>是的，她搭飛機去那裡。</u>

    (B) Yes, she took a train there. 是的，他搭火車去那裡。

    (C) No, she fed the horse there. 不，她在那裡餵馬。

* fly〔flaɪ〕*v.* 搭飛機　　Tokyo〔ˈtokɪ,o〕*n.* 東京【日本首都】
  by plane 搭飛機　　fed〔fɛd〕*v.* 餵【feed 的過去式】

6. (**B**)　There is something wrong with my easy card. The gate won't open. 我的悠遊卡有點問題。閘門不開。

(A) You can come to see me off if you like.
如果你願意，可以來幫我送行。

(B) Don't worry. I will ask the information desk for help.
別擔心，我來跟服務台求救。

(C) Happy birthday. 生日快樂。

* ***There's something wrong with*** ··· ···有問題
easy card 悠遊卡　　***gate*** 〔 get 〕 *n.* 出入口；門
see sb. off 幫某人送行　　***if you like*** 如果你願意
ask sb. for help 向某人求救　　***information desk*** 服務台

7. (**C**)　What is the time by your watch? 你的手錶顯示是幾點？

(A) It's June 8th. 六月八日。

(B) It's Tuesday. 是星期二。

(C) It's ten past three. 三點十分。

* time 〔 taɪm 〕 *n.* 時刻；時候　　by 〔 baɪ 〕 *prep.* 根據

8. (**B**)　Could you buy some sugar for me on your way home?
你回家路上可以幫我買一些糖嗎？

(A) Why are you hungry? 你為何會餓？

(B) Sure. 當然可以。

(C) How did it happen? 這怎麼發生的？

* sugar 〔 'ʃugɚ 〕 *n.* 糖　　***on one's way*** 在往···的路上
hungry 〔 'hʌŋgrɪ 〕 *adj.* 飢餓的

9. (**C**)　Exercise and good nutrition are important for people, especially for children.
運動和良好的營養對人是很重要的，特別是小孩。

(A) No, I don't think so. 不，我不覺得。

(B) Thanks, I don't like either of them.
謝謝，我兩個都不喜歡。

(C) Right. You can say that again. 的確。我非常同意。

* exercise〔'ɛksə,saɪz〕*n.* 運動
  nutrition〔nju'trɪʃən〕*n.* 營養
  important〔ɪm'pɔrtṇt〕*adj.* 重要的
  especially〔ə'spɛʃəlɪ〕*adv.* 特別是；尤其
  You can say that again. 你說的對；我同意。

10. (**A**) Peggy plans to get married before she turns 30. What do you think? 佩琪計畫在她三十歲前結婚。你覺得如何？

(A) I will congratulate her on her marriage.
我會恭喜她結婚。

(B) I don't think it is a good sign for her.
我不覺得這對她來說是個好徵兆。

(C) That's her birthday. 那是她的生日。

* plan〔plæn〕*v.* 計畫；打算　　***get married*** 結婚
  turn〔tɝn〕*v.* 變成　　***congratulate sb. on sth.*** 恭喜某人某事
  marriage〔'mærɪdʒ〕*n.* 結婚；婚姻
  sign〔saɪn〕*n.* 徵兆

第三部分：言談理解（第 11-20 題，共 10 題）

11. (**A**) W：Excuse me. Aren't you Gary?
女：對不起。你不是蓋瑞嗎？

M：Yes. Hi, Anna. Long time no see. How have you been?
男：是的。嗨，安娜。好久不見。你好嗎？

W：Not bad. Where are you going?
女：不錯。你要去哪裡？

M : I'm going to my girlfriend's place. By the way, how are your parents?

男：我正要去我女朋友家。對了，你父母親好嗎？

W : They are doing OK. How long will you stay in Taiwan this time?

女：他們過得還不錯。你這次在台灣要待多久？

M : Now I live in Tainan. I am tired of flying back and forth. And I have finished my studies in America.

男：我現在住在台南。我厭倦了來回飛來飛去。而且我已經完成了我美國的學業。

Question : Why did Gary stay in the U.S. before?

為何蓋瑞之前會住在美國？

(A) For further studies. 為了進修。

(B) On vacation. 度假。

(C) On business. 出差。

* *Excuse me*. 對不起。　　*Long time no see*. 好久不見。
Not bad. 不錯。　　girlfriend〔'gɝl,frɛnd〕*n.* 女朋友
place〔ples〕*n.* 地方；家　　*by the way* 順帶一提
do〔du〕*v.* (生活) 過得　　*be tired of* 厭倦
back and forth 來回地　　studies〔'stʌdɪz〕*n. pl.* 學業
further studies 進修；深造　　*on business* 因為公事

12. (**C**) W : What's the loud noise upstairs, Derek? Do you know it's already midnight? I have to get up early tomorrow.

女：樓上的噪音是怎麼回事，德瑞克？你知道現在已經半夜了嗎？我明天得早起。

M : Sorry, Mom. I'm afraid we forgot the time while we were practicing dancing.

男：對不起，媽。我恐怕我們在練舞的時候忘了時間。

W : You should be. You must stop the noise right now.

女：你們應該覺得抱歉。你們必須現在就停止那噪音。

M : Please give us ten more minutes. I promise we will quiet down by then.

男：請再給我們十分鐘。我保證我們會在那時候之前就會安靜下來。

W : All right, keep your promise or I'll cut off the power.

女：好的，要遵守你的承諾，不然我會切斷電源。

M : I see. You have my word.

男：我知道了。我保證。

Question : Which is true? 何者爲眞？

(A) The noise will stop in half hour.

噪音會再過半小時後會停止。

(B) Derek is practicing dancing on the first floor.

德瑞克正在一樓練習跳舞。

(C) Derek is practicing dancing at night.

<u>德瑞克在晚上練習跳舞。</u>

* loud〔laʊd〕*adj.* 大聲的　　noise〔nɔɪz〕*n.* 噪音
midnight〔'mɪd,naɪt〕*n.* 半夜　　***get up*** 起床
I'm afraid… 恐怕…　　***practice + V-ing*** 練習～
promise〔'prɑmɪs〕*v.* 保證；答應　　***quiet down*** 安靜下來
by〔baɪ〕*prep.* 在…之前　　then〔ðɛn〕*n.* 那時
all right. 好的　　***keep** one's* ***promise*** 遵守承諾
cut off 切斷　　power〔'paʊɚ〕*n.* 電力；電源
I see. 我知道；我了解。　　***You have my word.*** 我保證。

13. (**B**) W : Hey, Nilson. I heard that your bike was stolen.

女：嘿，尼爾森。我聽說你的腳踏車被偷了。

M : Yes, I guess it was stolen last night.

男：是的，我猜是昨晚被偷的。

W : I'm sorry to hear that. Then, how did you get to the office this morning?

女：很難過聽到那樣的事。那麼你今天早上怎麼到辦公室的？

M : I had to walk for more than a quarter of an hour.

男：我必須走超過十五分鐘的路。

W : How about going home on my motorcycle this afternoon?

女：今天下午坐我的摩托車回家如何？

M : Great. I'd appreciate that.

男：太棒了。很感謝妳。

Question : How long did it take Nilson to walk to the office this morning?

今天早上尼爾森花了多久的時間走到辦公室？

(A) About 10 minutes. 大約十分鐘。

(B) About 20 minutes. 大約二十分鐘。

(C) We don't know. 我們不知道。

* stolen〔'stolən〕 *v.* 偷【steal 的過去式】
  guess〔gɛs〕 *v.* 猜   *sorry to hear* 很難過聽到
  get to 到達   office〔'ɔfɪs〕 *n.* 辦公室
  quarter〔'kwɔrtɚ〕 *n.* 四分之一；十五分鐘
  How about + V-ing? ～如何？
  appreciate〔ə'priʃɪ,et〕 *v.* 感激

14. (**A**) W : Hello, Andy. Nice to see you.

女：哈囉，安迪。很高興見到你。

M : I'm glad to see you here, Wendy.

男：溫蒂，很高興看到妳在這。

W : Come join us and chat with your old friends.

女：來加入我們，和你的老朋友聊聊天。

M : No, thanks.　I can't stay too long.　I stopped in to get some coffee.　My manager is waiting in the car.

男：不，謝謝。我不能待太久。我只是順道來買點咖啡，我的經理正在車子裡等我。

W : Then why don't you come over to my apartment on Friday night?

女：那你何不週五晚上順道來我住的公寓呢？

M : I think you still live in the same place, right?　I'll be there by eight.

男：我想妳還是住在一樣的地方，是吧？我八點之前會到。

Question : Where did the dialogue happen?

　　　　　　對話發生在哪裡？

(A) At a café.　在咖啡店。

(B) At a bank.　在銀行。

(C) At a school.　在學校。

* **come + V.** 來~（= come to V. = come and V.）

　join〔dʒɔɪn〕v. 參加　　　chat〔tʃæt〕v. 聊天

　old friend 老朋友　　　**stop in** 中途停留

　get〔gɛt〕v. 買　　manager〔'mænɪdʒɚ〕n. 經理

　wait〔wet〕v. 等待　　**come over** 從遠道過來；順道來訪

　apartment〔ə'pɑrtmənt〕n. 公寓

　dialogue〔'daɪə,lɔg〕n. 對話

　café〔kə'fe〕n. 咖啡店　　bank〔bæŋk〕n. 銀行

15. (**A**) W : Jenny's interview is four blocks away and she still needs to walk with a cane.　I'm afraid that she might not be able to go for the interview.

女：珍妮的面試有四個街區遠，而且她還需要用枴杖走路。恐怕她可能無法去參加面試。

M : What did the doctor say?

男：醫生怎麼說？

W : She is much better but she had better not walk too much.

女：她好多了，但是她最好別走太多路。

M : Then we can drive her there.

男：那麼我們可以開車載她過去。

W : I hope she can learn a lesson from this accident.

女：我希望她可以從這次的意外學到教訓。

M : I believe she will. I'm sure she won't go through a red light again.

男：我相信她會的。我確定她不會再闖紅燈了。

Question : What happened to Jenny the other day?

前幾天珍妮發生什麼事？

(A) She had an accident. 她發生意外。

(B) She had the flu. 她得了流感。

(C) She missed an interview. 她錯過了一場面試。

* interview〔'ɪntɚ,vju〕*n.* 面試　　block〔blɑk〕*n.* 街區
cane〔ken〕*n.* 枴杖　　***be able to V.*** 能夠～
much〔mʌtʃ〕*adv.*（強調比較級）更加
had better 最好　　drive〔draɪv〕*v.* 開車載（某人）
learn a lesson 學到教訓　　accident〔'æksədənt〕*n.* 意外
believe〔bə'liv〕*v.* 相信　　***go through a red light*** 闖紅燈
the other day 前幾天（= *a few days ago*）
flu〔flu〕*n.* 流感（= *influenza*）　　miss〔mɪs〕*v.* 錯過

16. (**B**) W : What a delicious smell. Do you know where it is coming from?

女：好香的味道。你知道這香味哪裡來的嗎？

M : Oh! It's from my lunch box.

男：喔！是來自我的午餐盒。

W : Do you cook every day?

女：你每天煮飯嗎？

M : You bet. It's a piece of cake for me.

男：當然。這對我來說輕而易舉。

W : I used to cook but everything I cooked tasted awful,
so I gave up.

女：我以前常煮飯，但是所有我煮的東西都不好吃，所以我就放
棄了。

M : Come on. I think you will be a good cook with more
practice.

男：別這樣。我想妳多練習的話廚藝就會進步。

Question : Does the woman cook every day?

　　　　　女士每天煮飯嗎？

(A) No, she won't. 不，她不會。

(B) No, she doesn't. <u>不，她沒有。</u>

(C) Yes, she likes. 是的，她喜歡。

* delicious〔dɪ'lɪʃəs〕*adj.* 美味的；香的
　smell〔smɛl〕*n.* 味道　　***lunch box*** 午餐盒
　You bet. 的確；當然。　　***a piece of cake*** 簡單的事
　used to V. 以前常常　　taste〔test〕*v.* 嚐起來
　awful〔'ɔful〕*adj.* 很糟的　　***give up*** 放棄
　Come on. 算了吧；別這樣。
　cook〔kuk〕*v.* 煮菜　　*n.* 廚師　　practice〔'præktɪs〕*n.* 練習

17. (**C**) W : My goodness! I almost fell asleep during the meeting
in the morning.

女：天呀！我早上開會的時候幾乎要睡著了。

M : Why are you so sleepy? Didn't you sleep well
　　last night?

男：妳爲何這麼睏？妳昨晚沒睡好嗎？

W : No, I stayed up late because I was watching the
　　World Baseball Cup.

女：沒，我熬夜到很晚，因爲我在看世界盃棒球賽。

M : Really? I didn't know you were a baseball fan.

男：眞的嗎？我不知道妳是棒球迷。

W : I love sports. In fact, I often play baseball with
　　friends on weekends.

女：我喜歡運動。事實上，我常常和朋友在週末打棒球。

M : Wow, what a woman you are! How about playing
　　baseball together this weekend?

男：哇，妳眞是個了不起的女人！這週末一起打棒球如何？

Question : Who is interested in baseball?

　　　　　　誰對棒球有興趣？

(A) Either the man or the woman. 不是男士就是女士。

(B) Neither the man nor the woman. 男士和女士都沒有。

(C) Both the man and the woman. <u>男士和女士都有。</u>

* *My goodness*. 天呀。　　*fall asleep* 睡著
　meeting〔'mitɪŋ〕*n.* 會議　　sleepy〔'slipɪ〕*adj.* 想睡的；睏的
　stay up 熬夜　　late〔let〕*adv.* 晚地
　World Baseball Cup 世界盃棒球賽
　fan〔fæn〕*n.* 迷　　sport〔sport〕*n.* 運動
　in fact 事實上　　weekend〔'wik'ɛnd〕*n.* 週末
　interested〔'ɪntrɪstɪd〕*adj.* 感興趣的 < in >
　either A *or* B 不是 A 就是 B
　neither A *nor* B 既不是 A 也不是 B
　both A *and* B A 和 B 兩者

18. (**B**) W : Tom, it is almost lunchtime. Why are you so late?

女：湯姆，快到午餐時間了。你怎麼這麼晚？

M : I had a stomachache, so I went to the doctor before I came to school.

男：我肚子痛，所以我來學校前去看醫生。

W : Should I believe it? Is it another excuse?

女：我應該相信嗎？還是這只是另一個藉口？

M : I am telling the truth.

男：我說的是實話。

W : Not again.

女：又來了。

M : You can call my mom at once and find out the fact.

男：妳可以馬上打電話給我媽找出真相。

Question : Which is wrong?

何者為非？

(A) Tom missed the morning classes.

湯姆錯過了早上的課。

(B) Tom never went to school late before.

湯姆之前上學從未有遲到。

(C) Tom didn't feel well this morning.

湯姆今天早上覺得不舒服。

* lunchtime〔ˈlʌntʃˌtaɪm〕*n.* 午餐時間

stomachache〔ˈstʌməkˌek〕*n.* 胃痛；肚子痛

go to the doctor 去看醫生   believe〔bəˈliv〕*v.* 相信

excuse〔ɪkˈskjus〕*n.* 藉口   ***tell the truth*** 說實話

Not again. 又來了；不會吧。   ***at once*** 立刻；馬上

find out 找出；查明（真相）   fact〔fækt〕*n.* 事實

miss〔mɪs〕*v.* 錯過   well〔wɛl〕*adj.* 健康的；安好的

19. (**C**)　W : Honey, do you see my keys?

女：親愛的，你有看到我的鑰匙嗎？

M : Oh, no. Not again. This is the third time this week.

男：喔，不。不會吧。這是本週第三次了。

W : Sorry. I did put them away, but I just forgot where I put them.

女：抱歉。我真的有把它們收起來，但是我就是忘了放在哪。

M : I am afraid that we need to call for the locksmith again.

男：恐怕我們要再叫鎖匠了。

W : Please forgive me. I promise that I won't lose them again.

女：請原諒我，我保證我不會再弄丟了。

Question : What do the man and the woman need to do right now?

男士和女士現在需要做什麼？

(A) To open the door by themselves. 自己打開門。

(B) To find a place to hide their keys. 找個地方藏鑰匙。

(C) To ask a locksmith for help. 向鎖匠求救。

* honey〔ˈhʌnɪ〕*n.* (暱稱) 親愛的

  put away 把…收起來；放好

  forgot〔fəˈgɑt〕*v.* 忘記【forget 的過去式】

  call for 叫 (某人) 來

  locksmith〔ˈlɑk,smɪθ〕*n.* 鎖匠

  forgive〔fəˈgɪv〕*v.* 原諒

  promise〔ˈprɑmɪs〕*v.* 承諾；保證

  lose〔luz〕*v.* 遺失　　hide〔haɪd〕*v.* 隱藏

  ask sb. for help 向某人求救

20. (**C**) W：Look! Larry is showing off his new toys again.

女：你看！賴瑞又在炫耀他的新玩具了。

M：Right. I don't think it's a good way to make friends.

男：沒錯。我覺得這不是個交朋友的好方法。

W：It's not. I think showing off is what people do when they want to disguise their lack of self-confidence.

女：的確不是。我覺得炫耀是人們想要掩飾他們缺乏自信時才會做的事。

M：I couldn't agree with you more.

男：我非常同意。

Question：What is the man's attitude towards the woman's opinion?

男士對女士的意見有什麼看法？

(A) He can't agree with what the woman said.

他不同意女士所說的。

(B) He can't figure out what the woman was talking about. 他不了解女士在說什麼。

(C) He totally agrees with the woman.

他完全同意女士。

* ***show off*** 炫耀　　toy〔tɔɪ〕*n.* 玩具

make friends 交朋友

disguise〔dɪs'gaɪz〕*v.* 偽裝；掩飾

lack〔læk〕*n.* 缺乏

self-confidence〔ˏsɛlf'kɑnfədəns〕*n.* 自信

couldn't agree with sb. more 完全同意某人

figure out 了解

totally〔'totḷɪ〕*adv.* 完全地

TEST 4

第一部分：辨識句意（第 1-3 題，共 3 題）

作答說明： 第 1-3 題每題有三張圖片，請依據所聽到的內容，選出
符合描述的圖片，每題播放兩次。

示例題：你會看到

(A) 　　(B) 　　(C)

然後你會聽到……（播音）。依據所播放的內容，正確答案應該
選 A，請將答案卡該題「Ⓐ」的地方塗黑、塗滿，即：● Ⓑ Ⓒ

1. (A) 　　(B) 　　(C)

2. (A)　　　　　　(B)　　　　　　(C)

3. (A)　　　　　　(B)　　　　　　(C)

第二部分：基本問答（第 4-10 題，共 7 題）

作答說明： 第 4-10 題每題均有三個選項，請依據所聽到的內容，選出一個最適合的回應，每題播放兩次。

示例題：你會看到

(A) She is talking to the teacher.

(B) She is a student in my class.

(C) She is wearing a beautiful dress.

然後你會聽到……（播音）。依據所播放的內容，正確答案應該選 B，請將答案卡該題「Ⓑ」的地方塗黑、塗滿，即：Ⓐ ● Ⓒ

---

4. (A) So they are getting married soon?
   (B) What's wrong with her? Is she all right?
   (C) I know. She is on business as usual.

5. (A) Her leg hurts because she was hit by a truck last weekend.
   (B) She is talking on the phone.
   (C) Her ring is shiny.

6. (A) You'd better take it off.
   (B) Did she try asking at the shelter for animals?
   (C) I know. She must have been very excited.

7. (A) Don't mention it.
   (B) That's a good idea.
   (C) Now you are telling me.

8. (A) No kidding.
   (B) Sorry. It's my fault.
   (C) No problem.

9. (A) What? How could that be?
   (B) Of course not.
   (C) Of course. That's just a piece of cake.

10. (A) I don't believe it.
    (B) How come?
    (C) I love Hawaii.

第三部分：言談理解（第 11-20 題，共 10 題）

作答說明：第 11-20 題每題均有三個選項，請依據所聽到的內容，
　　　　　選出一個最適合的答案，每題播放兩次。

示例題：你會看到

(A) 9:50.　　(B) 10:00.　　(C) 10:10.

然後你會聽到……（播音）。依據所播放的內容，正確答案應該
選 B，請將答案卡該題「Ⓑ」的地方塗黑、塗滿，即：Ⓐ ● Ⓒ

---

11. (A) Surfing the Net.
    (B) She was shocked to
        see the mess in the
        man's room.
    (C) Some ways to clean
        his room up.

12. (A) Looking for his son.
    (B) Take the fifth
        elevator.
    (C) Find some stuff for
        sports.

13. (A) In the office.
    (B) In a restaurant.
    (C) In a cafeteria.

14. (A) To take care of the
        plants.
    (B) To paint his thumb
        green.
    (C) She wants to take
        care of the man.

15. (A) Yes, at the price of
        NT$3,800.
    (B) Yes, at the price of
        NT$3,000.
    (C) No, she didn't.

16. (A) To buy a new bracelet
        for his mom.
    (B) To apologize to Mary
        as soon as possible.
    (C) To be honest with his
        mom.

17. (A) Nobody.
    (B) Susan will.
    (C) Frank will.

18. (A) She needs to work to
        support the man.
    (B) She wants the man to
        find a part-time job for
        her.
    (C) She plans to study and
        work at the same time.

19. (A) Everything was great.
    (B) It was a trip by car.
    (C) It was a boat trip.

20. (A) They are going to have
        some coffee together.
    (B) They are going to drive
        to the Donut Café.
    (C) They are going to meet
        at the Donut Café.

TEST 4 詳解

第一部分:辨識句意(第 1-3 題,共 3 題)

1. (**C**) (A)　　　　　　(B)　　　　　　(C)

Jonny likes to go biking on weekends.
強尼喜歡週末去騎腳踏車。

* *go + V-ing* 去~　　bike〔baɪk〕*v.* 騎腳踏車
weekend〔'wik'ɛnd〕*n.* 週末

2. (**A**) (A)　　　　　　(B)　　　　　　(C)

Rose has been talking to her friend on the phone for half
an hour. 蘿絲和她的朋友講電話講了半小時。

* *talk on the phone* 講電話

3. (**C**) (A)　　　　　　(B)　　　　　　(C)

Superfoods include broccoli, spinach and green peppers,
and provide nutrition for human bodies.

超級食物包含花椰菜、菠菜和青椒,能提供人類身體養分。

* superfood〔'supɚ͵fud〕n. 超級食物【特別能促進健康的食物】
    include〔ɪn'klud〕n. 包含
    broccoli〔'brɑkəlɪ〕n. 花椰菜
    spinach〔'spɪnɪtʃ〕n. 菠菜   *green pepper* 青椒
    provide〔prə'vaɪd〕v. 提供
    nutrition〔nju'trɪʃən〕n. 營養   human〔'hjumən〕adj. 人的

第二部分:基本問答(第 4-10 題,共 7 題)

4.(**B**) Daisy has made an appointment with her doctor.

黛西和她的醫生有約診。

(A) So they are getting married soon?

所以他們很快要結婚了?

(B) What's wrong with her? Is she all right?

她怎麼了?她還好嗎?

(C) I know. She is on business as usual.

我知道。她跟平常一樣去出差。

* appointment〔ə'pɔɪntmənt〕n. 預約;約診
    get married 結婚   *What's wrong with…?* …怎麼了?
    all right 沒問題的
    on business 出差   *as usual* 如往常

5.(**A**) What's wrong with Judy? 茱蒂怎麼了?

(A) Her leg hurts because she was hit by a truck last
    weekend.

她腳痛,因為她上個週末被卡車撞倒。

(B) She is talking on the phone. 她在講電話。

(C) Her ring is shiny. 她的戒指很閃亮。

* hurt〔hɝt〕*v.* 疼痛　　hit〔hɪt〕*v.* 撞【hit 的過去分詞】
  truck〔trʌk〕*n.* 卡車　　weekend〔'wik'ɛnd〕*n.* 週末
  ring〔rɪŋ〕*n.* 戒指　　shiny〔'ʃaɪnɪ〕*adj.* 閃亮的

6. (**B**) Cindy looked everywhere for her pet dog, but in vain.
   辛蒂到處找她的寵物狗，但卻徒勞無功。

   (A) You'd better take it off. 你最好把這脫掉。

   (B) Did she try asking at the shelter for animals?
   <u>她有試過問看看動物收容所嗎？</u>

   (C) I know. She must have been very excited.
   　　我知道。她當時一定很興奮。

   * ***look for*** 尋找　　pet〔pɛt〕*n.* 寵物　*adj.*（作）寵物的
     in vain 徒勞無功　　***had better*** 最好
     take off 脫掉　　***try + V-ing*** 試試看～
     shelter〔'ʃɛltɚ〕*n.* 庇護所；收容所
     must have + p.p. 當時一定～
     excited〔ɪk'saɪtɪd〕*adj.* 興奮的

7. (**A**) Thanks for helping me out when I was in big trouble.
   謝謝你在我遇到大麻煩時幫助我。

   (A) Don't mention it. <u>不客氣。</u>

   (B) That's a good idea. 那是個好主意。

   (C) Now you are telling me. 我早就知道了。

   * ***thanks for***… 謝謝…　　***help*** *sb.* ***out*** 幫助某人
     be in trouble 身處困境；遭遇麻煩
     Don't mention it. 不客氣。
     You are telling me. 這還用你說；我早就知道了。

8. (**B**) Who broke the glass in my room?

誰打破了我房間的玻璃？

(A) No kidding. 這不是開玩笑的。

(B) Sorry. It's my fault. <u>抱歉，是我的錯。</u>

(C) No problem. 沒問題。

* broke〔brok〕*v.* 打破【break 的過去式】
glass〔glæs〕*n.* 玻璃
No kidding. 這不是開玩笑的；我是說真的。
fault〔fɔlt〕*n.* 過錯

9. (**B**) Kerry, do you mind buying me a loaf of bread on your way back?

凱瑞，你介意在你回來的路上幫我買條麵包嗎？

(A) What? How could that be?

什麼？那怎麼可能？

(B) Of course not. <u>當然不會。</u>

(C) Of course. That's just a piece of cake.

當然介意。那很容易。

* mind〔maɪnd〕*v.* 介意　　loaf〔lof〕*n.* 一條
on *one's* ***way back*** 在某人回來的路上
Of course. 當然。
a piece of cake 簡單的事；輕而易舉

10. (**A**) Do you think people will go to heaven after death?

你覺得人死後會上天堂嗎？

(A) I don't believe it. <u>我不相信。</u>

(B) How come? 為什麼？

(C) I love Hawaii. 我愛夏威夷。

* heaven〔ˈhɛvən〕*n.* 天堂
  go to heaven 上天堂　　death〔dɛθ〕*n.* 死亡
  believe〔bəˈliv〕*v.* 相信
  How come? 為什麼；怎麼會？(= *Why?*)
  Hawaii〔həˈwaɪji〕*n.* 夏威夷

第三部分：言談理解（第 11-20 題，共 10 題）

11. (**C**)　W : Joe, look at the mess in your room. You really need
      to tidy it up.

　　女：喬，你看看你的房間一團亂。你真的需要好好整理一下。

　　M : Yeah, I know. Do you have any suggestions?

　　男：是，我知道。妳有任何建議嗎？

　　W : I think you should get rid of the things you don't
      need, or you may sell them online.

　　女：我覺得你應該把你不需要的東西丟掉，或者是上網賣掉。

　　M : Right. That's a good idea indeed. Thank you.

　　男：妳說的對。那的確是個好主意。謝謝。

　　Question : What does the woman suggest?

　　　　　　女士建議什麼？

　　(A) Surfing the Net. 瀏覽網路。

　　(B) She was shocked to see the mess in the man's room.
      她看到男子房間一團亂很震驚。

　　(C) Some ways to clean his room up.
      一些整理他房間的方法。

　　* mess〔mɛs〕*n.* 混亂　　***tidy up*** 使整齊；收拾
    suggestion〔səgˈdʒɛstʃən〕*n.* 建議
    get rid of 除去；丟掉　　sell〔sɛl〕*v.* 賣
    online〔͵ɑnˈlaɪn〕*adv.* 在網路上

indeed〔ɪn'did〕*adv.* 的確   suggest〔səg'dʒɛst〕*v.* 建議
surf〔sɝf〕*v.* 瀏覽   *the Net* 網路（= *the Internet*）
shocked〔ʃɑkt〕*adj.* 震驚的   *clean up* 打掃；整理

12. (**C**) W : Hello, may I help you?

女：哈囉，需要我的幫忙嗎？

M : Hi! Well, I am looking for sporting goods.

男：嗨！嗯，我在找運動用品。

W : The sporting goods department is located on the fifth
floor. You can take the escalator or the elevator on
the left.

女：運動用品部在五樓。你可以搭電扶梯或是位於左側的電梯。

M : Thank you so much.

男：非常感謝妳。

W : You're welcome. Have a nice day.

女：不客氣。祝您有美好的一天。

Question : What will the man probably do?

男士可能會做什麼？

(A) Look for his son. 找他的兒子。

(B) Take the fifth elevator. 搭第五台電梯。

(C) Find some stuff for sports. <u>找運動用的東西。</u>

* well〔wɛl〕*interj.* 嗯   *look for* 尋找
goods〔gʊdz〕*n. pl.* 商品   *sporting goods* 運動用品
department〔dɪ'pɑrtmənt〕*n.* 部門
located〔lo'ketɪd〕*adj.* 位於…的
escalator〔'ɛskə,letɚ〕*n.* 電扶梯
elevator〔'ɛlə,vetɚ〕*n.* 電梯
Have a nice day. 祝你有個美好的一天。
probably〔'prɑbəblɪ〕*adv.* 可能
stuff〔stʌf〕*n.* 東西；物品   sport〔sport〕*n.* 運動

13. (**B**) M : May I take your order now?

男：我可以幫您點菜了嗎？

W : Yes, I'd like the sirloin steak with mashed potatoes and gravy.

女：好的，我想要沙朗牛排配馬鈴薯泥和肉汁。

M : OK! How would you like your steak? Medium or well-done?

男：好的！您的牛排要幾分熟呢？五分還是全熟？

W : Medium, please.

女：請給我五分熟的。

M : All right. I'll be back with your food shortly.

男：好的。我不久後會來送上您的食物。

Question : Where does the conversation probably occur?

這段對話可能發生在哪裡？

(A) In the office. 在辦公室。

(B) In a restaurant. 在餐廳。

(C) In a cafeteria. 在自助餐廳。

* ***take one's order*** 幫某人點菜
  would like 想要
  sirloin〔'sɜ˙lɔɪn〕*n.* 牛腰肉上部
  sirloin steak 沙朗牛排　　***mashed potatoes*** 馬鈴薯泥
  gravy〔'grevɪ〕*n.* 肉汁
  medium〔'midɪəm〕*adj.* 五分熟的
  well-done〔'wɛl'dʌn〕*adj.* 全熟的　　***All right.*** 好。
  shortly〔'ʃɔrtlɪ〕*adv.* 很快地；不久
  conversation〔͵kɑnvɚ'seʃən〕*n.* 對話
  probably〔'prɑbəblɪ〕*adv.* 可能　　occur〔ə'kɜ〕*v.* 發生
  office〔'ɔfɪs〕*n.* 辦公室　　restaurant〔'rɛstərənt〕*n.* 餐廳
  cafeteria〔͵kæfə'tɪrɪə〕*n.* 自助餐廳

14. (**A**) W：Jack, would you help me to water the plants on the
　　　　　　　balcony?

女：傑克，你可以幫我替陽台的植物澆水嗎？

M：OK! I'd love to.

男：好的！我很樂意。

W：Thanks. It's so kind of you to give me a hand.

女：謝謝。你人真好，願意幫我忙。

M：Never mind. I love to take care of the plants
　　anyway.

男：沒關係，反正我喜歡照顧植物。

W：Right. No wonder everybody says you have a
　　green thumb.

女：沒錯。難怪每個人都說你擅長園藝。

Question：What does the woman want the man to do?
　　　　　　女士要男士做什麼？

(A) To take care of the plants. 照顧植物。

(B) To paint his thumb green. 把他的大拇指塗成綠色。

(C) She wants to take care of the man.
　　　她想要照顧男士。

* help〔hɛlp〕v. 幫助　　water〔ˋwɔtɚ〕v. 給…澆水
plant〔plænt〕n. 植物　　balcony〔ˋbælkənɪ〕n. 陽台
would love to V. 願意～
It's kind of sb. ***to V.*** 某人真好願意～
give sb. ***a hand*** 幫助某人
Never mind. 別在意；沒關係。　　***take care of*** 照顧
anyway〔ˋɛnɪˏwe〕adv. 無論如何；反正
thumb〔θʌm〕n. 大拇指
have a green thumb 擅長園藝
paint〔pet〕v. 油漆；（用顏料）畫

15. (**C**) W : Excuse me. How much is this dress?

女：對不起，這件洋裝多少錢？

M : It's NT$3,800.

男：台幣 3,800 元。

W : Can you give me a discount? How about NT$3,000.

女：你可以給我折扣嗎？3,000 元如何？

M : Sorry. This is the best price.

男：很抱歉，這是最優惠的價格了。

W : But I don't really have that much money with me.

女：但是我真身上的沒有那麼多錢。

M : I'm really sorry then.

男：那麼我真的很抱歉。

Question : Did the woman get the dress?

女士有買那件洋裝嗎？

(A) Yes, at the price of NT$3,800.

有，以台幣 3,800 元的價格。

(B) Yes, at the price of NT$3,000.

有，以台幣 3,000 元的價格。

(C) No, she didn't. <u>沒有，她沒買。</u>

* ***Excuse me.*** 對不起。【用於引起對方注意】
  dress〔drɛs〕*n.* 洋裝　　***NT$*** 新台幣（ *= New Taiwan Dollar* ）
  discount〔dɪsˈkaʊnt〕*n.* 折扣
  the best price 最優惠的價格
  How about…? …如何？　　get〔gɛt〕*v.* 買
  at the price of 以…的價格

16. (**C**) M : Mary, I need your advice.

男：瑪麗，我需要妳的建議。

W : What's up?

女：怎麼了？

M : I broke my mother's favorite bracelet by accident and I don't know what to do.

男：我意外地打破我媽媽最愛的手鐲，我現在不知道該怎麼辦。

W : That's easy. Just go apologize to her as soon as possible and ask for her forgiveness.

女：那很簡單。只要儘快去跟你母親道歉並請求原諒。

M : But I am afraid that she will be mad at me.

男：但我害怕她會生我的氣。

W : Ted, trust me. Honesty is the best policy. You'd better tell her the truth yourself.

女：泰德，相信我。誠實為上策。你最好自己跟她說實話。

Question : What does the woman want the man to do?

　　　　　 女士建議男士做什麼？

(A) To buy a new bracelet for his mom.

　　 去買個新手鐲給他的母親。

(B) To apologize to Mary as soon as possible.

　　 儘快跟瑪麗道歉。

(C) To be honest with his mom.

　　 去跟他的母親說實話。

* advice〔əd'vaɪs〕n. 勸告；建議

What's up? 發生什麼事；怎麼了？

favorite〔'fevərɪt〕adj. 最喜愛的

bracelet〔'breslɪt〕n. 手鐲

by accident 意外地　　apologize〔ə'palə,dʒaɪz〕v. 道歉

as soon as possible 儘快　　**ask for** 請求

forgiveness〔 fə'gɪvnɪs 〕 *n.* 原諒

mad〔 mæd 〕 *adj.* 生氣的 < *at* >

Honesty is the best policy. 誠實爲上策。

had better V. 最好　　　truth〔 truθ 〕 *n.* 眞相；事實

honest〔'ɑnɪst 〕 *adj.* 誠實的 < *with* >

17. (**C**)　W：Hello, this is Susan Lee.　May I speak to Frank?

　　　　女：哈囉，我是李蘇珊。我可以和法蘭克說話嗎？

　　　　M：Sorry, he went out ten minutes ago.　Would you like to leave a message for him?

　　　　男：很抱歉，他十分鐘前出去了。妳想要留言給他嗎？

　　　　W：OK.　Please tell him to pick up Mary at 10:30 at the train station tomorrow.

　　　　女：好的。請告訴他明天 10 點 30 分要去火車站接瑪麗。

　　　　M：Is that all?

　　　　男：就這樣嗎？

　　　　W：Yes.　Thank you very much.

　　　　女：是的，很感謝你。

　　　　M：You're welcome.

　　　　男：不客氣。

　　　　Question：Who will pick up Mary at 10:30 at the train station tomorrow?

　　　　　　　　　誰明天 10 點 30 分要去火車站接瑪麗？

　　　　(A) Nobody. 沒人。

　　　　(B) Susan will. 蘇珊。

　　　　(C) Frank will. 法蘭克。

* ***This is*** ~. 我是～。【用於講電話時】

　would like to V. 想要～

　leave a message for *sb.* 留言給某人　　***pick up*** *sb.* 接某人

18. (**C**) M : What do you plan to do after graduation?

男：妳畢業後打算做什麼？

W : I plan to find a job to support myself.

女：我打算找個工作養活自己。

M : Oh! I see. What kind of job do you want to do?
　　A full-time job? Or a part-time job?

男：喔！我知道了。妳想要做哪種工作？全職工作還是兼職？

W : Maybe a part-time job is suitable for me because I
　　plan to attend a graduate school to do further study.

女：或許兼職的工作適合我，因為我打算唸研究所繼續進修。

Question：What is true about the woman?

關於女士何者為真？

(A) She needs to work to support the man.

她需要工作來養活男士。

(B) She wants the man to find a part-time job for her.

她要男士幫她找份兼職工作。

(C) She plans to study and work at the same time.

她打算半工半讀。

* plan〔plæn〕*v.* 計畫；打算
  graduation〔‚grædʒʊ'eʃən〕*n.* 畢業
  job〔dʒɑb〕*n.* 工作
  support〔sə'port〕*v.* 支持；扶養
  support *oneself* 謀生；養活自己　　*I see.* 我知道了。
  full-time〔'fʊl'taɪm〕*adj.* 全職的
  part-time〔'pɑrt'taɪm〕*adj.* 兼職的
  maybe〔'mebɪ〕*adv.* 或許
  suitable〔'sutəbḷ〕*adj.* 適合的
  attend〔ə'tɛnd〕*v.* 上（學）　　***graduate school*** 研究所
  further study 進修　　***at the same time*** 同時

19. (**B**) W : Oliver, how was your trip to Nantou?

女: 奧利佛,你的南投之旅如何?

M : Not bad. Everything was great, but....

男: 不錯。一切都很好除了…。

W : What happened?

女: 發生什麼事?

M : I was caught in a traffic jam on the freeway on the first day. Except for that, the trip was fun.

男: 我第一天在高速公路上遇到塞車。除了那件事,這是趟有趣的旅遊。

W : Did anything interesting happen?

女: 有發生什麼有趣的事嗎?

M : Oh, yes. I made some new friends.

男: 喔,有的。我交了一些新朋友。

Question : What is true about the trip?

關於旅遊何者為真?

(A) Everything was great. 所有的事情都很棒。

(B) It was a trip by car. <u>這趟旅遊是開車去的。</u>

(C) It was a boat trip. 這是乘船的旅遊。

* trip〔trɪp〕*n.* 旅遊   ***Not bad.*** 不錯。
  great〔gret〕*adj.* 很棒的
  be caught in 遇到   ***a traffic jam*** 塞車
  freeway〔'fri,we〕*n.* 高速公路
  except for 除了…之外   fun〔fʌn〕*adj.* 有趣的
  interesting〔'ɪntrəstɪŋ〕*adj.* 有趣的
  make friends 交朋友
  by car 開車   boat〔bot〕*n.* 船

20. (**B**) W : I can't wait to see Lora tonight; we haven't met each other for years.

女：我等不急今晚要看到洛拉；我們已經好幾年沒看到彼此了。

M : Wow! You must be very excited. When and where will you meet tonight?

男：哇！妳一定非常興奮。妳們今晚何時何地要見面？

W : Yeah! We plan to meet at 7:00 at the Donut Café near the museum.

女：是的！我們打算七點在博物館附近的多那咖啡店見面。

M : I know the place. I can take you there.

男：我知道那個地方，我可以載妳去。

W : That would be great. Thanks for the ride.

女：那真是太棒了。謝謝你的便車。

Question : What are the two persons going to do?

　　　　　這兩個人即將要做什麼？

(A) They are going to have some coffee together.

他們要一起去喝點咖啡。

(B) They are going to drive to the Donut Café.

他們要開車去多那咖啡店。

(C) They are going to meet at the Donut Café.

他們要在多那咖啡店見面。

* **can't wait to V**. 等不及~　　excited〔ɪk'saɪtɪd〕*adj.* 興奮的
plan〔plæn〕*v.* 計畫；打算　　meet〔mit〕*v.* 會面
donut〔'do,nʌt〕*n.* 甜甜圈　　café〔kə'fe〕*n.* 咖啡店
museum〔mju'ziəm〕*n.* 博物館
place〔ples〕*n.* 地方　　ride〔raɪd〕*n.* 搭車；便車
have〔hæv〕*v.* 吃；喝　　drive〔draɪv〕*v.* 開車

TEST 5

第一部分：辨識句意（第1-3題，共3題）

作答說明：第1-3題每題有三張圖片，請依據所聽到的內容，選出符合描述的圖片，每題播放兩次。

示例題：你會看到

(A) 　　(B) 　　(C)

然後你會聽到……（播音）。依據所播放的內容，正確答案應該選A，請將答案卡該題「Ⓐ」的地方塗黑、塗滿，即：● Ⓑ Ⓒ

1. (A) 　　(B) 　　(C)

2. (A)　　　　　　　(B)　　　　　　　(C)

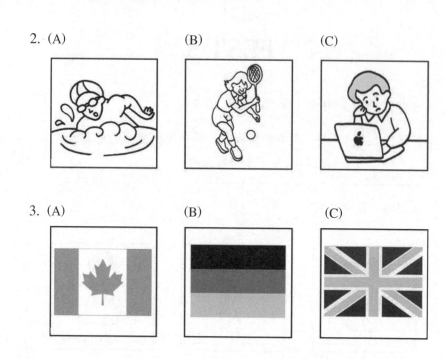

3. (A)　　　　　　　(B)　　　　　　　(C)

第二部分：基本問答（第 4-10 題，共 7 題）

作答說明： 第 4-10 題每題均有三個選項，請依據所聽到的內容，選出一個最適合的回應，每題播放兩次。

示例題：你會看到

(A) She is talking to the teacher.

(B) She is a student in my class.

(C) She is wearing a beautiful dress.

然後你會聽到……（播音）。依據所播放的內容，正確答案應該選 B，請將答案卡該題「Ⓑ」的地方塗黑、塗滿，即：Ⓐ ● Ⓒ

4. (A) I am sorry. I forgot to take you there.
   (B) It's very convenient.
   (C) It usually takes twenty minutes.

5. (A) Don't mention it.
   (B) Here you are.
   (C) Great! Let's have a celebration.

6. (A) She is really good at drawing.
   (B) It's not surprising. Her brother draws well.
   (C) Lily has studied drawing since she was five.

7. (A) But it doesn't look like rain. Why bother?
   (B) Don't worry. I will ask others for help.
   (C) All right. I will take a rain check.

8. (A) Good idea.
   (B) I enjoyed the food very much.
   (C) You are comfortable.

9. (A) It took me an hour.
   (B) Believe it or not.
   (C) You can say that again.

10. (A) It was difficult.
    (B) Sure. It's about time!
    (C) You must be patient.

第三部分：言談理解（第 11-20 題，共 10 題）

作答說明： 第 11-20 題每題均有三個選項，請依據所聽到的內容，選出一個最適合的答案，每題播放兩次。

示例題：你會看到

(A) 9:50.   (B) 10:00.   (C) 10:10.

然後你會聽到……（播音）。依據所播放的內容，正確答案應該選 B，請將答案卡該題「Ⓑ」的地方塗黑、塗滿，即：Ⓐ ● Ⓒ

11. (A) She can understand why the boy is interested in playing with the smartphone.
   (B) She was angry to see the boy play with the smartphone.
   (C) She wants to learn how to use smartphones.

12. (A) She suggests the man keep his own dog.
   (B) She suggests the man play with the dog.
   (C) She suggests the man leave the dog alone.

13. (A) Some crops.
   (B) How to make traditional Hakka tea.
   (C) The origin of traditional Hakka tea.

14. (A) In an elementary school.
   (B) In a university.
   (C) In a cafeteria.

15. (A) To brush her teeth.
   (B) To brush his teeth.
   (C) To see a dentist.

16. (A) The man should work hard.
   (B) The man should take time to dream.
   (C) The man should take life easy.

17. (A) In the bathroom.
   (B) In the garage.
   (C) In the kitchen.

18. (A) He was sent to the hospital.
   (B) He had bad luck.
   (C) He found his car.

19. (A) It's common.
   (B) It's as good as can be.
   (C) It's like a home.

20. (A) About one year.
   (B) About three years.
   (C) About one week.

TEST 5 詳解

第一部分：辨識句意（第 1-3 題，共 3 題）

1. (**A**) (A)  (B)  (C)

Somebody, call an ambulance. People got hurt in an accident. 來人呀，叫救護車。有人發生意外受傷了。

＊ call〔kɔl〕v. 叫　　ambulance〔ˈæmbjələns〕n. 救護車
get hurt 受傷　　accident〔ˈæksədənt〕n. 意外事故

2. (**A**) (A)  (B)  (C)

Jack enjoys swimming. He usually swims five times a week. 傑克喜歡游泳。他通常一週游五次。

＊ **enjoy + V-ing** 喜歡～　　usually〔ˈjuʒʊəlɪ〕adv. 通常
time〔taɪm〕n. 次

3. (**B**) (A)  (B)  (C)

I have made a pen-pal recently.　She is from Germany.

我最近交了一個筆友。她來自德國。

* pen-pal〔ˈpɛnˈpæl〕 n. 筆友　　recently〔ˈrisṇtlɪ〕 adv. 最近
Germany〔ˈdʒɝmənɪ〕 n. 德國

第二部分：基本問答（第 4-10 題，共 7 題）

4. (**C**) Excuse me.　How long will it take to get from here to the
MRT station?　對不起。從這裡到捷運站要多久？

    (A) I am sorry.　I forgot to take you there.
      我很抱歉。我忘了要帶你去那裡。

    (B) It's very convenient.　這很方便。

    (C) It usually takes twenty minutes.　<u>通常要花二十分鐘。</u>

    * ***Excuse me***. 對不起。【用於引起對方注意】
      take〔tek〕 v. 花（時間）
      MRT 捷運（ = *mass rapid transit* ）
      forgot〔fəˈgɑt〕 v. 忘記【forget 的過去式】
      convenient〔kənˈvɪnjənt〕 adj. 方便的

5. (**B**) John, please fetch me the thermometer.　I'm feeling
under the weather.

約翰，請幫我拿溫度計過來。我覺得身體不舒服。

    (A) Don't mention it.　不客氣。

    (B) Here you are.　<u>拿去吧。</u>

    (C) Great!　Let's have a celebration.
      太棒了！我們來慶祝一下。

    * fetch〔fɛtʃ〕 v. 把（東西）拿來
      thermometer〔θəˈmɑmətɚ〕 n. 溫度計
      under the weather 身體不舒服　　***Don't mention it***. 不客氣。
      Here you are. 你要的東西在這裡；拿去吧。
      Let's ~. 我們～吧。　　have〔hæv〕 v. 舉辦
      celebration〔ˌsɛləˈbreʃən〕 n. 慶祝；活動

6. (**B**) Lily's drawing is worse than her brother's.

莉莉畫的圖比她弟弟的還糟糕。

(A) She is really good at drawing. 她真的很擅長畫畫。

(B) It's not surprising. Her brother draws well.

這不令人驚訝。她弟弟畫得很好。

(C) Lily has studied drawing since she was five.

莉莉自從她五歲開始就學習畫畫。

* drawing〔'drɔ‧ɪŋ〕*n.* 畫　***be good at*** 擅長
surprising〔sə'praɪzɪŋ〕*adj.* 令人驚訝的
study〔'stʌdɪ〕*v.* 學習

7. (**A**) Honey, don't forget to take an umbrella with you in case of rain. 親愛的,別忘了帶支雨傘,以防下雨。

(A) But it doesn't look like rain. Why bother?

但看起來不像會下雨。何必麻煩呢?

(B) Don't worry. I will ask others for help.

別擔心。我會跟他人求助。

(C) All right. I will take a rain check.

沒關係。我改到下一次。

* honey〔'hʌnɪ〕*n.*(暱稱)親愛的　　forget〔fə'gɛt〕*v.* 忘記
umbrella〔ʌm'brɛlə〕*n.* 雨傘
in case of 以防萬一;唯恐　***look like*** 看起來像;有可能出現
bother〔'baðə〕*v.* 費事　***ask sb. for help*** 向某人求助
All right. 沒關係。　***take a rain check*** 改天;改到下一次

8. (**A**) Why don't we throw a party to welcome Sally back from Canada? 我們何不舉辦個派對歡迎莎莉從加拿大回來?

(A) Good idea. 好主意。

(B) I enjoyed the food very much. 我很喜歡這個食物。

(C) You are comfortable. 你很自在。

* ***throw a party*** 舉辦派對　　welcome〔'wɛlkəm〕*v.* 歡迎
Canada〔'kænədə〕*n.* 加拿大
enjoy〔ɪn'dʒɔɪ〕*v.* 享受；喜歡
comfortable〔'kʌmfətəbl̩〕*adj.* 舒服的；自在的

9. (**C**) The movie is so interesting that I feel like watching it
again and again.
電影如此有趣，以致於我想反覆看好幾次。

　(A) It took me an hour. 這花了我一個小時。

　(B) Believe it or not. 信不信由你。

　(C) You can say that again. 我非常同意。

* movie〔'muvɪ〕*n.* 電影　　interesting〔'ɪntrɪstɪŋ〕*adj.* 有趣的
feel like + V-ing 想要~　　***again and again*** 反覆地
take〔tek〕*v.* 花（時間）　　***Believe it or not.*** 信不信由你。
You can say that again. 我非常同意。

10. (**B**) We had better prepare for the final exam now.
我們最好現在準備期末考。

　(A) It was difficult. 這很困難。

　(B) Sure. It's about time! 當然。是時候了！

　(C) You must be patient. 你一定很有耐心。

* ***had better + V.*** 最好~
prepare〔prɪ'pɛr〕*v.* 準備 *< for >*
final exam 期末考　　difficult〔'dɪfəˌkʌlt〕*adj.* 困難的
It's about time. 時間差不多了；是時候了。
patient〔'peʃənt〕*adj.* 有耐心的

第三部分：言談理解（第 11-20 題，共 10 題）

11. (**A**) W：Ted, stop playing with your smart phone, will you?
女：泰德，停止玩你的智慧型手機，可以嗎？

M : But why? Mom! It's too interesting to stop. You
　　can do lots of things with a smartphone.

男：但是爲什麼？媽！這太有趣了，無法停下來。妳可以用智慧
　　型手機做很多事情。

W : Like what?

女：像是什麼？

M : You can take photos, listen to music, watch videos,
　　play games, and do some online shopping.

男：妳可以照相、聽音樂、看影片、玩遊戲，和線上購物。

W : Sounds like fun. No wonder you are hooked on it.

女：聽起來很有趣。難怪你會沈迷。

Question : What does the woman mean?

　　　　　　女士說的話是什麼意思？

(A) She can understand why the boy is interested in
　　playing with the smartphone.
　　她可以了解爲何男孩對玩智慧型手機有興趣。

(B) She was angry to see the boy play with the
　　smartphone. 她很生氣看到男孩玩智慧型手機。

(C) She wants to learn how to use smartphones.
　　要想要學會如何使用智慧型手機。

* smartphone〔'smɑrt,fon〕 n. 智慧型手機
　interesting〔'ɪntrɪstɪŋ〕 adj. 有趣的
　too…to~　太…而不~　　**take photos** 照相
　video〔'vɪdɪ,o〕 n. 影片　　**do some + V-ing** 做些~
　online〔,ɑn'laɪn〕 adj. 線上的
　sound〔saʊnd〕 v. 聽起來　　fun〔fʌn〕 adj. 有趣的
　no wonder 難怪　　**be hooked on** 迷上
　mean〔min〕 v. 意思是　　**be interested in** 對…感興趣
　use〔juz〕 v. 使用

12. (**C**)　W : Look! There is a dog on the MRT.

　　　女：你看！有一隻狗在捷運上。

　　　M : But a dog is not allowed to get on the public
　　　　　transportation system, is it?

　　　男：但是狗是不允許上大眾運輸系統的，是吧？

　　　W : No. I think it's a guide dog.

　　　女：不。我覺得那是隻導盲犬。

　　　M : A what?

　　　男：一隻什麼？

　　　W : A guide dog is a dog which is trained to lead and
　　　　　help the blind.

　　　女：導盲犬是訓練來引導和幫助盲人的狗。

　　　M : I see. It is so cute. Let's go play with it.

　　　男：我知道了。牠好可愛。我們來跟牠玩吧。

　　　W : Wait! Don't. We can't play with guide dogs while
　　　　　they are working.

　　　女：等等！不行。我們不能在導盲犬工作時跟牠玩。

　　　Question : What does the woman suggest?

　　　　　　　女士建議什麼？

　　(A)　She suggests the man keep his own dog.
　　　　她建議男士自己養一隻狗。

　　(B)　She suggest the man play with the dog.
　　　　她建議男士去和狗玩。

　　(C)　She suggests the man leave the dog alone.
　　　　她建議男士不要去打擾那隻狗。

* **_MRT_**　捷運（= _mass rapid transit_）
　　allow〔ə'laʊ〕_v._ 允許　　_**get on**_　上（公車、火車等）
　　public〔'pʌblɪk〕_adj._ 大眾的
　　transportation〔͵trænspə'teʃən〕_n._ 運輸

system〔'sɪstəm〕*n.* 系統　　***guide dog*** 導盲犬
train〔tren〕*v.* 訓練　　lead〔lid〕*v.* 引導
help〔hɛlp〕*v.* 幫助　　***the blind*** 盲人
I see. 我知道了；我了解了。　　***Let's ~*** . 我們一起～吧。
work〔wɝk〕*v.* 工作　　suggest〔səg'dʒɛst〕*v.* 建議
keep〔kip〕*v.* 養　　***leave⋯alone*** 不打擾⋯

13. (**B**) M : Hm, the tea tastes different.

男：嗯，這茶嘗起來不一樣。

W : Yes, it is a traditional Hakka drink called "leicha" in Chinese.

女：是的，這是傳統的客家飲料，中文叫做「擂茶」。

M : "Leicha"?

男：「擂茶」？

W : Right. It is also known as "ground tea."

女：沒錯。也稱作「地茶」。

M : Ground tea?

男：地茶？

W : Yes. We put a variety of grains, beans, seeds, nuts and tea leaves into a bowl and then we use a stick to grind it.

女：是的。我們放了很多種穀物、豆子、種子、堅果，和茶葉到茶缽裡，然後用擂棒研磨。

M : And you just stir all the stuff in hot water.

男：然後妳只是把所有這些東西用熱水攪拌？

W : Correct. It's very tasty. Would you like to try some?

女：沒錯。這很好喝。你想要喝一些嗎？

Question : What are the two people talking about?

這兩個人在討論什麼？

(A) Some crops. 一些農作物。

(B) How to make traditional Hakka tea.
如何製作傳統的客家茶。

(C) The origin of traditional Hakka tea.
傳統客家茶的起源。

* hm〔hm〕*interj.*（講話時停頓）嗯　　tea〔ti〕*n.* 茶
taste〔test〕*v.* 嚐起來　　traditional〔trə'dɪʃənḷ〕*adj.* 傳統的
drink〔drɪŋk〕*n.* 飲料　　Chinese〔tʃaɪ'niz〕*n.* 中文
be known as 被稱為　　**a variety of** 各種的
grain〔gren〕*n.* 穀物　　bean〔bin〕*n.* 豆子
seed〔sid〕*n.* 種子　　nut〔nʌt〕*n.* 堅果
tea leaf 茶葉　　bowl〔bol〕*n.* 碗；缽
stick〔stɪk〕*n.* 棍；棒　　grind〔graɪnd〕*v.* 磨
stir〔stɝ〕*v.* 攪拌　　stuff〔stʌf〕*n.* 東西
tasty〔'testɪ〕*adj.* 美味的　　**would like to V.** 想要
crop〔krɑp〕*n.* 農作物　　origin〔'ɔrədʒɪn〕*n.* 起源

14. (**A**)　M : Hello, welcome to our school. Let me introduce our facilities to you.

男：哈囉，歡迎來到我們的學校。讓我跟妳介紹我們的設施。

W : Wow, look at the huge playground.

女：哇，看看那巨大的操場。

M : Yes, you can see children enjoy playing games and running around on it. And on your right hand side is our gym, where children can play sports after school.

男：是的，妳可以看到孩子們在那裡快樂地玩遊戲和到處跑。而且在你的右手邊是我們的體育館，孩子們可以在放學後在那裡運動。

W : Yes, playing sports is good for their health.

女：是的，運動對他們的健康有益。

M : And the library is on your left hand side. Children can borrow books they like to read.

男：而且圖書館就在你的左手邊。孩子們可以借他們喜歡讀的書。

W : Yes, that's wonderful.

女：是的，那很棒。

M : Now it's about time to have lunch in the cafeteria. Follow me, please?

男：現在該是在自助餐廳吃午餐的時候了。請跟我來，好嗎？

Question : Where does the conversation probably occur?

這對話可能發生在哪裡？

(A) In an elementary school. 在小學裡。

(B) In a university. 在大學裡。

(C) In a cafeteria. 在自助餐廳裡。

* introduce〔͵ɪntrə'djus〕*v.* 介紹
  facilities〔fə'sɪlətɪz〕*n. pl.* 設施   huge〔hjudʒ〕*adj.* 巨大的
  playground〔'ple͵graʊnd〕*n.* 運動場
  enjoy + V-ing 享受～   **right hand side** 右手邊
  gym〔dʒɪm〕*n.* 體育館   **play sports** 運動
  after school 放學後   health〔hɛlθ〕*n.* 健康
  library〔'laɪ͵brɛrɪ〕*n.* 圖書館   **left hand side** 左手邊
  borrow〔'bɑro〕*v.* 借（入）
  wonderful〔'wʌndəfəl〕*adj.* 很棒的
  it's about time to V. 該是…的時候了   have〔hæv〕*v.* 吃
  cafeteria〔͵kæfə'tɪrɪə〕*n.* 自助餐廳
  conversation〔͵kɑnvə'seʃən〕*n.* 對話
  probably〔'prɑbəblɪ〕*adv.* 可能   occur〔ə'kɝ〕*v.* 發生
  elementary school 小學   university〔͵junə'vɝsətɪ〕*n.* 大學

15. (**B**) W : Jeff, don't forget to brush your teeth before going to bed.

女：傑夫。別忘了睡覺前要刷牙。

M : But Mom, I don't like to brush my teeth. Can I skip it just once?

男：但是，媽，我不喜歡刷牙。我可以就一次不要刷嗎？

W : You'd better not, unless you want to see a dentist.

女：你最好別這麼做，除非你想要看牙醫。

M : All right, all right. I am on my way now.

男：好吧，好吧。我現在去。

Question : What does the woman want the man to do?

女士要男士做什麼？

(A) To brush her teeth 去刷她的牙。

(B) To brush his teeth. <u>去刷他的牙。</u>

(C) To see a dentist. 去看牙醫。

* forget〔fɚˈgɛt〕*v.* 忘記　　brush〔brʌʃ〕*v.* 刷
  teeth〔tiθ〕*n. pl.* 牙齒【單數為 tooth】　　***go to bed*** 去睡覺
  skip〔skɪp〕*v.* 省去；跳過不做　　***had better not*** 最好不要
  dentist〔ˈdɛntɪst〕*n.* 牙醫　　***All right.*** 好吧。
  on one's way 在路上；動身前往

16. (**C**) M : I had a dream last night.

男：我昨晚做了一個夢。

W : Really? What did you dream of?

女：真的嗎？你夢到什麼？

M : In my dream, I was engaged in working nonstop.

男：在夢裡，我不停地工作。

W : You appear to be giving yourself too much pressure.
    You just need to take some time off and relax.

女：你似乎給你自己太多壓力了。你只是需要放假和休息。

Question : What does the woman mean?

女士的話是什麼意思？

(A) The man should work hard.

　　男士應該努力工作。

(B) The man should take time to dream.

　　男士應該挪出時間做夢。

(C) The man should take life easy. 男士應該放輕鬆。

* ***have a dream*** 做夢　　***dream of*** 夢到；夢見

　be engaged in 從事；忙於　　nonstop〔nɑn'stɑp〕*adv.* 不停地

　appear〔ə'pɪr〕*v.* 似乎（= *seem*）

　pressure〔'prɛʃɚ〕*n.* 壓力　　***take···off*** 放···的假

　relax〔rɪ'læks〕*v.* 放鬆；休息　　mean〔min〕*v.* 意思是

　take time to V. 挪出時間（做）　　***take···easy*** 輕鬆看待···

17. (**B**) W：Come on, Jimmy, come and help me.

　　女：來吧，吉米，來幫我。

　　M：OK! What are you going to do, Mom?

　　男：好的！媽，那妳要做什麼？

　　W：I want to wash my car. And I think you can wash

　　　　your bike, too.

　　女：我要洗車。我覺得你也可以洗你的腳踏車。

　　M：Wonderful. I can play with the water.

　　男：太棒了。我可玩水。

　　W：Don't get too wet, all right?

　　女：不要弄得濕答答的，好嗎？

　　M：Don't worry, Mom.

　　男：別擔心，媽。

　　Question：Where is the mother? 媽媽在哪裡？

　　(A) In the bathroom. 在浴室。

　　(B) In the garage. 在車庫。

　　(C) In the kitchen. 在廚房。

* **come on** 快點；來吧　　wash〔waʃ〕 v. 洗
  bike〔baɪk〕 n. 腳踏車　　wonderful〔'wʌndɚfəl〕 adj. 很棒的
  wet〔wɛt〕 adj. 濕的　　**All right?** 好嗎；可以嗎？
  bathroom〔'bæθ,rum〕 n. 浴室
  garage〔gə'rɑdʒ〕 n. 車庫　　kitchen〔'kɪtʃɪn〕 n. 廚房

18. (**B**)　W：Oh, my! Are you OK, Leo?

　　　女：喔，唉呀！李歐，你還好嗎？

　　　M：Today is not my day. My car wouldn't start so I had
　　　　to walk 50 minutes to work.

　　　男：我今天真不順。我的車發動不了，所以我必須走五十分鐘的
　　　　路來上班。

　　　W：Why are you all wet?

　　　女：為何你全身濕透？

　　　M：On my way to work, I fell in a pond.

　　　男：在我來上班的路上，我跌入池塘裡。

　　　W：Were you hurt?

　　　女：你有受傷嗎？

　　　M：A little. I sprained my ankle.

　　　男：有一點。我扭傷腳踝。

　　　Question：How was Leo today?　李歐今天如何？

　　　(A) He was sent to the hospital. 他被送去醫院。

　　　(B) He had bad luck. <u>他運氣不好。</u>

　　　(C) He found his car. 他找到了他的車。

* **my**〔maɪ〕 interj. 唉呀　　**not** one's **day** 不如意；不順利
  start〔stɑrt〕 v. 發動　　wet〔wɛt〕 adj. 濕的
  on one's **way to**… 在往…的路上　　pond〔pɑnd〕 n. 池塘
  be hurt 受傷　　sprain〔spren〕 v. 扭傷
  ankle〔'æŋkl̩〕 n. 腳踝　　hospital〔'hɑspɪtl̩〕 n. 醫院
  bad luck 運氣不好

19. (**B**) W : This is the most wonderful hotel I have ever been to.

女：這是我去過最棒的飯店了。

M : It is called the King's Garden. Everything here is excellent.

男：這間叫作國王花園。這裡所有的東西都很棒。

W : I couldn't agree with you more. The food and the service are amazing.

女：我非常同意你。食物和服務真令人吃驚。

M : That's true! I have never had a more tasty lunch!

男：沒錯！我沒有吃過如此美味的午餐。

W : Why not spend our Valentine's Day here?

女：何不在這裡過情人節？

M : That sounds great.

男：那聽起來很棒。

Question : How is the hotel? 旅館如何？

(A) It's common. 很普通。

(B) It's as good as can be. 非常好。

(C) It's like a home. 像家一樣。

* wonderful〔'wʌndəfəl〕 *adj.* 很棒的
hotel〔ho'tɛl〕 *n.* 旅館；飯店　　***have ever been to*** 曾經去過
excellent〔'ɛksḷənt〕 *adj.* 極好的
couldn't agree with *sb.* ***more*** 非常同意某人
service〔'sɝvɪs〕 *n.* 服務
amazing〔ə'mezɪŋ〕 *adj.* 令人吃驚的
true〔tru〕 *adj.* 真實的；確實的　　tasty〔'testɪ〕 *adj.* 美味的
Why not V.? 何不～？　　spend〔spɛnd〕 *v.* 度過
Valentine's Day 情人節　　sound〔saʊnd〕 *v.* 聽起來
common〔'kɑmən〕 *adj.* 普通的
as…as can be 再…不過了；非常（＝*very*）

20. (**A**) W：Ronald hasn't found his lost pet, has he?

女：羅納德還沒找到他走失的寵物，是吧？

M：No, not yet. He prays that it will come back to him soon.

男：不，還沒。他祈禱牠會早日回到他身邊。

W：He used to walk his dog and feed it every day after work. He must be very sad now.

女：他以前會每天下班去遛狗並餵牠。他現在一定很難過。

M：Yes, it was his present last Children's Day. They have been together every day since then.

男：是的，這是他去年兒童節的禮物。他們自從那時起每天都一起。

W：What can we do for him?

女：我們可以為他做點什麼？

M：Perhaps we can ask all our friends to help him.

男：或許我們可以請所有的朋友來幫他。

Question：How long did Ronald keep the dog?

羅納德養他的狗多久了？

(A) About one year. 大約一年。

(B) About three years. 大約三年。

(C) About one week. 大約一週。

* lost〔lɔst〕*adj.* 走失的　　pet〔pɛt〕*n.* 寵物
  not yet 還沒　　pray〔pre〕*v.* 祈禱
  used to V. 以前常常～　　***walk one's dog*** 遛狗
  feed〔fid〕*v.* 餵　　***after work*** 下班後
  present〔'prɛznt〕*n.* 禮物　　last〔læst〕*adj.* 上次的
  Children's Day 兒童節
  perhaps〔pɚ'hæps〕*adv.* 可能；或許

TEST 6

第一部分：辨識句意（第1-3題，共3題）

作答說明：第1-3題每題有三張圖片，請依據所聽到的內容，選出
符合描述的圖片，每題播放兩次。

示例題：你會看到

(A) 　　　(B) 　　　(C)

然後你會聽到……（播音）。依據所播放的內容，正確答案應該
選A，請將答案卡該題「Ⓐ」的地方塗黑、塗滿，即：● Ⓑ Ⓒ

1. (A) 　　　(B) 　　　(C)

2. (A)　　　　　(B)　　　　　(C)

3. (A)　　　　　(B)　　　　　(C)

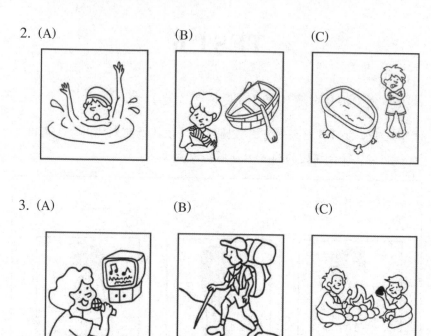

第二部分：基本問答（第 4-10 題，共 7 題）

作答說明： 第 4-10 題每題均有三個選項，請依據所聽到的內容，選出一個最適合的回應，每題播放兩次。

示例題：你會看到

(A) She is talking to the teacher.

(B) She is a student in my class.

(C) She is wearing a beautiful dress.

然後你會聽到……（播音）。依據所播放的內容，正確答案應該選 B，請將答案卡該題「Ⓑ」的地方塗黑、塗滿，即：Ⓐ ● Ⓒ

---

4. (A) Yes, he loves music.
   (B) Yes, he bought a cooking book.
   (C) No, his ears are hurt.

5. (A) Not at all.
   (B) Let's go.
   (C) Cool. See you later.

6. (A) My mom will go there, too.
   (B) They don't have time for it.
   (C) Yes. It's me.

7. (A) It's too beautiful to be true.
   (B) Why not?
   (C) The yellow one, please.

8. (A) How about some backpacks?
   (B) Take it easy. Just have a good sleep.
   (C) Sneakers are a good idea.

9. (A) OK, here you are.
   (B) Sorry, I have no skates.
   (C) Learn how to balance first.

10. (A) OK. Then I will have to take the first flight.
    (B) Yes. The weather in Taipei is wonderful.
    (C) Oh, how about taking a taxi with me?

第三部分：言談理解（第 11-20 題，共 10 題）

作答說明：第 11-20 題每題均有三個選項，請依據所聽到的內容，選出一個最適合的答案，每題播放兩次。

示例題：你會看到

(A) 9:50.　　(B) 10:00.　　(C) 10:10.

然後你會聽到……（播音）。依據所播放的內容，正確答案應該選 B，請將答案卡該題「Ⓑ」的地方塗黑、塗滿，即：Ⓐ ● Ⓒ

11. (A) The boots are not
    big enough for the
    woman.
    (B) The man wants to
    buy boots for the
    woman.
    (C) The man likes the
    boots and wants to
    buy them.

12. (A) About 20.
    (B) About 8.
    (C) About 50.

13. (A) Singing.
    (B) Dancing.
    (C) Magic.

14. (A) She was caught in
    heavy traffic.
    (B) She ran through
    a red light.
    (C) She was stopped
    by a policeman.

15. (A) The mountains.
    (B) The beach.
    (C) The mall.

16. (A) He doesn't agree with
    what the woman is doing.
    (B) He has had the experience
    of losing weight himself.
    (C) He does think the woman
    has to lose some weight
    for the sake of her health.

17. (A) Computers.
    (B) Music.
    (C) Languages.

18. (A) In the man's car.
    (B) By taxi.
    (C) On foot.

19. (A) 0926-571-786.
    (B) 0927-157-876.
    (C) 0926-156-867.

20. (A) They will do some
    shopping in the
    department store.
    (B) They like the stinky tofu.
    (C) Both of them will buy
    things in the night market.

TEST 6 詳解

第一部分：辨識句意（第 1-3 題，共 3 題）

1. (**A**) (A)   (B)   (C)

The girl trained her bird to say hello.

女孩訓練她的鳥說哈囉。

* train〔tren〕v. 訓練　　hello〔həˈlo〕interj. 哈囉

2. (**C**) (A)   (B)   (C)

I can't take a hot bath now because there isn't any gas.

我現在無法洗熱水澡，因為沒有瓦斯。

* **take a bath** 洗澡　　gas〔gæs〕n. 瓦斯

3. (**C**) (A)   (B)   (C)

They were having fun together around the campfire.
他們圍著營火玩得很愉快。

* **have fun** 玩得愉快　　campfire〔'kæmp,faɪr〕*n.* 營火

第二部分：基本問答（第 4-10 題，共 7 題）

4. (**A**) Andy really has an ear for good music.
安迪真的能夠鑑賞好音樂。

(A) Yes, he loves music. 是的，他喜愛音樂。

(B) Yes, he bought a cooking book.
　　是的，他買了一本食譜。

(C) No, his ears are hurt. 不，他的耳朵受傷了。

* **have an ear for** 對…聽覺靈敏；有…鑑賞力
　　music〔'mjuzɪk〕*n.* 音樂
　　cooking book 食譜（= *cookbook*）　　**be hurt** 受傷

5. (**A**) Peter said I'm too short for the basketball team.
彼得說我太矮了，不能加入籃球隊。

(A) Not at all. 完全不會。

(B) Let's go. 我們走吧。

(C) Cool. See you later. 好酷喔。待會兒見。

* **too…for N.** 太…而無法　　basketball〔'bæskɪt,bɔl〕*n.* 籃球
　　team〔tim〕*n.* 隊　　**Not at all.** 一點也不；完全不會。
　　Let's ~. 我們一起~吧。　　**See you later.** 待會兒見。

6. (**C**) Are you the host of the party tonight?
你是今晚派對的主辦人嗎？

(A) My mom will go there, too. 我媽媽也會去。

(B) They don't have time for it. 他們沒時間參加。

(C) Yes. It's me. 是的。我是。

* host〔host〕*n.* 主人　　party〔'partɪ〕*n.* 派對
have no time for N. 沒時間（做）

7. (**B**) I don't like the small plant pot. 我不喜歡這個小盆栽。

(A) It's too beautiful to be true. 這太漂亮了，不像真的。

(B) Why not? 為什麼不？

(C) The yellow one, please. 請給我黃色的。

* ***plant pot*** 盆栽　　***too…to~*** 太…以致於不~
yellow〔'jɛlo〕*adj.* 黃色的

8. (**B**) I am so nervous about tomorrow's speech contest.
對於明天的演講比賽我感到很緊張。

(A) How about some backpacks? 一些背包如何？

(B) Take it easy. Just have a good sleep.
放輕鬆。好好睡一覺。

(C) Sneakers are a good idea. 運動鞋是個好主意。

* nervous〔'nɝvəs〕*adj.* 緊張的　　speech〔spitʃ〕*n.* 演講
contest〔'kɑntɛst〕*n.* 比賽　　***How about~?*** ~如何？
backpack〔'bæk,pæk〕*n.* 背包　　***take it easy*** 放輕鬆
sneakers〔'snikɚz〕*n. pl.* 運動鞋

9. (**C**) Can you give me some tips for skating?
你可以告訴一些我溜冰的訣竅嗎？

(A) OK, here you are. 好的，拿去吧。

(B) Sorry, I have no skates. 抱歉，我沒有溜冰鞋。

(C) Learn how to balance first. 一開始先學習如何保持平衡。

* tip〔tɪp〕*n.* 秘訣；訣竅
skate〔sket〕*v.* 溜冰　*n. pl.* 溜冰鞋
Here you are. 你要的東西在這；拿去吧。
learn〔lɝn〕*v.* 學習　　balance〔'bæləns〕*v.* 保持平衡

10. (**A**) Is it possible for you to arrive here earlier tomorrow?

你明天能早一點到這裡嗎？

(A) OK. Then I will have to take the first flight.

好的。那我就得搭到第一班的飛機。

(B) Yes. The weather in Taipei is wonderful.

是的。台北的天氣很棒。

(C) Oh, how about taking a taxi with me?

喔，跟我一起搭計程車如何？

* possible〔'pɑsəbḷ〕*adj.* 可能的 arrive〔ə'raɪv〕*v.* 到達
flight〔flaɪt〕*n.* 班機 weather〔'wɛðɚ〕*n.* 天氣
wonderful〔'wʌdəfəl〕*adj.* 很棒的
How about~? ~如何？ taxi〔'tæksɪ〕*n.* 計程車

第三部分：言談理解（第 11-20 題，共 10 題）

11. (**A**) W : Look, George, shall I return these boots?

女：你看，喬治，我該退還這雙靴子嗎？

M : Honey, what's wrong with them?

男：親愛的，它們有什麼問題嗎？

W : They are too small.

女：它們太小了。

M : Did you try them on before you paid the bill?

男：妳付帳前有試穿過嗎？

W : No, I didn't. I just took a look and I bought them.

女：不，沒有。我只是看了一下就買了。

M : OK. When will you go? I can go with you.

男：好的。妳何時要去？我可以跟妳去。

W : You are so sweet.

女：你真好。

Question : What's true according to the dialogue?

根據對話，何者爲眞？

(A) The boots are not big enough for the woman.

靴子對女士來說不夠大。

(B) The man wants to buy boots for the woman.

男士想要買靴子給女士。

(C) The man likes the boots and wants to buy them.

男士喜歡那雙靴子，想要買下來。

* return 〔 rɪ'tɜn 〕 v. 退還　　boots 〔 buts 〕 n. pl. 靴子
honey 〔 'hʌnɪ 〕 n. (暱稱) 親愛的
What's wrong with ~? ～有問題嗎？　　*try on* 試穿
pay 〔 pe 〕 v. 支付　　bill 〔 bɪl 〕 n. 帳單
take a look 看一下
bought 〔 bɔt 〕 v. 買【buy 的過去式】
sweet 〔 swit 〕 adj. 溫柔的；善良的

12. (**A**) W : Dear, take good care of yourself in Tainan.

女：親愛的，在台南要好好照顧你自己。

M : I will. It's time to say goodbye. Here comes the train.

男：我會的。該是說再見的時候了。火車來了。

W : Anyway, I hope you'll study hard at college.

女：無論如何，我希望你在大學能用功讀書。

M : I'll try my best. There goes the whistle. Goodbye,
Mom.

男：我會盡力。汽笛聲響了。再見，媽。

W : All right, keep your promise.

女：好的，要遵守你的承諾。

M : See you!

男：再見！

Question：How old is the man? 男士幾歲？

(A) About 20. 大約二十歲。

(B) About 8. 大約八歲。

(C) About 50. 大約五十歲。

* ***take good care of*** 好好照顧
   it's time to V. 該是～的時候了
   anyway〔ˈɛnɪ,we〕*adv.* 無論如何　　***study hard*** 用功讀書
   hard〔hɑrd〕*adv.* 努力地　　college〔ˈkɑlɪdʒ〕*n.* 大學
   whistle〔ˈhwɪsl̩〕*n.* 汽笛；鳴聲
   go〔go〕*v.* 響　　***All right.*** 好的。
   keep *one's* ***promise*** 信守承諾　　***See you.*** 再見。

13. (**A**)　W：How was the talent show, Billy?

女：選秀節目如何，比利？

M：It was wonderful, Sara. It was beyonds words.

男：很棒，莎拉。無法用言語形容。

W：What a pity. I wish I had been able to take part in it.
   In fact, I was busy finishing my science report.

女：真可惜。真希望我當時能夠參加。事實上，我忙著做我的科
   學報告。

M：Don't worry. You still have another chance next year.

男：別擔心。妳明年還有機會。

W：That's true.

女：沒錯。

M：You can sing and I can dance, then.

男：那麼，妳可以唱歌，我可以跳舞。

Question：What is Sara good at?

　　　　　莎拉擅長什麼？

(A) Singing. 唱歌。

(B) Dancing. 跳舞。

(C) Magic. 魔術。

* **talent show** 選秀節目　　wonderful (ˈwʌdəfəl) *adj.* 很棒的
  beyond words 無法用言語形容
  pity (ˈpɪtɪ) *n.* 可惜的事　　**be able to V.** 能夠～
  take part in 參加　　**in fact** 事實上
  be busy + V-ing 忙於～　　science (ˈsaɪəns) *n.* 科學
  report (rɪˈport) *n.* 報告　　worry (ˈwɝɪ) *v.* 擔心
  chance (tʃæns) *n.* 機會　　**That's true.** 真的；你說的對。
  sing (sɪŋ) *v.* 唱歌　　dance (dæns) *v.* 跳舞
  be good at 擅長　　magic (ˈmædʒɪk) *n.* 魔術

14. (**C**) W : Dad, I was given a ticket this morning.

女： 爸爸，我今早被開罰單了。

M : How come, Tina?

男： 為什麼，蒂娜？

W : I was talking on the cellphone in the car and I didn't
see the policeman.

女： 我在車裡講手機，而且沒有看到警察。

M : It's your fault.

男： 這是妳的錯。

W : I see.　I have learned a lesson.

女： 我知道了。我學到教訓了。

M : You should keep it in mind for good.

男： 妳要應該永遠牢記在心中。

Question : What happened to Tina this morning?

蒂娜今天早上發生什麼事？

(A) She was caught in heavy traffic.

她遇到交通壅塞。

(B) She ran through a red light. 她闖紅燈。

(C) She was stopped by a policeman.

她被警察攔下來。

* *give sb. a ticket* 開某人罰單　　*How come?* 怎麼會；為什麼？
talk on the phone 講電話　　policeman〔pə'lismən〕*n.* 警察
fault〔fɔlt〕*n.* 過錯　　*I see.* 我知道了。
learn a lesson 學到教訓
keep…in mind 把…牢記在心　　*for good* 永遠
be caught in 遇到　　*heavy traffic* 交通壅塞
run through a red light 闖紅燈

15. (**B**) W : Leo, may I borrow a backpack from you?

女：李歐，我可以跟你借背包嗎？

M : Sure, Fiona. Here it is.

男：當然，費歐娜。拿去吧。

W : I also need a cap and sunglasses. May I borrow them from you, too?

女：我也需要一頂帽子和太陽眼鏡。我也可以跟你借這些嗎？

M : All right. When do you need them?

男：好的。妳什麼時候需要？

W : How about this Friday?

女：這星期五如何？

M : No problem. By the way, you may need a swimming suit, too.

男：沒問題。順便一提，妳可能也需要泳衣。

Question : Where may Fiona go? 費歐娜可能會去哪？

(A) The mountains. 山上。

(B) The beach. 海灘。

(C) The mall. 購物中心。

* borrow〔'bɔro〕*v.* 借（入）　　backpack〔'bæk,pæk〕*n.* 背包
sure〔ʃur〕*adv.* 當然　　***Here it is.*** 你要的東西在這裡；拿去吧。
cap〔kæp〕*n.*（無邊的）帽子
sunglasses〔'sʌn,glæsɪz〕*n. pl.* 太陽眼鏡　　***All right.*** 好的。
How about…? …如何？　　***No problem.*** 沒問題。
by the way 順便一提　　***swimming suit*** 泳衣
mall〔mɔl〕*n.* 購物中心

16. (**A**) M : Time for lunch. Will you come have lunch with me, Sara?

男：該是吃午餐的時候了。妳要來跟我吃午餐嗎，莎拉？

W : I'd like to, but I can't.

女：我很想，但不行。

M : Why not? Are you ill?

男：為何不行？妳生病了嗎？

W : No. It's just because I am on a diet now.

女：不。是因為我在節食。

M : Again? So you decided not to eat anything for days?

男：又來了？所以妳決定好幾天都不吃東西？

W : I'm afraid so. Do you have any other suggestion on how to lose weight?

女：恐怕是如此。你有任何可以減肥的建議嗎？

M : You bet. Eating properly and exercising regularly are a healthful way to keep in good shape.

男：當然。適當的飲食和規律的運動是可以讓妳保持健康的方式。

Question : What does the man imply?

男士暗示什麼？

(A) He doesn't agree with what the woman is doing.

<u>他不同意女士的做法。</u>

(B) He has had the experience of losing weight himself.

他自己有減肥的經驗。

(C) He thinks the woman has to lose some weight for the sake of her health.

他覺得女士應該為了健康而減些體重。

* *Time for N.* 該是…的時候了。(= *It's time for N.*)
have〔hæv〕*v.* 吃　　*would like to V.* 想要～
ill〔ɪl〕*adj.* 生病的　　*be on a diet* 節食
decide〔dɪˋsaɪd〕*v.* 決定　　*I'm afraid so.* 恐怕是如此。
suggestion〔səgˋdʒɛstʃən〕*n.* 建議　　on〔ɑn〕*prep.* 關於
weight〔wet〕*n.* 體重　　*lose weight* 減肥；減重
You bet. 當然。　　properly〔ˋprɑpəlɪ〕*adv.* 適當地
exercise〔ˋɛksəˏsaɪz〕*v.* 運動
regularly〔ˋrɛgjələlɪ〕*adv.* 規律地
healthful〔ˋhɛlθfəl〕*adj.* 健康的
keep in good shape 保持健康良好
imply〔ɪmˋplaɪ〕*v.* 暗示
agree〔əˋgri〕*v.* 同意 < *with* >
experience〔ɪkˋspɪrɪəns〕*n.* 經驗
for the sake of 為了　　health〔hɛlθ〕*n.* 健康

17. (**C**) W：Dad, I want to learn Japanese.

女：爸爸，我想要學日文。

M：What? You have learned French and German.

男：什麼？妳已經學了法文跟德文了。

W：I know. But I'm very interested in languages.

女：我知道。但是我對學語言很有興趣。

M：But you learned them only for a few months and then you quit.

男：但是妳只學了幾個月就放棄了。

W : This time I am serious. I really like Japanese.

女：這一次我是認真的。我真的喜歡日文。

M : I need to think about it.

男：我需要考慮一下。

Question : What is the woman interested in?

女士對什麼有興趣？

(A) Computers. 電腦。

(B) Music. 音樂。

(C) Languages. 語言。

* learn〔lɜn〕*v.* 學習　　Japanese〔͵dʒæpəˊniz〕*n.* 日文
French〔frɛntʃ〕*n.* 法文　　German〔ˊdʒɜmən〕*n.* 德文
be interested in 對…有興趣
language〔ˊlæŋgwɪdʒ〕*n.* 語言
quit〔kwɪt〕*v.* 放棄　　time〔taɪm〕*n.* 次
serious〔ˊsɪrɪəs〕*adj.* 認真的　　**think about** 考慮
computer〔kəmˊpjutɚ〕*n.* 電腦
music〔ˊmjuzɪk〕*n.* 音樂

18. (**B**) W : Josh, when will the taxi arrive?

女：喬希，計程車何時會到？

M : I guess it is on the way. Let me call the taxi company.

男：我想已經在路上了。我來打給計程車公司。

W : What did they say?

女：他們說什麼？

M : They said the taxi driver is caught in a traffic jam now.

男：他們說現在計程車司機遇到塞車。

W : Then we will be late for Lina's wedding.

女：那莉娜的婚禮我們會遲到。

M：I'm afraid so.　But my car broke down and it's too far to walk there.　All we can do is to wait for the taxi.

男：恐怕是如此。但我的車故障了，而且那裡太遠了，無法走路去。我們能做的就是等計程車。

Question：How will they go to Lina's wedding?

他們要如何去莉娜的婚禮？

(A) In the man's car. 開男士的車。

(B) By taxi. 搭計程車。

(C) On foot. 步行。

* taxi〔'tæksɪ〕n. 計程車

　arrive〔ə'raɪv〕v. 到達

　guess〔gɛs〕v. 推測；猜想

　be on the way 在路上

　call〔kɔl〕v. 打電話（給）

　company〔'kʌmpənɪ〕n. 公司

　driver〔'draɪvɚ〕n. 司機

　be caught in 遇到　**a traffic jam** 塞車

　late〔let〕adj. 遲到的 < for >

　wedding〔'wɛdɪŋ〕n. 婚禮

　I'm afraid so. 恐怕是如此。

　break down 故障；拋錨

　too…to ~ 太…以致於不~

　all one **can do is** (to) **V.** 某人所能做的就是~

　wait〔wet〕v. 等待 < for >

　by + 交通工具　搭乘…　　**on foot** 步行

19. (**C**) W：Excuse me.　I want to book a table for two.

女：對不起。我想要訂兩人的桌子。

M：Is it for tonight?

男：是今晚的嗎？

W : Yes. At about 8:00 p.m.

女：是的。大約晚上八點。

M : OK. What's your name?

男：好的。請問您的大名是？

W : Wang Li-hone.

女：王力宏。

M : And your cellphone number, please.

男：請留下您的手機號碼。

W : 0926-156-867.

女：0926-156-867。

Question : What's Mr. Wang's cellphone number?

王先生的手機號碼是幾號？

(A) 0926-571-786. 0926-571-786。

(B) 0927-157-876. 0927-157-876。

(C) 0926-156-867. 0926-156-867。

* book〔buk〕*v.* 預訂
  a table for 一張（幾人）的桌子
  p.m. 午後（= *post meridiem*）
  cellphone number 手機號碼

20. (**A**) W : Eric, let's go to the night market for dinner this evening.

女：艾瑞克，我們今晚去夜市吃晚餐吧。

M : Sounds great. I like the stinky tofu there.

男：聽起來很棒。我喜歡那裡的臭豆腐。

W : Me, too. And we can do some shopping after dinner.

女：我也是。而且我們可以吃完晚餐後買些東西。

M : Yes. I need new socks.

男：是的。我需要新的襪子。

W : And I want to buy new clothes.

女：而我想要買新衣服。

M : Everything seems much cheaper in the night market than in the department store.

男：在夜市乎所有的東西裡都比百貨公司便宜很多。

Question : What's *not* true according to the dialogue?

　　　　根據對話，何者「不是」真的？

(A) They will do some shopping in the department store.

　　他們會去百貨公司買點東西。

(B) They like the stinky tofu.

　　他們喜歡臭豆腐。

(C) Both of them will buy things in the night market.

　　他們兩人都會在夜市買東西。

* *Let's ~.* 我們一起~吧。

night market 夜市

sound〔saʊnd〕v. 聽起來

great〔gret〕adj. 很棒的

stinky〔'stɪŋkɪ〕adj. 臭的

tofu〔'tofu〕n. 豆腐

do some shopping 買點東西

socks〔sɑks〕n. pl. 襪子

clothes〔kloz〕n. pl. 衣服

seem〔sim〕v. 似乎

cheap〔tʃip〕adj. 便宜的

department store 百貨公司

according to 根據

dialogue〔'daɪə,lɔg〕n. 對話

TEST 7

第一部分：辨識句意（第 1-3 題，共 3 題）

作答說明：第 1-3 題每題有三張圖片，請依據所聽到的內容，選出
符合描述的圖片，每題播放兩次。

示例題：你會看到

(A) 　　　(B) 　　　(C)

然後你會聽到……（播音）。依據所播放的內容，正確答案應該
選 A，請將答案卡該題「Ⓐ」的地方塗黑、塗滿，即：● Ⓑ Ⓒ

---

1. (A) 　　　(B) 　　　(C)

2. (A)　　　　　(B)　　　　　(C)

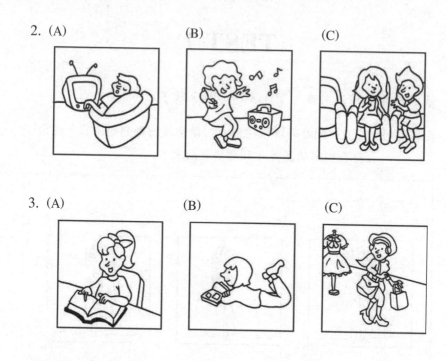

3. (A)　　　　　(B)　　　　　(C)

第二部分：基本問答（第 4-10 題，共 7 題）

作答說明：第 4-10 題每題均有三個選項，請依據所聽到的內容，選出一個最適合的回應，每題播放兩次。

示例題：你會看到

(A) She is talking to the teacher.

(B) She is a student in my class.

(C) She is wearing a beautiful dress.

然後你會聽到……（播音）。依據所播放的內容，正確答案應該選 B，請將答案卡該題「Ⓑ」的地方塗黑、塗滿，即：Ⓐ ● Ⓒ

---

4. (A) It is Wednesday.
   (B) It is Friday.
   (C) It is Sunday.

5. (A) Lots of things. I mostly use it to watch movies.
   (B) Lots of things. I mostly use it to cool me down.
   (C) I don't think so.

6. (A) Don't forget to put on your coat.
   (B) Yes. I feel sweaty today.
   (C) Be careful. Don't touch it.

7. (A) You are too big for it.
   (B) Never mind.
   (C) It's my pleasure.

8. (A) Well, I would need a good cook.
   (B) Well, I love sandwiches and salads.
   (C) Well, I'm getting mostly A's and B's.

9. (A) He is handsome.
   (B) He is really lazy.
   (C) He really works hard.

10. (A) Anything good happened?
    (B) She eats too much.
    (C) She is overweight.

第三部分：言談理解（第 11-20 題，共 10 題）

作答說明： 第 11-20 題每題均有三個選項，請依據所聽到的內容，
　　　　　選出一個最適合的答案，每題播放兩次。

示例題：你會看到

(A) 9:50.　　(B) 10:00.　　(C) 10:10.

然後你會聽到……（播音）。依據所播放的內容，正確答案應該
選 B，請將答案卡該題「Ⓑ」的地方塗黑、塗滿，即：Ⓐ ● Ⓒ

---

11. (A) We can recycle
        bottles.
    (B) We can buy more
        paper bags.
    (C) We can eat out more
        often.

12. (A) Because everything
        is cheaper.
    (B) Because many
        people live around it.
    (C) Because its food is
        fresh.

13. (A) By 5:00.
    (B) By 5:45.
    (C) By 4:15.

14. (A) May.
    (B) August.
    (C) December.

15. (A) The doctor put some
        ice on her head.
    (B) The doctor gave her
        some medicine.
    (C) The doctor gave her
        a shot.

16. (A) A story.
    (B) A plant.
    (C) An animal.

17. (A) Who should clean the
        room.
    (B) Parents' right to their
        kids' things.
    (C) Children' right to
        privacy.

18. (A) At a concert.
    (B) At a bus stop.
    (C) At a supermarket.

19. (A) Hank.
    (B) Ivy.
    (C) Ms. Pan.

20. (A) She thinks the man
        should make a decision
        quickly.
    (B) She thinks the man
        should take her
        advice.
    (C) She thinks the man
        can ask for others'
        opinions.

TEST 7 詳解

第一部分：辨識句意（第 1-3 題，共 3 題）

1. (**B**) (A)　　　　　　(B)　　　　　　(C)

  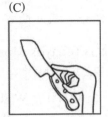

Don't touch the vase. It breaks easily.

不要碰那花瓶。它很容易破。

* touch〔tʌtʃ〕v. 觸摸；碰　　vase〔ves〕n. 花瓶
　break〔brek〕v. 破裂　　easily〔'izḷɪ〕adv. 容易地

2. (**C**) (A)　　　　　　(B)　　　　　　(C)

You should keep your voice down when you see a movie.

當妳看電影的時候，應該降低音量。

* ***keep down*** 使小聲　　voice〔vɔɪs〕n. 聲音
　see a movie 看電影

3. (**A**) (A)　　　　　　(B)　　　　　　(C)

Having correct study habits is important for students.

有正確的讀書習慣對學生是很重要的。

* correct〔kə'rɛkt〕*adj.* 正確的　　study〔'stʌdɪ〕*n.* 讀書
habit〔'hæbɪt〕*n.* 習慣　　important〔ɪm'pɔrtn̩t〕*adj.* 重要的

第二部分：基本問答（第 4-10 題，共 7 題）

4. (**A**) Today is Monday. What day is the day after tomorrow?

今天是星期一。後天是星期幾？

(A) It is Wednesday. 星期三。

(B) It is Friday. 星期五。

(C) It is Sunday. 星期日。

* **the day after tomorrow** 後天

5. (**A**) This phone is so cool. What do you use it for?

這電話好酷喔。你用這個做什麼？

(A) Lots of things. I mostly use it to watch movies.

很多事情。我大多用它來看電影。

(B) Lots of things. I mostly use it to cool me down.

很多事情。我大多用這來讓我自己冷靜下來。

(C) I don't think so. 我不這麼認為。

* phone〔fon〕*n.* 電話　　**lots of** 很多
mostly〔'mostlɪ〕*adv.* 大多；主要地
watch movies 看電影　　**cool** sb. **down** 使某人冷靜下來
I don't think so. 我不這麼認為。

6. (**B**) Gosh! It is scorching hot today.

唉呀！今天真是酷熱。

(A) Don't forget to put on your coat.

別忘了要穿上外套。

(B) Yes. I feel sweaty today.

是的。我今天覺得汗流浹背。

(C) Be careful. Don't touch it. 小心。別碰它。

* gosh〔gɑʃ〕*interj.*（表示驚訝）唉呀
scorching〔'skɔrtʃɪŋ〕*adv.* 酷熱地　　forget〔fɚ'gɛt〕*v.* 忘記
put on 穿上　　coat〔kot〕*n.* 外套
sweaty〔'swɛtɪ〕*adj.* 冒汗的；汗流浹背的
careful〔'kɛrfəl〕*adj.* 小心的　　touch〔tʌtʃ〕*v.* 觸摸；碰

7. (**B**) My classmates call me "chicken." I feel sad about it.

我的同班同學叫我「膽小鬼」。我覺得很難過。

(A) You are too big for it. 你的體型太大了，不適合。

(B) Never mind. 別介意。

(C) It's my pleasure. 這是我的榮幸。

* classmate〔'klæs,met〕*n.* 同班同學
chicken〔'tʃɪkən〕*n.* 雞；膽小鬼
sad〔sæd〕*adj.* 難過的　　mind〔maɪnd〕*v.* 介意
Never mind. 不要介意；沒關係。　　pleasure〔'plɛʒɚ〕*n.* 榮幸

8. (**C**) How's school going? 學校課業還好吧？

(A) Well, I would need a good cook.

嗯，我會需要一位好廚師。

(B) Well, I love sandwiches and salads.

嗯，我喜歡三明治跟沙拉。

(C) Well, I'm getting mostly A's and B's.

嗯，我成績大多拿 A 和 B。

* school〔skul〕*n.* 學校；學業　　go〔go〕*v.* 進展
cook〔kʊk〕*n.* 廚師　　sandwich〔'sændwɪtʃ〕*n.* 三明治
salad〔'sæləd〕*n.* 沙拉　　mostly〔'mostlɪ〕*adv.* 大多；主要地
A〔e〕*n.*（五個等第中的）甲（等）【複數型是 A's】
B〔bi〕*n.*（學校成績的）乙（等）【複數型是 B's】

9. (**C**) Tom works around the clock to finish his social studies report. 湯姆夜以繼日地工作，爲了完成社會研究報告。

(A) He is handsome. 他很帥。

(B) He is really lazy. 他眞的很懶惰。

(C) He really works hard. 他眞的很努力工作。

* work〔wɜk〕v. 工作　***around the clock*** 夜以繼日地
social〔ˈsoʃəl〕adj. 社會的　studies〔ˈstʌdɪs〕n. pl. 研究
report〔rɪˈport〕n. 報告　handsome〔ˈhænsəm〕adj. 英俊的
lazy〔ˈlezɪ〕adj. 懶惰的　hard〔hɑrd〕adv. 努力地

10. (**A**) Helen is as happy as a pig in mud. 海倫快樂無比。

(A) Something good happened? 有什麼好事情發生嗎？

(B) She eats too much. 她吃太多。

(C) She is overweight. 她過重。

* pig〔pɪg〕n. 豬　mud〔mʌd〕n. 泥
as happy as a pig in mud 快樂無比
overweight〔ˈovəˌwet〕adj. 過重的

第三部分：言談理解（第 11-20 題，共 10 題）

11. (**A**) W：What are we going to do with the garbage?

女：我們要怎麼處理這垃圾？

M：I've got an idea. We can recycle some of it to reduce the garbage.

男：我有一個想法。我們可以回收一些來減少垃圾量。

W：Please explain your idea, Vincent.

女：請解釋你的想法，文生。

M：For example, we can recycle glass drinking bottles, milk cartons, plastic bags, cans, and so on.

男：舉例來說，我們可以回收玻璃瓶、牛奶盒、塑膠袋、罐子等等。

W : Ooh, I have another good point. We can reuse all that we can.

女：喔，我有另一個好點子。我們可以重複使用那些可用的。

M : Right, recycling and reusing can help to reduce the amount of garbage. Then I won't have to take out so much garbage every day.

男：沒錯，回收和重複使用可以幫助減少垃圾量。然後我就不需要每天丟這麼多的垃圾了。

Question : According to the reading, what can we do to reduce the amount of garbage?

根據這段文章，我們可以如何減少垃圾量？

(A) We can recycle bottles. 我們可以回收瓶子。

(B) We can buy more paper bags.
我們可以買更多的紙袋。

(C) We can eat out more often. 我們可以更常吃外食。

* garbage (ˈgɑrbɪdʒ) n. 垃圾 **get an idea** 有一個想法
recycle (riˈsaɪkl̩) v. 回收 reduce (rɪˈdjus) v. 減少
explain (ɪkˈsplen) v. 解釋；說明 **for example** 舉例來說
glass (glæs) n. 玻璃 bottle (ˈbɑtl̩) n. 瓶子
milk (mɪlk) n. 牛奶 carton (ˈkɑrtn̩) n. 紙盒
plastic (ˈplæstɪk) adj. 塑膠的 bag (bæg) n. 袋子
can (kæn) n. 罐子 **and so on** 等等 ooh (u) interj. 嗚；喔
point (pɔɪnt) n. 觀點；看法 reuse (riˈjuz) v. 再使用
take out the garbage 丟垃圾 **eat out** 在外吃飯；吃外食

12. (**C**) W : Wow.... There are so many people in this market.

女：哇…。這市場人好多。

M : Yes. This is the busiest market around here.

男：是的。這是這附近最熱鬧的市場。

W : I agree. It's not only crowded but also noisy.

女：我同意。這不只是最擁擠，也是最吵鬧的。

M : But the food here is very fresh.

男：但是這裡的食物很新鮮。

W : That's why it's famous.

女：那就是為何它會有名的原因。

M : Look! The fruit at the stand is big and it looks delicious, too.

男：妳看！那一攤位的水果很大，而且看起來也很好吃。

Question : Why is the market very famous?

　　　　　為何這個市場非常有名？

(A) Because everything is cheaper.

　　因為所有的東西都比較便宜。

(B) Because many people live around it.

　　因為有很多人住附近。

(C) Because its food is fresh.

　　因為食物很新鮮。

* market〔'mɑrkɪt〕*n.* 市場　　***around here*** 這周圍；這附近
agree〔ə'gri〕*v.* 同意　　***not only⋯but also~*** 不僅⋯而且~
crowded〔'kraʊdɪd〕*adj.* 擁擠的　　noisy〔'nɔɪzɪ〕*adj.* 吵鬧的
fresh〔frɛʃ〕*adj.* 新鮮的　　famous〔'feməs〕*adj.* 有名的
stand〔stænd〕*n.* 攤位　　look〔lʊk〕*v.* 看起來
delicious〔dɪ'lɪʃəs〕*adj.* 好吃的　　cheap〔tʃip〕*adj.* 便宜的

13. (**B**) W : Hey, Sam. It's already 5:00 p.m. Let's call it a day.

女：嘿，山姆。已經五點了。今天就到此為止吧。

M : See you, Dina. I need to work on the papers which Mr. Huang needs for tomorrow's meeting.

男：再見，蒂娜。我需要繼續做黃先生明天會議需要的文件。

W : Poor you. Do you need my help?

女：眞可憐。你需要我的幫忙嗎？

M : No, thanks! I only need to deal with some numbers.
I can finish them by quarter to six.

男：不，謝謝！我只需要處理一些數字。我五點四十五分前可以
完成。

W : Let me help you; then we can have dinner together.

女：讓我幫你；然後我們可以一起吃晚餐。

M : Good idea. It's my treat tonight.

男：好主意。今晚我請客。

Question : When will Sam finish the papers?

　　　　　山姆何時可以完成文件？

(A) By 5:00. 五點之前。

(B) By 5:45. 五點四十五分之前。

(C) By 4:15. 四點十五分之前。

* *p.m.* 午後（= *post meridiem*）
　　call it a day 今天到此爲止；收工　　*See you*. 再見。
　　work on 做　　papers〔'pepɚz〕*n. pl.* 文件
　　meeting〔'mitɪŋ〕*n.* 會議　　*deal with* 處理
　　number〔'nʌmbɚ〕*n.* 數字　　finish〔'fɪnɪʃ〕*v.* 完成
　　by〔baɪ〕*prep.* 在…之前　　quarter〔'kwɔrtɚ〕*n.* 一刻；十五分鐘
　　a quarter to six 差十五分就六點；五點四十五分
　　Good idea. 好主意。　　treat〔trit〕*n.* 請客

14. (**A**) W : Honey, we need to book a restaurant. Mother's Day
　　　　　　　is coming.

女：親愛的，我們需要預訂餐廳。母親節要到了。

M : I see. I will work on it. I'll try my best to get us a
fine restaurant.

男：我知道了。我來做這件事。我會盡力訂到一間好餐廳。

W : And I'll order a big cake.

女：而我會訂一個大蛋糕。

M : Good. Don't forget to invite Mom to come.

男：很好。別忘了邀請媽來。

W : OK. Andy and I will pick her up.

女：好的。安迪和我會去接她。

M : We can also buy a gift for Mom.

男：我們也可以買一個禮物給媽。

Question : What month is it? 這是幾月？

(A) May. 五月。

(B) August. 八月。

(C) December. 十二月。

* honey〔'hʌnɪ〕*n.*（暱稱）親愛的　　book〔bʊk〕*v.* 預訂
restaurant〔'rɛstərənt〕*n.* 餐廳　　***Mother's Day*** 母親節
I see. 我知道了。　　***try one's best*** 盡力
order〔'ɔrdɚ〕*v.* 訂（購）　　cake〔kek〕*n.* 蛋糕
invite〔ɪn'vaɪt〕*v.* 邀請　　***pick sb. up*** 接某人
gift〔gɪft〕*n.* 禮物

15. (**A**) W : Why do you look worried?

女：為何你看起來很擔心？

M : Because I am worried about our daughter's bad cold.

男：因為我很擔心我們女兒的重感冒。

W : Don't worry. I took her to the hospital and the doctor gave her a shot. She will get better now.

女：別擔心。我帶她去醫院了，而且醫生給她打了一針。她現在比較好了。

M : Really? Now I can finally stop worrying and focus on my work.

男：真的嗎？現在我終於可以不用擔心而專心工作了。

W : Yes.　The doctor also gave her some medicine.

女：是的。醫生也給了她一些藥。

M : Then, please remind her to take the medicine.

男：那麼請提醒她要吃藥。

Question：What DIDN'T the doctor do for their
daughter?　醫生「沒有」替他們的女兒做什麼？

(A) The doctor put some ice on her head.

　　醫生在她頭上冰敷。

(B) The doctor gave her some medicine.

　　醫生給了她一些藥。

(C) The doctor gave her a shot.　醫生給她打了一針。

* worried〔'wɜɪd〕*adj.* 擔心的 < *about* >
　cold〔kold〕*n.* 感冒　***bad cold*** 重感冒
　hospital〔'hɑspɪtl〕*n.* 醫院　　doctor〔'dɑktɚ〕*n.* 醫生
　give sb. a shot 給某人打一針　　***focus on*** 專注於
　medicine〔'mɛdəsn〕*n.* 藥　　remind〔rɪ'maɪnd〕*v.* 提醒
　take medicine 吃藥　　ice〔aɪs〕*n.* 冰

16. (**C**)　W : Kyle, do you know the word "salmon"?

　　女：凱爾，你知道"salmon"這個字嗎？

　　M : Sorry.　I have no idea.　Why?

　　男：抱歉。我不知道。爲何問這個？

　　W : I am reading a story, and I don't know what it means.

　　女：我正在讀一個故事，而我不知道這個字是什麼意思。

　　M : Did you look it up in the dictionary?

　　男：妳有查字典嗎？

　　W : Not yet.　I'll look it up right now.　Here.　It's a kind
of fish.

　　女：還沒。我現在查。在這裡。它是一種魚。

Question : What is "salmon"? 什麼是"salmon"？

(A) A story. 一個故事。

(B) A plant. 一種植物。

(C) An animal. 一種動物。

* salmon〔'sæmən〕*n.* 鮭魚　　*have no idea* 不知道
mean〔min〕*v.* 意思是　　*look up* 查閱
dictionary〔'dɪkʃən,ɛrɪ〕*n.* 字典　　*Not yet.* 還沒。
right now 現在　　story〔'storɪ〕*n.* 故事
plant〔plænt〕*n.* 植物　　animal〔'ænəml〕*n.* 動物

17. (**C**) M : Mom, did you tidy up my room again?

男：媽，妳又清理了我的房間嗎？

W : Yeah. It was a mess.

女：是的。你的房間亂七八糟。

M : Mom, didn't I tell you just leave my room alone? I need some privacy.

男：媽，我不是跟妳說過不要碰我的房間？我需要一些隱私。

W : I am your mother. Of course I have the right to see what my boy is doing.

女：我是你的母親。我當然有權利看看我兒子在做什麼。

M : I know you did this for my own good. But I've grown up. So please stop treating me like a child. I need some respect.

男：我知道妳這麼做是為了我好。但是我已經長大了。所以請不要把我當作小孩子。我需要一點尊重。

Question : What are the man and the woman arguing about?

男士和女士在爭論什麼？

(A) Who should clean the room. 誰該清理房間。

(B) Parents' right to their kids' things.

父母對孩子東西的權利。

(C) Children's right to privacy. <u>小孩的隱私權。</u>

* **tidy up** 清理；收拾　　room〔rum〕*n.* 房間

　yeah〔jæ〕*adv.* 是（= *yes*）

　mess〔mɛs〕*n.* 混亂；亂七八糟

　leave…alone 不管…；不碰…

　privacy〔'praɪvəsɪ〕*n.* 隱私　　*of course* 當然

　right〔raɪt〕*n.* 權利　　*for one's own good* 爲了某人好

　grow up 長大　　treat〔trit〕*v.* 對待

　respect〔rɪ'spɛkt〕*n.* 尊重　　argue〔'ɑrgjʊ〕*v.* 爭論

　clean〔klin〕*v.* 清理；打掃　　parents〔'pɛrənts〕*n. pl.* 父母

　right to N. …的權利

18. (**B**)　W：Mike, stop pushing me.

女：麥可，不要推我。

M：Sorry. I didn't mean to.

男：抱歉。我不是故意的。

W：What's the matter, then?

女：那你是怎麼了？

M：I didn't see a hole in the ground and fell forward.

男：我沒有看到地上有一個洞，所以就向前仆倒了。

W：I see. Are you all right?

女：我知道了。你還好吧？

M：I'm OK. Let's get on the bus.

男：我沒事。我們上公車吧。

Question：Where are the man and the woman?

男士和女士在哪裡？

(A) At a concert. 在演唱會。

(B) At a bus stop. 在公車站。

(C) At a supermarket. 在超級市場。

* push〔puʃ〕v. 推

  mean to V. 有意～；故意～

  What's the matter? 怎麼了？

  then〔ðɛn〕adv. 那麼

  hole〔hol〕n. 洞　　**fall forward** 向前倒

  I see. 我知道了。　　**all right** 安然無恙的

  get on 上（公車、火車等）　　bus〔bʌs〕n. 公車

  concert〔'kɑnsɝt〕n. 音樂會；演唱會

  bus stop 公車站

  supermarket〔'supɚˌmɑrkɪt〕n. 超級市場

19. (**C**) W：Thanks for your help, Hank. We finally got the deal with Pineapple Company.

女：謝謝你的幫忙，漢克。我們最後拿到了鳳梨公司的生意。

M：I'm glad I helped. Ivy, you also played an important part in it.

男：我很高興我有幫上忙。艾薇，在這件事當中，妳也扮演了重要的角色。

W：To be honest, I think your ideas were the key point in this success.

女：老實說，我覺得你的想法是這次成功的關鍵。

M：In fact, I didn't come up with the ideas. They are Ms. Pan's ideas.

男：事實上，這些想法不是我想出來的。是潘小姐的想法。

W：So Ms. Pan helped us make these wise decisions the most.

女：所以潘小姐幫我們最多，做了這些明智的決定。

M : You can say that again.

男：妳說對了。

Question : Who helped the most with the deal?

對於這次的生意誰幫了最大的忙？

(A) Hank. 漢克。

(B) Ivy. 艾維。

(C) Ms. Pan. 潘小姐。

* *thanks for…* 謝謝…   help (hɛlp) *n.* 幫助

finally (ˈfaɪnḷɪ) *adv.* 最後；終於

deal (dil) *n.* 交易；生意

pineapple (ˈpaɪnˌæpḷ) *n.* 鳳梨

company (ˈkʌmpənɪ) *n.* 公司

glad (glæd) *adj.* 高興的

play an important part 扮演重要的角色

to be honest 老實說   key (ki) *adj.* 關鍵的

key point 關鍵點；重點   success (səkˈsɛs) *n.* 成功

in fact 事實上   *come up with* 想出

wise (waɪz) *adj.* 明智的   decision (dɪˈsɪʒən) *n.* 決定

You can say that again. 我非常同意；你說對了。

20. (**C**) W : Have you decided what to major in when you attend university?

女：你決定好了上大學要主修什麼嗎？

M : Well, actually, no. I think it's hard to make a decision.

男：嗯，事實上，還沒。我覺得很難做決定。

W : Right. Maybe you need some help.

女：沒錯。或許你需要一些幫助。

M : But I don't know where to ask.

男：但我不知道哪裡可以求助。

W : You may turn to your parents, school counselors or friends for advice. But you also need to take your interests into consideration.

女：你可以求助於你父母、學校的輔導員，或是朋友，聽聽他們的建議。但是你也需要考量到你的興趣。

Question : What does the woman suggest the man do?

　　　　　女士建議男士做什麼？

(A) She thinks the man should make a decision quickly.

　　她覺得男生應該快點做決定。

(B) She thinks the man should take her advice.

　　她覺得男士應該採用她的建議。

(C) She thinks the man can ask for others' opinions.

　　她覺得男士可以尋求他人的意見。

* decide〔dɪ'saɪd〕v. 決定
 major〔'meʒɚ〕v. 主修 < in >
 attend〔ə'tɛnd〕v. 上（學）
 well〔wɛl〕interj.（講話停頓）嗯
 actually〔'æktʃʊəlɪ〕adv. 事實上
 hard〔hɑrd〕adj. 困難的
 make a decision 做決定
 maybe〔'mebɪ〕adv. 或許；可能
 help〔hɛlp〕n. 幫助
 turn to sb. **for** sth. 求助於某人某事
 counselor〔'kaʊnslɚ〕n. 輔導員
 advice〔əd'vaɪs〕n. 建議
 take…into consideration 把…列入考慮；考量到…
 interest〔'ɪntrɪst〕n. 興趣　　suggest〔səg'dʒɛst〕v. 建議
 quickly〔'kwɪklɪ〕adv. 很快地
 take〔tek〕v. 接受；採用　　**ask for** 要求
 opinion〔ə'pɪnjən〕n. 意見

TEST 8

第一部分：辨識句意（第1-3題，共3題）

作答說明： 第1-3題每題有三張圖片，請依據所聽到的內容，選出符合描述的圖片，每題播放兩次。

示例題：你會看到

(A) 　　(B) 　　(C)

然後你會聽到……（播音）。依據所播放的內容，正確答案應該選A，請將答案卡該題「Ⓐ」的地方塗黑、塗滿，即：● Ⓑ Ⓒ

---

1. (A) 　　(B) 　　(C)

2. (A)   (B)   (C)

3. (A)   (B)   (C)

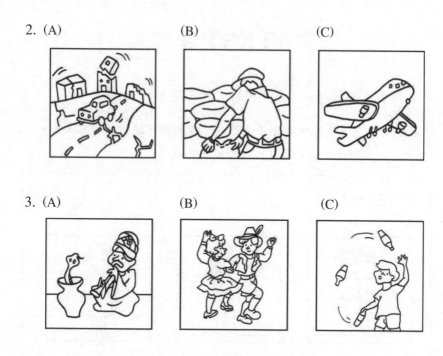

第二部分：基本問答（第 4-10 題，共 7 題）

作答說明： 第 4-10 題每題均有三個選項，請依據所聽到的內容，選出一個最適合的回應，每題播放兩次。

示例題：你會看到

(A) She is talking to the teacher.

(B) She is a student in my class.

(C) She is wearing a beautiful dress.

然後你會聽到……（播音）。依據所播放的內容，正確答案應該選 B，請將答案卡該題「Ⓑ」的地方塗黑、塗滿，即：Ⓐ ● Ⓒ

---

4. (A) I have been eating more than before.
   (B) The rain isn't heavy.
   (C) Thank you for the gift.

5. (A) It's kind of you.
   (B) Not a chance.
   (C) I don't get it.

6. (A) I can't hear him.
   (B) He ate lunch with Joe.
   (C) I spoke to him at lunchtime.

7. (A) Your new watch looks cool.
   (B) That's enough.
   (C) You had better spend more time studying.

8. (A) I like to play games on the computer.
   (B) I can't believe it.
   (C) He doesn't have green fingers.

9. (A) Don't run too fast.
   (B) I'm hungry, too.
   (C) Let's get to the nearest gas station.

10. (A) Sure. Tell me which part you have problem with?
    (B) Yes, you can finish it on your own.
    (C) Of course, you don't have to hand it in tomorrow.

第三部分：言談理解（第 11-20 題，共 10 題）

作答說明：第 11-20 題每題均有三個選項，請依據所聽到的內容，選出一個最適合的答案，每題播放兩次。

示例題：你會看到

(A) 9:50.　　(B) 10:00.　　(C) 10:10.

然後你會聽到……（播音）。依據所播放的內容，正確答案應該選 B，請將答案卡該題「Ⓑ」的地方塗黑、塗滿，即：Ⓐ ● Ⓒ

11. (A) Tuesday.
    (B) Wednesday.
    (C) Thursday.

12. (A) Mason's sister.
    (B) Mason's mother.
    (C) Mason.

13. (A) It was $560,000.
    (B) It was over 100
        million dollars.
    (C) It was free.

14. (A) She thinks people
        need to draw pictures
        to get the meaning of
        the literary works.
    (B) She holds positive
        attitude towards
        reading literature.
    (C) She wonders why the
        man doesn't know
        the value of literature.

15. (A) He's going on a date.
    (B) He likes to see
        movies.
    (C) He met an old friend.

16. (A) Sandwiches.
    (B) Hamburgers.
    (C) Hot milk tea.

17. (A) NT$5,000.
    (B) NT$3,000.
    (C) NT$2,000.

18. (A) Witney has stayed in
        a foreign country for
        some time.
    (B) Leon has stayed in a
        foreign country for
        some time.
    (C) Witney has a cold.

19. (A) The man is harming
        the woman.
    (B) The man wants to
        help the woman.
    (C) The man and the
        woman are best
        friends.

20. (A) He failed in doing the
        project.
    (B) He is proud.
    (C) He is hard-working.

TEST 8 詳解

第一部分：辨識句意（第 1-3 題，共 3 題）

1. (**C**) (A)   (B)   (C)

 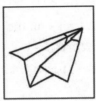 

My art class is about how to turn straws into a dragon.

我的美術課是關於如何把吸管變成龍。

* art〔ɑrt〕*n.* 藝術   *art class* 美術課
  turn A *into* B 把 A 變成 B
  straw〔strɔ〕*n.* 吸管
  dragon〔'drægən〕*n.* 龍

2. (**B**) (A)   (B)   (C)

A typhoon is coming. We have to do something to reduce the damage.

颱風要來了。我們必須做些事情來減少損失。

* typhoon〔taɪ'fun〕*n.* 颱風
  reduce〔rɪ'djus〕*v.* 減少
  damage〔'dæmɪdʒ〕*n.* 破壞；損失

3. (**C**) (A)　　　　　　　(B)　　　　　　　(C)

The kid did some tricks on the stage.

那個小孩在舞台上表演特技。

* kid〔kɪd〕*n.* 小孩　　　trick〔trɪk〕*n.* 把戲；特技
　stage〔stedʒ〕*n.* 舞台

第二部分：基本問答（第 4-10 題，共 7 題）

4. (**A**) You seem to be a little heavier these days.

你最近似乎重了一點。

(A) I have been eating more than before.

<u>我現在吃得比以前多。</u>

(B) The rain isn't heavy. 雨不大。

(C) Thank you for the gift. 謝謝你的禮物。

* seem〔sim〕*v.* 似乎　　***a little*** 有點　　heavy〔'hɛvɪ〕*adj.* 重的
　these days 最近　　rain〔ren〕*n.* 雨
　thank sb. for sth. 謝謝某人某事　　gift〔gɪft〕*n.* 禮物

5. (**A**) It looks like rain. Let me drive you home.

看起來好像要下雨了。讓我開車載你回家吧。

(A) It's kind of you. <u>你人真好。</u>

(B) Not a chance. 休想。

(C) I don't get it. 我不懂。

* ***look like*** 看起來像；很可能出現
　drive〔draɪv〕*v.* 開車載（某人）
　Not a chance. 一點機會都沒有；休想。　　***get it*** 了解；懂

6. (**C**) When did you talk to Albert? 你何時跟艾伯特說話的？

 (A) I can't hear him. 我聽不到他說的話。

 (B) He ate lunch with Joe. 他和喬一起吃午餐。

 (C) I spoke to him at lunchtime.

 我午餐時間跟他說過話。

 * lunchtime〔'lʌntʃˌtaɪm〕*n.* 午餐時間

7. (**C**) Dad wants me not to watch too much TV.

 爸爸要我不要看太多電視。

 (A) Your new watch looks cool.

 你的新手錶看起來很酷。

 (B) That's enough. 夠了。

 (C) You had better spend more time studying.

 你最好花多點時間讀書。

 * *watch TV* 看電視　watch〔watʃ〕*n.* 手錶
 look〔lʊk〕*v.* 看起來　cool〔kul〕*adj.* 酷的
 had better V. 最好~　study〔'stʌdɪ〕*v.* 讀書

8. (**B**) Danny can't use the computer. He never surfs the Net.

 丹尼不會用電腦。他從不瀏覽網路。

 (A) I like to play games on the computer.

 我喜歡在電腦上玩遊戲。

 (B) I can't believe it. 我不相信。

 (C) He doesn't have green fingers. 他不擅長園藝。

 * use〔juz〕*v.* 使用　computer〔kəm'pjutɚ〕*n.* 電腦
 surf〔sɝf〕*v.* 瀏覽　*the Net* 網路（= *the Internet*）
 believe〔bə'liv〕*v.* 相信　*have green fingers* 擅長園藝

9. (**C**) We are running out of gas now.
   我們現在油快沒了。

   (A) Don't run too fast. 別跑太快。
   (B) I'm hungry, too. 我也很餓。
   (C) Let's get to the nearest gas station.
      我們到最近的加油站去吧。

   * ***run out of*** 用光　　gas〔gæs〕*n.* 汽油
   　hungry〔'hʌŋgrɪ〕*adj.* 餓的
   　get to 到達　　***gas station*** 加油站

10. (**A**) Can you help me with my science report?
    你可以幫我做科學報告嗎？

    (A) Sure. Tell me which part you have a problem with.
       當然。告訴我你哪個部分有問題。
    (B) Yes, you can finish it on your own.
       好的，你可以自己完成。
    (C) Of course, you don't have to hand it in tomorrow.
       當然，你不需要明天交。

    * ***help*** *sb.* ***with*** *sth.* 幫助某人某事
    　science〔'saɪəns〕*n.* 科學
    　report〔rɪ'port〕*n.* 報告　　part〔pɑrt〕*n.* 部分
    　have problem with 有…的問題
    　on *one's* ***own*** 獨自地　　***of course*** 當然
    　hand in 繳交

第三部分：言談理解（第 11-20 題，共 10 題）

11. (**B**) W : Mickey. The final exam is coming. Have you studied
       for it?

       女：米奇，期末考要到了。你書讀完了嗎？

M : No. I forgot about it. What date is the final exam?

男：不。我忘了。期末考是哪一天？

W : It's on June 23 and 24. You still have time to prepare.

女：六月二十三和二十四日。你還有時間可以準備。

M : What day is the final exam?

男： 期末考是星期幾？

W : On Wednesday and Thursday.

女：星期三和星期四。

M : I'm very poor at English. I'm afraid I can't do well.

男：我英文很差。我恐怕無法考得好。

W : Don't worry. I can help you with it.

女：別擔心。我可以幫助你。

M : I know I can always count on you.

男： 我知道我總是可以指望妳。

Question : What day is June 23?

六月二十三日是星期幾？

(A) Tuesday. 星期二。

(B) Wednesday. 星期三。

(C) Thursday. 星期四。

* **final exam** 期末考　　study〔ˈstʌdɪ〕*v.* 讀書
  forget about 忘記　　date〔det〕*n.* 日期
  prepare〔prɪˈpɛr〕*v.* 準備
  be poor at 不擅長　　***I'm afraid***… 恐怕…
  do well 考得好　　worry〔ˈwɝɪ〕*v.* 擔心
  help *sb.* **with** *sth.* 幫助某人某事　　***count on*** 依靠；指望

12. (**A**) M : Hey, Mom. Why do you look worried?

男：嘿，媽。為何妳看起來很擔心？

W : Your little sister had a fever at the cram school.

女：你的妹妹在補習班發燒了。

M : Should I take her home now?

男：我現在要去帶她回家嗎？

W : Thank you, Mason, but your dad took her to the hospital half an hour ago.

女：謝謝，麥森，但你爸爸半小時前帶她去醫院了。

M : What did the doctor say? We should call them.

男：醫生怎麼說？我們應該打電話給他們。

W : I called your dad five minutes ago, but he didn't answer the call.

女：我五分鐘前打打電話給你爸爸了，但是他沒有接。

M : Let me get my bicycle. I'll ride to the hospital now.

男：讓我去騎我的腳踏車。我現在要騎去醫院。

Question : Who is sick in the dialogue?

　　　　　對話中誰生病了？

(A) Mason's sister. 麥森的妹妹。

(B) Mason's mother. 麥森的媽媽。

(C) Mason. 麥森。

* worried ('wɜɪd) *adj.* 擔心的　　fever ('fivɚ) *n.* 發燒
  have a fever 發燒　　***cram school*** 補習班
  hospital ('hɑspɪt!) *n.* 醫院
  doctor ('dɑktɚ) *n.* 醫生
  answer ('ænsɚ) *v.* 接 (電話)
  bicycle ('baɪ,sɪk!) *n.* 腳踏車
  sick (sɪk) *adj.* 生病的　　dialogue ('daɪə,lɔg) *n.* 對話

13. (**C**) W : I won the lottery last night.

女：我昨晚贏了樂透。

M : Congratulations. How much did you win?

男：恭喜。妳贏了多少錢？

W : Over 100 million dollars.

女：超過一億元。

M : Wow.... What a fortune! How I envy you. You are always luckier than I am.

男：哇…好大的一筆錢！我真羨慕妳。妳總是比我幸運。

W : I don't think so. You won the biggest prize of our company last year. Remember? You got a new car for nothing.

女：我不這麼覺得。你去年贏得了我們公司最大的獎。記得嗎？你免費得到一輛新車。

M : That's true.

男：的確。

Question : How much was the new car? 那部新車多少錢？

(A) It was $560,000. $560,000 元。

(B) It was over 100 million dollars. 超過一億元。

(C) It was free. <u>免費</u>。

* won〔wʌn〕v. 贏【三態為：win-won-won】
  lottery〔'lɑtərɪ〕n. 彩券；樂透
  congratulations〔kən͵grætʃə'leʃənz〕n. pl. 恭喜
  million〔'mɪljən〕n. 百萬
  fortune〔'fɔrtʃən〕n. 鉅款；大筆錢
  envy〔'ɛnvɪ〕v. 羨慕   lucky〔'lʌkɪ〕adj. 幸運的
  I don't think so. 我不這麼認為。
  prize〔praɪz〕n. 獎   company〔'kʌmpənɪ〕n. 公司
  car〔kɑr〕n. 汽車
  for nothing 免費（= *for free* = *free of charge*）
  That's true. 是真的；的確。   free〔fri〕adj. 免費的

14. (**B**)　M：I believe I have a hard time reading English poems.

男：我相信我讀英文詩遇到了困難。

W：Why?　What's wrong?

女：為什麼？怎麼了？

M：I try very hard to remember the lines, but in vain.

男：我很努力試著去記住詩句，但卻徒勞無功。

W：I think first you need to understand the meaning of each poem.　It helps form a picture of it in your mind.　Then read it out loud several times till you get really familiar with it.

女：我覺得你首先需要了解每首詩的意思。這可以幫助你心中有個詩的想像。然後出聲唸幾遍，直到你熟悉這首詩。

M：I see.　But sometimes I just have no idea why we need to spend time reading poems or some other literary works.

男：我知道了。但是有時候我就是不了解，為何我們需要花時間讀詩，或者是一些其他文學作品。

W：I think it is cool to read books or some other materials because we can learn about others' opinions and values through the works.　It's like exploring the world through words.

女：我覺得讀詩或者是其他的資料是很酷的，因為我們可以透過作品知道他人的想法和價值觀。這就像是用文字探索世界。

Question：What does the woman think of literary works?

　　　　　女士對文學作品有什麼看法？

(A) She thinks people need to draw pictures to get the meaning of the literary works.

她覺得人需要畫圖來了解文學作品的意思。

(B) She holds positive attitude towards reading literature.

她對讀文學作品抱持正面的態度。

(C) She wonders why the man doesn't know the value of literature.

她想知道為何男子不知道文學的價值。

* believe ﹝bə'liv﹞ v. 相信

have a hard time V-ing 做～有困難

poem ﹝'po·ɪm﹞ n. 詩　　***What's wrong?*** 怎麼了？

try ﹝traɪ﹞ v. 嘗試　　hard ﹝hɑrd﹞ adv. 努力地

remember ﹝rɪ'mɛmbɚ﹞ v. 記住

line ﹝laɪn﹞ n. (詩的) 一行　　***in vain*** 徒勞無功

meaning ﹝'minɪŋ﹞ n. 意思　　form ﹝fɔrm﹞ v. 形成

picture ﹝'pɪktʃɚ﹞ n. 想像；形象

mind ﹝maɪnd﹞ n. 心　　read ﹝rid﹞ v. 朗讀

out loud 出聲地

familiar ﹝fə'mɪljɚ﹞ adj. 熟悉的 < with >

I see. 我知道了。　　***have no idea*** 不知道

literary ﹝'lɪtə,rɛrɪ﹞ adj. 文學的

work ﹝wɝk﹞ n. 作品　　cool ﹝kul﹞ adj. 很酷的

material ﹝mə'tɪrɪəl﹞ n. 資料；材料

opinion ﹝ə'pɪnjən﹞ n. 意見；看法

values ﹝'væljuz﹞ n. pl. 價值觀

through ﹝θru﹞ prep. 透過　　explore ﹝ɪk'splor﹞ v. 探索

word ﹝wɝd﹞ n. 文字　　***think of*** 覺得；認為

draw ﹝drɔ﹞ v. 畫　　hold ﹝hold﹞ v. 抱持 (想法)

positive ﹝'pɑzətɪv﹞ adj. 正面的

attitude ﹝'ætə,tjud﹞ n. 態度；看法

towards ﹝'tordz﹞ prep. 對於

literature ﹝'lɪtərətʃɚ﹞ n. 文學 (作品)

wonder ﹝'wʌndɚ﹞ v. 想知道

value ﹝'vælju﹞ n. 價值

15. (**A**) W : Good morning, Anson. You look happy.

女：早安，安森。你看起來很高興。

M : Thank you.

男：謝謝。

W : Anything special going on?

女：有發生任何特別的事情嗎？

M : You bet. I'm going to a movie with Rita.

男：沒錯。我要和瑞塔去看電影。

W : Who's Rita?

女：誰是瑞塔？

M : She's a girl I met on the bus.

男：她是我在公車上認識的女孩。

W : You met a girl... on the bus? That's interesting.

女：你…在公車認識一位女孩？眞是有趣。

M : Yeah. It's like a dream to me.

男：是的。這對我來說就像一場夢。

W : Good luck to you.

女：祝你好運。

Question : Why does Anson look happy?

　　　　爲何安森看起來很高興？

(A) He's going on a date. 他要去約會。

(B) He likes to see movies. 他喜歡看電影。

(C) He met an old friend. 他遇到老朋友。

* happy〔'hæpɪ〕*adj.* 高興的　　special〔'spɛʃəl〕*adj.* 特別的
　go on 發生　　***You bet.*** 的確；沒錯。
　go to a movie 去看電影　　interesting〔'ɪntrɪstɪŋ〕*adj.* 有趣的
　yeah〔jæ〕*interj.* 是的（= *yes*）　　dream〔drim〕*n.* 夢
　Good luck to you. 祝你好運。　　date〔det〕*n.* 約會
　go on a date 去約會　　***old friend*** 老朋友

16. (**A**) W : The weather is becoming colder and colder. Let's
go into the convenience store and get something
warm to eat.

女：天氣越來越冷了。我們進去便利商店買些熱的東西吃吧。

M : The sandwiches and rice burgers are yummy and
cheap. Hey, aren't you thirsty?

男：三明治和米漢堡很好吃又便宜。嘿，妳不渴嗎？

W : Yes, I feel thirsty, but I have no money left now.

女：是，我覺得渴，但我現在沒剩下半毛錢了。

M : That's OK. I can share my hot milk tea with you.

男：沒關係。我可以分妳喝熱奶茶。

W : Wow! It tastes great. Where did you get it?

女：哇！喝起來太棒了。你哪裡買的？

M : My mom made it for me.

男：我媽做給我的。

Question : What did they buy in the convenience store?

他們在便利商店買了什麼？

(A) Sandwiches. 三明治。

(B) Hamburgers. 漢堡。

(C) Hot milk tea. 熱奶茶。

* weather〔'wɛðɚ〕*n.* 天氣
become colder and colder 變得越來越冷
Let's* ~ .** 我們一起 ~ 吧。   ***convenience store 便利商店
get〔gɛt〕*v.* 買   sandwich〔'sændwɪtʃ〕*n.* 三明治
rice〔raɪs〕*n.* 米飯   burger〔'bɜgɚ〕*n.* 漢堡
yummy〔'jʌmɪ〕*adj.* 好吃的   cheap〔tʃip〕*adj.* 便宜的
thirsty〔'θɜstɪ〕*adj.* 渴的   left〔lɛft〕*adj.* 剩下的
That's OK. 沒關係。   share〔ʃɛr〕*v.* 分享   ***milk tea*** 奶茶
wow〔waʊ〕*interj.* 哇！   taste〔test〕*v.* 嚐起來

17. (**C**) W : Hi, Peter! What are you busy with?

　　　女：嗨，彼得！你在忙什麼？

　　　M : I want to put an ad on the Internet.

　　　男：我想要在網路上登廣告。

　　　W : What for?

　　　女：為什麼？

　　　M : I want to sell my digital camera.

　　　男：我想要把我的數位相機賣掉。

　　　W : Your digital camera? Don't you like it?

　　　女：你的數位相機？你不是很喜歡？

　　　M : No, I don't. It's too big for me. I want to buy a
　　　　　smaller one.

　　　男：不，我不喜歡。對我來說太大了。我想要買小一點的。

　　　W : I see. How much are you going to sell it for?

　　　女：我知道了。你想要賣多少錢？

　　　M : NT$2,000.

　　　男：台幣兩千元。

　　　W : Are you kiddding? The price is too low. How about
　　　　　NT$5,000?

　　　女：你在開玩笑嗎？這價格太低了。台幣五千元如何？

　　　M : No. NT$2,000 is fine.

　　　男：不。台幣兩千元就可以了。

　　　Question : How much will the digital camera be sold for?

　　　　　　　　那台數位相機會賣多少錢？

　　(A) NT$5,000. 台幣五千元。

　　(B) NT$3,000. 台幣三千元。

　　(C) NT$2,000. <u>台幣兩千元。</u>

* **be busy with** 忙於　　**What for?** 為什麼？（= *Why?*）
put an ad 登廣告　　ad〔æd〕*n.* 廣告（= *advertisement*）
Internet〔'ɪntɚˌnɛt〕*n.* 網際網路
sell〔sɛl〕*v.* 賣　　digital〔'dɪdʒɪtl̩〕*adj.* 數位的
camera〔'kæmərə〕*n.* 相機
I see. 我知道了。　　**sell for** 賣（多少錢）；以…價格出售
NT$ 新台幣（= *New Taiwan Dollar*）
be kidding 開玩笑　　price〔praɪs〕*n.* 價格
How about ~? ~如何？

18. (**A**)　W：Leon, how do I look?

　　女：李昂，我看起來如何？

　　M：Witney, you look awful. What's the matter?

　　男：惠妮，妳看起來很糟糕。怎麼了？

　　W：I have jet lag.

　　女：我有時差。

　　M：We are going to talk about the marketing plan for
　　　　next year. Can you join us?

　　男：我們要談談明年的行銷計畫。妳可以加入我們嗎？

　　W：Sure. I just need some coffee.

　　女：當然。我只是需要一點咖啡。

　　M：No problem. Help yourself.

　　男：沒問題。請自行取用。

　　Question：What can we infer from the dialogue?

　　　　　　　我們可以從對話中推論出什麼？

　　(A)　Witney has stayed in a foreign country for some time.

　　　　　惠妮在國外度過一段時間。

　　(B)　Leon has stayed in a foreign country for some time.

　　　　　李昂在國外待過一段時間。

　　(C)　Witney has a cold. 威特妮感冒了。

* awful (ˈɔfʊl) *adj.* 很糟的
What's the matter? 怎麼了？　　***jet lag*** 時差
marketing (ˈmɑrkɪtɪŋ) *adj.* 行銷的
plan (plæn) *n.* 計畫　　coffee (ˈkɔfɪ) *n.* 咖啡
help *oneself* 自行取用　　infer (ɪnˈfɝ) *v.* 推論
dialogue (ˈdaɪəˌlɔg) *n.* 對話
foreign (ˈfɔrɪn) *adj.* 外國的
country (ˈkʌntrɪ) *n.* 國家　　***have a cold*** 感冒

19. (**B**) W : Oh! I have a terrible headache. I think I need to take some aspirin.

女：噢！我頭痛很嚴重。我覺得我需要吃些阿斯匹靈。

M : No. You shouldn't take medicine without a doctor's prescription.

男：不。妳不該沒拿醫生處方就吃藥。

W : But it's really inconvenient to see a doctor. Besides, it works every time when I feel ill.

女：但是看醫生真的很不方便。此外，每次我覺得生病的時候這都很有效。

M : You know you will pay for this because taking the wrong medicine will cause serious side effects and even harm your body.

男：妳知道妳將會為此付出代價，因為吃錯藥會有副作用，而且甚至會傷害妳的身體。

W : All right. I should listen to you and see a doctor later.

女：好吧。我應該聽你的，等一下去看醫生。

Question : What can we infer from this conversation?

我們可以從對話中推論出什麼？

(A) The man is harming the woman.

男士在傷害女士。

(B) The man wants to help the woman.

男士想要幫助女士。

(C) The man and the woman are best friends.

男士和女士是最要好的朋友。

* terrible〔'tɛrəbḷ〕*adj.* 糟糕的;劇烈的
  take〔tek〕*v.* 吃(藥)
  aspirin〔'æspərɪn〕*n.* 阿斯匹靈【退燒鎮痛劑】
  medicine〔'mɛdəsṇ〕*n.* 藥
  prescription〔prɪ'skrɪpʃən〕*n.* 處方
  inconvenient〔ˌɪnkən'vinjənt〕*adj.* 不方便的
  see a doctor 看醫生　　besides〔bɪ'saɪdz〕*adv.* 此外
  work〔wɜk〕*v.* 有效　　ill〔ɪl〕*adj.* 不舒服的;生病的
  pay for 為…付出代價　　cause〔kɔz〕*v.* 造成
  side effect 副作用　　harm〔hɑrm〕*v.* 傷害
  body〔'bɑdɪ〕*n.* 身體　　later〔'letɚ〕*adv.* 之後;等一下
  infer〔ɪn'fɝ〕*v.* 推論
  conversation〔ˌkɑnvɚ'seʃən〕*n.* 對話
  help〔hɛlp〕*v.* 幫助

20. (**C**)　W：Tom, I heard that you did a good job on this project.

女：湯姆,我聽說你這次的企畫做得很好。

M：Thanks. I think I was just doing my job.

男：謝謝。我覺得我只是在做我的工作。

W：You always stick to your goal, and you overcome difficulties successfully.

女：你總是堅持你的目標,而且你成功克服困難。

M：Thanks for your praise. I believe hard work is the key to success.

男：謝謝妳的讚美。我相信努力是成功的關鍵。

W : You are sure to be a bright star in our company.

女：你一定會成爲我們公司的閃亮之星。

Question : What's true about Tom?

關於湯姆何者爲眞？

(A) He failed in doing the project.

他企畫做失敗了。

(B) He is proud.　他很驕傲。

(C) He is hard-working. <u>他工作很努力。</u>

* ***do a good job***　做得好
　project (ˈprɑdʒɛkt) *n.* 企畫
　stick to　堅持　　goal (gol) *n.* 目標
　overcome (ˌovəˈkʌm) *v.* 克服
　difficulty (ˈdɪfəˌkʌltɪ) *n.* 困難
　successfully (səkˈsɛsfəlɪ) *adv.* 成功地
　thanks for …　謝謝…　　praise (prez) *n.* 稱讚
　believe (bəˈliv) *v.* 相信　　***hard work***　努力
　key (ki) *n.* 關鍵 < to >　　success (səkˈsɛs) *n.* 成功
　be sure to V.　一定會～
　bright (braɪt) *adj.* 發光的；閃亮的
　star (stɑr) *n.* 星星　　company (ˈkʌmpənɪ) *n.* 公司
　fail (fel) *v.* 失敗 < in >　　proud (praʊd) *adj.* 驕傲的
　hard-working (ˌhɑrdˈwɝkɪŋ) *adj.* 努力工作的

TEST 9

第一部分：辨識句意（第1-3題，共3題）

作答說明：　第1-3題每題有三張圖片，請依據所聽到的內容，選出
符合描述的圖片，每題播放兩次。

示例題：你會看到

(A)　　　　　　　(B)　　　　　　　(C)

然後你會聽到……（播音）。依據所播放的內容，正確答案應該
選A，請將答案卡該題「Ⓐ」的地方塗黑、塗滿，即：● Ⓑ Ⓒ

1. (A)　　　　　　　　(B)　　　　　　　(C)

2. (A)   (B)   (C)

3. (A)   (B)   (C)

第二部分：基本問答（第 4-10 題，共 7 題）

作答説明： 第 4-10 題每題均有三個選項，請依據所聽到的內容，選出一個最適合的回應，每題播放兩次。

示例題：你會看到

(A) She is talking to the teacher.

(B) She is a student in my class.

(C) She is wearing a beautiful dress.

然後你會聽到……（播音）。依據所播放的內容，正確答案應該選 B，請將答案卡該題「Ⓑ」的地方塗黑、塗滿，即：Ⓐ ● Ⓒ

---

4. (A) That's true. What a
       brave thing they did!
   (B) I want to be a
       firefighter when I
       grow up.
   (C) You should not have
       done that again.

5. (A) No way. I have only
       two hands myself.
   (B) Sure. No problem.
   (C) I'd love to, but I
       can't cut myself.

6. (A) Did they get married?
   (B) That's wonderful.
       They're so romantic.
   (C) How much do I need
       to pay for this?

7. (A) It couldn't be worse.
   (B) It is impossible.
   (C) Please give my
       congratulations to her.

8. (A) I usually go to the
       cinema with my wife.
   (B) I usually go to the
       cinema by bus.
   (C) About twice a month.

9. (A) Go ahead.
   (B) No, I can't.
   (C) I don't get it.

10. (A) Yes, I'll need an
        umbrella.
    (B) Thanks. I will.
    (C) No. It's not rainy.

第三部分：言談理解（第 11-20 題，共 10 題）

作答說明： 第 11-20 題每題均有三個選項，請依據所聽到的內容，
          選出一個最適合的答案，每題播放兩次。

示例題：你會看到

(A) 9:50.　　(B) 10:00.　　(C) 10:10.

然後你會聽到……（播音）。依據所播放的內容，正確答案應該
選 B，請將答案卡該題「Ⓑ」的地方塗黑、塗滿，即：Ⓐ ● Ⓒ

11. (A) Buy a new smartphone.
　　(B) Try using a smartphone himself.
　　(C) Become a smartphone addict.

12. (A) His father will pick him up.
　　(B) His mother will pick him up.
　　(C) He will walk home by himself.

13. (A) They will buy a cake for their mom.
　　(B) They will send their mom a bunch of flowers.
　　(C) They would cook a meal for their mom.

14. (A) The man is inviting the woman to go to a dance with him.
　　(B) The man is going to teach the woman how to dance.
　　(C) The woman doesn't like to go with the man any more.

15. (A) He is worried about something.
　　(B) He gets mad easily.
　　(C) He gets along with his classmates.

16. (A) A snake.
　　(B) A tiger.
　　(C) A pet.

17. (A) A foreigner who is visiting Taiwan.
　　(B) A tour guide in Taiwan.
　　(C) He is good at bargaining at markets.

18. (A) Ms. Li's cook.
　　(B) Ms. Li's daughter.
　　(C) Ms. Li's husband.

19. (A) A hospital.
　　(B) A hotel.
　　(C) A supermarket.

20. (A) Valentine's Day.
　　(B) Thanksgiving.
　　(C) Halloween.

TEST 9 詳解

第一部分：辨識句意（第1-3題，共3題）

1. (**C**) (A)   (B)   (C)

How I wish I could watch TV!
我真希望我可以看電視!
* *How I wish* + 假設語氣 我真希望～!
  watch TV 看電視

2. (**B**) (A)   (B)   (C)

I like the merry-go-round. 我喜歡旋轉木馬。
* merry-go-round〔'mɛrɪɡo,raʊnd〕*n.* 旋轉木馬

3. (**A**) (A)   (B)   (C)

I prefer Chinese food to Western food.
我喜歡中式食物勝過西式食物。

* *prefer* A *to* B 喜歡 A 甚於 B
  Chinese〔tʃaɪˈniz〕*adj.* 中國的;中式的
  Western〔ˈwɛstən〕*adj.* 西方的;西式的

第二部分:基本問答(第4-10題,共7題)

4. (**A**) I should thank the firefighters for saving my family from the fire. 我應該要感謝消防隊員拯救我的家人免於火災。

   (A) That's true. What a brave thing they did!
   <u>的確。他們做了一件很勇敢的事!</u>

   (B) I want to be a firefighter when I grow up.
   當我長大,我想要當一位消防隊員。

   (C) You should not have done that again.
   你當時不該再那樣做。

   * *thank sb. for sth.* 感謝某人某事
     firefighter〔ˈfaɪr͵faɪtə〕*n.* 消防隊員(= *fireman*)
     save〔sev〕*v.* 拯救　　*save sb. from sth.* 拯救某人免於某事
     fire〔faɪr〕*n.* 火災　　*That's true.* 是真的;的確。
     brave〔brev〕*adj.* 勇敢的　　*grow up* 長大
     should not have p.p. 當時不該~

5. (**B**) Excuse me. I need some help. Could you give me a hand? 對不起。我需要幫忙。你可以幫我嗎?

   (A) No way. I have only two hands myself.
   不行。我自己只有兩隻手。

   (B) Sure. No problem. <u>當然。沒問題。</u>

   (C) I'd love to, but I can't cut myself.
   我很樂意,但是我不能割傷我自己。

* ***Excuse me***. 對不起。【用於引起注意】
  help〔hɛlp〕*n.* 幫助　　***give sb. a hand*** 幫助某人
  No way. 不行。　　***No problem***. 沒問題。
  I'd love to. 我很樂意。　　cut〔kʌt〕*v.* 切；割傷

6. (**B**) My parents are going to celebrate their wedding
  anniversary this weekend.
  我的父母這週末即將要慶祝他們的結婚週年紀念。

  (A) Did they get married?　他們結婚了嗎？

  (B) That's wonderful.　They're so romantic.
  <u>太棒了。他們真浪漫。</u>

  (C) How much do I need to pay for this?
  我需要付多少錢來買這個？

  * parents〔'pɛrənts〕*n. pl.* 父母
  celebrate〔'sɛlə,bret〕*v.* 慶祝　　wedding〔'wɛdɪŋ〕*n.* 婚禮
  anniversary〔,ænə'vɝsərɪ〕*n.* 週年紀念
  weekend〔'wik'ɛnd〕*n.* 週末　　***get married*** 結婚
  wonderful〔'wʌndəfəl〕*adj.* 很棒的
  romantic〔ro'mæntɪk〕*adj.* 浪漫的　　***pay for*** 為…付錢；買

7. (**C**) Renee is getting married to a man she has known for
  seven years.　芮妮要嫁給一位她認識七年的人。

  (A) It couldn't be worse.　真是遭透了。

  (B) It is impossible.　這是不可能的。

  (C) Please give my congratulations to her.
  <u>請幫我恭喜她。</u>

  * ***get married to*** 和…結婚
  couldn't be + 形容詞　不能再…；非常…
  impossible〔ɪm'pasəbl̩〕*adj.* 不可能的
  congratulations〔kən,grætʃə'leʃənz〕*n. pl.* 恭喜

8. (**C**) How often do you see a movie at a cinema?

你多久去電影院看一次電影？

(A) I usually go to the cinema with my wife.

我通常和我老婆去看電影。

(B) I usually go to the cinema by bus.

我通常搭公車去看電影。

(C) About twice a month. 大約一個月兩次。

* ***How often~?*** ～多久一次？　　***see a movie*** 看電影
cinema (ˈsɪnəmə) *n.* 電影院　　***go to the cinema*** 看電影
wife (waɪf) *n.* 妻子；老婆　　***by bus*** 搭公車
twice (twaɪs) *adv.* 兩次

9. (**A**) Sir, may I use your bathroom?

先生，我可以用你的廁所嗎？

(A) Go ahead. 請便。

(B) No, I can't. 不，我不行。

(C) I don't get it. 我不懂。

* use (juz) *v.* 使用　　bathroom (ˈbæθˌrum) *n.* 浴室；廁所
Go ahead. 請便。　　***I don't get it.*** 我不懂。

10. (**B**) It's freezing cold outside. Why not take a coat with you?

外面很冷。你何不帶件外套？

(A) Yes, I'll need an umbrella.

好的，我需要一把雨傘。

(B) Thanks. I will. 謝謝。我會的。

(C) No. It's not rainy. 不。沒在下雨。

* freezing (ˈfrizɪŋ) *adv.* 冷凍般地
freezing cold 極冷的；冰冰冰的　　outside (ˈaʊtˈsaɪd) *adv.* 外面
Why not V.? 何不～？ (= *Why don't you V.?*)
coat (kot) *n.* 外套

第三部分：言談理解（第 11-20 題，共 10 題）

11. (**B**) M : I don't see why so many people spend lots of time on
their smartphones or iPads.

男：我不懂爲何這麼多人花很多時間在他們的智慧型手機或 iPad
上。

W : Grandpa, are you talking about the smartphone
addicts?

女：爺爺，你在講的是低頭族嗎？

M : I don't know what that is, but I just can't see why those
smartphones are so attractive.

男：我不知道那是什麼，但我只是不懂爲何智慧型手機如此吸引
人。

W : Grandpa, smartphones are really useful devices.
People can do lots of things, such as make phone
calls, take pictures, watch films, and play games.
Above all, we can surf the Net anytime
anywhere to connect with the world.

女：爺爺，智慧型手機眞的是很有用的東西。人們可以做很多事
情，像是打電話、照相、看影片，和玩遊戲。最重要的是，
我們可以在任何時間任何地點瀏覽網路，和世界連結。

M : In other words, we can do almost anything with a
smartphone.

男：換句話說，我們幾乎可以用智慧型手機做任何事。

W : Bingo. Do you want to give it a try? You are going
to get hooked on it.

女：答對了。你想要試看看嗎？你會上癮的。

Question : What does the woman suggest the man do?

女士暗示男士做什麼？

(A) Buy a new smartphone. 買新的智慧型手機。

(B) Try using a smartphone himself.

試著自己用看看智慧型手機。

(C) Become a smartphone addict. 變成低頭族。

* see〔si〕*v.* 知道；了解　　***lots of*** 很多的
smartphone〔'smɑrt͵fon〕*n.* 智慧型手機
iPad iPad 平板電腦　　addict〔'ædɪkt〕*n.* 上癮者
smartphone addict 智慧型手機上癮者；低頭族
attractive〔ə'træktɪv〕*adj.* 吸引人的
useful〔'jusfəl〕*adj.* 有用的
device〔dɪ'vaɪs〕*n.* 裝置；精巧的東西
make phone calls 打電話　　***take pictures*** 照相
film〔fɪlm〕*n.* 電影；影片　　***above all*** 最重要的是
surf〔sɝf〕*v.* 瀏覽　　***the Net*** 網路（= *the Internet*）
connect〔kə'nɛkt〕*v.* 連結 < *with* >
in other words 換句話說
bingo〔'bɪŋgo〕*interj.*（表示驚訝）你猜對了
give it a try 試試看　　***get hooked on*** 對⋯上癮
suggest〔səg'dʒɛst〕*v.* 建議　　***try + V-ing*** 試試看～

12. (**B**) M : Helen, I want to make sweet and sour chicken.

　　　　Can you buy some things for me on your way home?

　　男：海倫，我想要做糖醋雞柳。妳在回家的路上可以幫我買點東
　　　　西嗎？

W : Sure. What do you need, Tommy?

女：當然。你需要什麼，湯米？

M : Sugar and chicken will do.

男：糖和雞肉就可以了。

W : How much sugar do you need?

女：你需要多少糖？

M : Please buy one pound of sugar.

男：請買一磅的糖。

W : How much chicken do you need?

女：你需要多少雞肉？

M : A whole chicken. By the way, can you pick up David
   on your way home?

男：一隻全雞。順帶一提，妳回家的路上可以去接大衛嗎？

Question : How will David get home? 大衛要如何回家？

(A) His father will pick him up. 他的父親會接他。

(B) His mother will pick him up. 他的母親會接他。

(C) He will walk home by himself. 他會自己走回家。

* sweet〔swit〕*adj.* 甜的   sour〔saur〕*adj.* 酸的
  chicken〔'tʃɪkən〕*n.*（不可數）雞肉：（可數）雞
  on** one's **way 在往…的路上
  sugar〔'ʃʊgɚ〕*n.* 糖   do〔du〕*v.* 可以；足夠
  pound〔paund〕*n.* 磅   whole〔hol〕*adj.* 整個的
  by the way 順帶一提   ***pick** sb. **up*** 接某人

13. (**C**) W : You know Mother's Day is around the corner.

女：你知道母親節要到了嗎？

M : Right. Do you have any plans for that day?

男：沒錯。妳那天有什麼計畫嗎？

W : I suggest that we buy Mom a cake as well as a
   bunch of carnations.

女：我建議我們買一個蛋糕和一束康乃馨給媽。

M : Sounds great. But do you have the money?

男：聽起來很棒。但是妳有錢嗎？

W : Well, actually, I am running out of my allowance.

女：嗯，事實上，我零用錢要花光了。

M : Then we need to take plan B. That is to cook a big meal by ourselves and help Mom do the household chores.

男：那我們需要採用 B 計畫。也就是自己煮一個大餐，和幫媽媽做家事。

Question : What will the man and the woman do to celebrate Mother's Day?

男士和女士要怎麼慶祝母親節？

(A) They will buy a cake for their mom.

他們會買一個蛋糕給他們的母親。

(B) They will send their mom a bunch of flowers.

他們會送一束花給他們的母親。

(C) They will cook a meal for their mom.

他們會煮一頓大餐給他們的母親。

* ***Mother's Day*** 母親節　　***be around the corner*** 即將到來
 suggest〔səg'dʒɛst〕*v.* 建議　　***as well as*** 以及
 bunch〔bʌntʃ〕*n.* 一束　　carnation〔kɑr'neʃən〕*n.* 康乃馨
 sound〔saʊnd〕*v.* 聽起來　　well〔wɛl〕*interj.* （說話停頓）嗯
 actually〔'æktʃʊəlɪ〕*adv.* 實際上　　***run out of*** 用光
 allowance〔ə'laʊəns〕*n.* 零用錢　　take〔tek〕*v.* 採用
 meal〔mil〕*n.* 一餐　　household〔'haʊs,hold〕*adj.* 家庭的
 chores〔tʃorz〕*n. pl.* （家庭）雜事
 celebrate〔'sɛlə,bret〕*v.* 慶祝

14. (**A**) M : Lisa, I am wondering if you can go to the prom with me tomorrow night.

男：麗莎，我想知道妳明天晚上是否可以和我去舞會。

W : Well, I am afraid not. I can't dance actually.

女：嗯，恐怕不行。事實上我不會跳舞。

M : It's easy. All you need to do is to shake your body to the music.

男：這很容易。妳所需要做的就是隨著音樂搖擺身體。

W : Really! I hope I won't embarrass you in front of your friends.

女：眞的！我希望我不會讓你在朋友面前尷尬。

M : You won't. So I will pick you up at 6:00. OK?

男：妳不會的。那我明天六點去接妳。好嗎？

W : See you then.

女：到時候見。

Question : What do we know from the dialogue?

從對話中，我們知道什麼？

(A) The man is inviting the woman to go to a dance with him. <u>男士正在邀請女士和他去參加舞會。</u>

(B) The man is going to teach the woman how to dance.

男士要敎女士如何跳舞。

(C) The woman doesn't like to go with the man any more.

女士不想再跟男士去了。

* wonder〔ˈwʌndɚ〕v. 想知道
prom〔prɑm〕n. (高中生、大學生主辦的) 舞會 (= *promenade*)
well〔wɛl〕*interj.* (說話停頓) 嗯
I am afraid not. 恐怕不行。　　dance〔dæns〕v. 跳舞
actually〔ˈæktʃuəlɪ〕*adv.* 實際上；事實上
All one ***need to do is*** *(to) V.* 某人所必須要做的就是～
shake〔ʃek〕v. 搖動；搖擺　　***to the music*** 隨著音樂
hope〔hop〕v. 希望　　embarrass〔ɪmˈbærəs〕v. 使尷尬
pick *sb.* ***up*** 接某人　　***See you then.*** 到時候見。
dialogue〔ˈdaɪəˌlɔg〕*n.* 對話　　invite〔ɪnˈvaɪt〕v. 邀請
go to a dance 去參加舞會　　***not…any more*** 不再…

15. (**B**) W : Please have a seat, Mr. Chen. Let's have a talk about your son.

女：請坐，陳先生。我們來談談關於你兒子的事。

M : To tell the truth, I already know what you are going to tell me.

男：老實說，我已經知道妳要跟我說什麼了。

W : That's great. I am worried about his emotional control. He seems to get mad easily.

女：那很好。我擔心他的情緒控制問題。他似乎容易動怒。

M : Hm, I understand. What can I do to solve the problem?

男：嗯，我了解。我可以怎麼做來解決問題？

W : Maybe you can take him to see a psychiatrist.

女：或許你應該帶他去看精神科醫生。

M : Thanks for your advice. I will do that.

男：謝謝妳的建議。我會那麼做的。

Question : What's wrong with Mr. Chen's son?

陳先生的兒子有什麼問題？

(A) He is worried about something. 他在擔心某事。

(B) He gets mad easily. 他容易動怒。

(C) He gets along with his classmates.

他和他的同班同學和睦相處。

* *have a seat* 坐下   *talk about* 談論
to tell the truth 說實話
worried ('wɜɪd) *adj.* 擔心的 < *about* >
emotional (ɪ'moʃənḷ) *adj.* 情緒的   control (kən'trol) *n.* 控制
seem (sim) *v.* 似乎   get (gɛt) *v.* 變得
mad (mæd) *adj.* 生氣的   hm (hm) *interj.* (說話停頓) 嗯
solve (sɑlv) *v.* 解決   problem ('prɑbləm) *n.* 問題

psychiatrist〔saɪˈkaɪətrɪst〕*n.* 精神科醫生
thanks for… 謝謝…　　advice〔ədˈvaɪs〕*n.* 建議
What's wrong with…? …怎麼了；…有什麼問題？
get along with 和…和睦相處

16. (**B**)　M：We are going to have a field trip this Friday.

男：這個星期五我們要去戶外教學。

W：Oh! Really? Where will you go?

女：喔！真的喔？你們要去哪？

M：The Taipei zoo. Isn't it amazing?

男：台北市立動物園。這不是很棒嗎？

W：Yes. It's a wonderful place for both children and adults to visit.

女：是的。這對孩童和成人來說都是參觀的好地方。

M：I want to see some lions, tigers, giraffes, and elephants.

男：我想要看一些獅子、老虎、長頸鹿，和大象。

W：You can also feed and touch animals at the petting zoo.

女：你也可以在寵物動物園區餵食和撫摸動物。

Question：What animal does the man want to see at the zoo? 男士想要在動物園看什麼動物？

(A) A snake. 蛇。

(B) A tiger. 老虎。

(C) A pet. 寵物。

* ***field trip*** 戶外教學　　amazing〔əˈmezɪŋ〕*adj.* 驚人的；很棒的
wonderful〔ˈwʌndɚfəl〕*adj.* 很棒的
visit〔ˈvɪzɪt〕*v.* 拜訪；參觀　　lion〔ˈlaɪən〕*n.* 獅子
tiger〔ˈtaɪgɚ〕*n.* 老虎　　giraffe〔dʒəˈræf〕*n.* 長頸鹿
elephant〔ˈɛləfənt〕*n.* 大象　　feed〔fid〕*v.* 餵
petting zoo 寵物動物園　　snake〔snek〕*n.* 蛇
pet〔pɛt〕*n.* 寵物

17. (**A**)　M：I've heard how interesting it is to shop at night
markets in Taiwan.

男：我有聽說在台灣的夜市購物是很有趣的。

W：Yes, it's surely a fun and interesting thing you must
try while visiting Taiwan.

女：是的，這確實是好玩又有趣的事，你去台灣的時候一定要試
看看。

M：What is so special about the night markets here?

男：這裡的夜市有什麼特別的？

W：Well, you can find lots of interesting stuff here such
as delicious local food, inexpensive clothes,
accessories, toys and fun games.　You can also enjoy
the fun of bargaining with the vendors.

女：嗯，你可以找到很多有趣的東西，像是當地好吃的食物、便
宜的衣服、配件、玩具，和有趣的遊戲。你也可以享受和攤
販討價還價的樂趣。

M：Sounds really interesting.

男：聽起來真的很有趣。

W：Right.　No visit to Taiwan is complete without
a visit to a night market.

女：沒錯。去台灣沒有去夜市就不算是一趟完整的旅行。

Question：What do you think the man probably is?

你覺得男士的身份可能是什麼？

(A) A foreigner who is visiting Taiwan.

要去台灣遊覽的外國人。

(B) A tour guide in Taiwan.　台灣的導遊。

(C) He is good at bargaining at markets.

他擅長在市場討價還價。

* interesting (ˈɪntrɪstɪŋ) *adj.* 有趣的   shop (ʃɑp) *v.* 購物
night market 夜市   surely (ˈʃʊrlɪ) *adv.* 確實；無疑地
fun (fʌn) *v.* 有趣的；好玩的   *n.* 樂趣
special (ˈspɛʃəl) *adj.* 特別的
well (wɛl) *interj.* (說話停頓) 嗯   **lots of** 很多的
stuff (stʌf) *n.* 東西   delicious (dɪˈlɪʃəs) *adj.* 好吃的
local (ˈlokḷ) *adj.* 當地的
inexpensive (ˌɪnɪkˈspɛnsɪv) *adj.* 不貴的；便宜的
clothes (kloz) *n. pl.* 衣服
accessory (ækˈsɛsərɪ) *n.* 配件   toy (tɔɪ) *n.* 玩具
enjoy (ɪnˈdʒɔɪ) *v.* 享受   bargain (ˈbɑrgɪn) *v.* 討價還價
vendor (ˈvɛndɚ) *n.* 小販   sound (saʊnd) *v.* 聽起來
complete (kəmˈplit) *adj.* 完整的
without (wɪðˈaʊt) *prep.* 沒有   probably (ˈprɑbəblɪ) *adv.* 可能
foreigner (ˈfɔrɪnɚ) *n.* 外國人   **tour guide** 導遊
be good at 擅長

18. (**B**) Ms. Li owns a café. One day, two of her three cooks quit the job because the pay is not much. Ms. Li was very worried because the spring vacation was coming, and the café would be very busy then. During the spring vacation, many people came to the café. The only cook got sick because of being too tired. Luckily, one of Ms. Li's childen, Sophia, told Ms. Li that she could help in the kitchen. Ms. Li was very happy and made Sophia a cook at the café.

李小姐有一家咖啡店。有一天，她的三位廚師中，有兩位辭職了，因為薪水不多。李小姐很擔心，因為春假要來了，而咖啡店那時候會很忙碌。在春假時，很多人會來咖啡店。唯一的廚師因為太累而生病了。幸運的是，李小姐的一個孩子，蘇菲亞，跟李小姐說她可以在廚房幫忙。李小姐很高興，讓蘇菲亞在廚房當廚師。

Question : Who helped Ms. Li solve her problem in the café? 誰幫助李小姐解決咖啡店的問題？

(A) Ms. Li's cook. 李小姐的廚師。

(B) Ms. Li's daughter. 李小姐的女兒。

(C) Ms. Li's husband. 李小姐的丈夫。

* own〔on〕v. 擁有　　café〔kə'fe〕n. 咖啡店
　cook〔kʊk〕n. 廚師　　quit〔kwɪt〕v. 停止；放棄；辭（職）
　job〔dʒɑb〕n. 工作　　pay〔pe〕n. 薪水
　worried〔'wɝɪd〕adj. 擔心的　　*spring vacation* 春假
　busy〔'bɪzɪ〕adj. 忙碌的　　*get sick* 生病
　because of 因為　　tired〔taɪrd〕adj. 疲勞的
　luckily〔'lʌkɪlɪ〕adv. 幸運地　　help〔hɛlp〕v. 幫忙
　solve〔sɑlv〕v. 解決　　husband〔'hʌzbənd〕n. 丈夫

19. (**B**) Do you like nature? Nature can keep us from getting burned out. Hereton Villa is a wonderful place to get close to nature. Why not find some time to enjoy the blue sky or the blue river, or just lie down on the grass near our villa? You are sure to enjoy many wonderful things outside of the city. So plan a trip here to get away from your busy days and take a break in the arms of nature. Come visit our website or contact Mr. Huang at 0925642312!

你喜歡大自然嗎？大自然可以讓我們免於過度勞累。亨瑞頓別墅是個能夠接近大自然很棒的地方。你何不找時間享受藍色的天空或是河流，或只是躺在別墅附近的草地上？你一定會享受到許多城市之外的美妙事物。所以計畫來這裡一趟，遠離你忙碌的日子，並在大自然的懷抱中休息一下。來看看我們的網站，或是打電話聯絡黃先生：0925642312！

Question : What is "Hereton Villa"?

"Hereton Villa"是什麼？

(A) A hospital. 醫院。

(B) A hotel. 飯店。

(C) A supermarket. 超市。

* nature〔'netʃɚ〕*n.* 大自然　***keep sb. from V-ing*** 使某人不會~

get〔gɛt〕*v.* 變得　***be burned out*** 筋疲力盡

villa〔'vɪlə〕*n.* 別墅　wonderful〔'wʌndɚfəl〕*adj.* 很棒的

get close to 接近

Why not~? 何不~？（=*Why don't you~?*）

enjoy〔ɪn'dʒɔɪ〕*v.* 享受　lie〔laɪ〕*v.* 躺

grass〔græs〕*n.* 草地　***be sure to V.*** 一定~

outside of 在…之外　city〔'sɪtɪ〕*n.* 城市

plan〔plæn〕*v.* 計畫　trip〔trɪp〕*n.* 旅行

get away from 離開　***take a break*** 休息

in the arms of 在…的懷裡

come V. 來~（=*come to V.* = *come and V.*）

website〔'wɛb,saɪt〕*n.* 網站　contact〔'kɑntækt〕*v.* 聯絡

hospital〔'hɑspɪtḷ〕*n.* 醫院　hotel〔ho'tɛl〕*n.* 飯店；旅館

supermarket〔'supɚ,mɑrkɪt〕*n.* 超市

20. (**C**) October is John's favorite month. He can make jack-o'-lanterns with his friends. They also decorate their rooms with scary toys. In the evening, John and his friends will put on their special costumes, and all the children of the town will, too. They will go to costume parties or go from door to door. They will shout, "Trick or treat!" The people in the houses will open the doors and give them some candy. John and his friends are happy because they always get the most candy.

十月是約翰最喜愛的月份。他可以和朋友一起做南瓜燈。他們也可
以用可怕的玩具佈置他們的房間。晚上的時候,約翰和他的朋友
會穿上特別的服裝,而城裡所有的小孩也會。他們會去化妝舞會,
或是挨家挨戶去拜訪。他們會大喊:「不給糖就搗蛋!」房子裡的
人會打開門,並給他們一些糖果。約翰和他的朋友很高興,因
為他們總是得到最多的糖果。

Question : What holiday is it? 這是什麼節日?

(A) Valentine's Day. 情人節。

(B) Thanksgiving. 感恩節。

(C) Halloween. 萬聖節。

* favorite〔'fevərɪt〕*adj.* 最喜愛的
　jack-o'-lantern〔'dʒækə,læntən〕*n.* 杰克燈;南瓜燈
　decorate〔'dɛkə,ret〕*v.* 裝飾;佈置
　room〔rum〕*n.* 房間　　scary〔'skɛrɪ〕*adj.* 可怕的;嚇人的
　toy〔tɔɪ〕*n.* 玩具　　***put on*** 穿上
　special〔'spɛʃəl〕*adj.* 特別的　　costume〔'kɑstum〕*n.* 服裝
　costume party 化妝舞會　　***from door to door*** 挨家挨戶
　shout〔ʃaut〕*v.* 大叫;呼喊　　***Trick or treat.*** 不給糖就搗蛋。
　candy〔'kændɪ〕*n.* 糖果　　holiday〔'hɑlə,de〕*n.* 假日;節日
　Valentine's Day 情人節
　Thanksgiving〔,θæŋks'gɪvɪŋ〕*n.* 感恩節
　Halloween〔,hælo'in〕*n.* 萬聖節前夕【10月31日】

TEST 10

第一部分：辨識句意（第1-3題，共3題）

作答說明：第1-3題每題有三張圖片，請依據所聽到的內容，選出
　　　　　符合描述的圖片，每題播放兩次。

示例題：你會看到

(A)　　　　　　　　(B)　　　　　　　　(C)

然後你會聽到……（播音）。依據所播放的內容，正確答案應該
選 A，請將答案卡該題「Ⓐ」的地方塗黑、塗滿，即：● Ⓑ Ⓒ

---

1. (A)　　　　　　　　(B)　　　　　　　　(C)

2. (A)  (B)  (C)

3. (A)  (B)  (C)

第二部分：基本問答（第 4-10 題，共 7 題）

作答說明： 第 4-10 題每題均有三個選項，請依據所聽到的內容，選
出一個最適合的回應，每題播放兩次。

示例題：你會看到

(A) She is talking to the teacher.

(B) She is a student in my class.

(C) She is wearing a beautiful dress.

然後你會聽到……（播音）。依據所播放的內容，正確答案應該
選 B，請將答案卡該題「Ⓑ」的地方塗黑、塗滿，即：Ⓐ ● Ⓒ

4. (A) What do you feel like doing?
   (B) I'm sorry. I don't have a CD.
   (C) Great! Can I come?

5. (A) Good. I'm starving.
   (B) It's late for dinner.
   (C) I'd like to take you out to dinner.

6. (A) Does that mean you want to own a business?
   (B) Business is business.
   (C) Why do you run fast?

7. (A) Yes, I have done my homework.
   (B) Not too much.
   (C) Yes, there's a lot.

8. (A) Every day. I don't drive, so I have to take the bus.
   (B) Of course! I enjoy it.
   (C) The public transportation is safe.

9. (A) Oh, sorry, I'm free tonight.
   (B) Oh, sorry, I'm not free tonight.
   (C) Oh, thanks, I'm playing a video game.

10. (A) Sure. I hope you feel better.
    (B) Oh? What's the matter with you?
    (C) Thanks. I am fine.

第三部分：言談理解（第 11-20 題，共 10 題）

作答說明： 第 11-20 題每題均有三個選項，請依據所聽到的內容，
選出一個最適合的答案，每題播放兩次。

示例題：你會看到

(A) 9:50.　　(B) 10:00.　　(C) 10:10.

然後你會聽到……（播音）。依據所播放的內容，正確答案應該
選 B，請將答案卡該題「Ⓑ」的地方塗黑、塗滿，即：Ⓐ ● Ⓒ

11. (A) She is a doctor.
    (B) She is a dentist.
    (C) She is an artist.

12. (A) She is trying to get close to the kitchen.
    (B) She is trying to cook a new dish.
    (C) She is trying to write a book.

13. (A) She looks sad.
    (B) She looks funny.
    (C) She looks happy.

14. (A) They are going to wear raincoats.
    (B) They are going to a theater.
    (C) They are going to buy birds.

15. (A) They are going to take a taxi.
    (B) They are going to get small change ready.
    (C) They are going to take a bus.

16. (A) She went to see a movie.
    (B) She took her son to see a doctor.
    (C) She made an appointment for her son.

17. (A) 9:00 a.m. to 3:00 p.m.
    (B) 9:00 a.m. to 1:00 p.m.
    (C) 9:00 a.m. to 5:00 p.m.

18. (A) In a bank.
    (B) In a supermarket.
    (C) In a shopping mall.

19. (A) They both did.
    (B) The woman did.
    (C) The man did.

20. (A) She was doing the housework.
    (B) She was cutting a hole.
    (C) She was putting the knife down.

TEST 10 詳解

第一部分：辨識句意（第1-3題，共3題）

1. (**A**) (A)  (B) (C)

The post office is across from the bank. 郵局在銀行對面。

* *post office* 郵局　　*across from* 在…的對面
　bank〔bæŋk〕*n.* 銀行

2. (**C**) (A)  (B)  (C)

The traffic sign means "No right turns."
這交通號誌的意思是：「禁止右轉。」

* *traffic sign* 交通號誌　　mean〔min〕*v.* 意思是
　turn〔tɜn〕*n.* 轉彎

3. (**B**) (A)  (B)  (C)

I tie back my hair when I'm cooking.

我煮飯的時候會把頭髮綁到腦後。

* tie〔taɪ〕*v.* 綁　　cook〔kʊk〕*v.* 烹調；做飯

第二部分：基本問答（第 4-10 題，共 7 題）

4. (**C**) We are going to a concert. 我們正要去演唱會。

　　(A) What do you feel like doing? 你想要做什麼？

　　(B) I'm sorry. I don't have a CD. 很抱歉。我沒有 CD。

　　(C) <u>Great! Can I come?</u> <u>太棒了！我可以去嗎？</u>

　　* concert〔ˈkɑnsɝt〕*v.* 演唱會　　***feel like V-ing*** 想要~
　　　CD CD 唱片（= *compact disc*）　　great〔gret〕*adj.* 很棒的

5. (**A**) Dinner's ready! 晚餐準備好了！

　　(A) <u>Good. I'm starving.</u> <u>很好。我好餓。</u>

　　(B) It's late for dinner. 太晚吃晚餐了。

　　(C) I'd like to take you out to dinner.

　　　　我想要帶你去外面吃晚餐。

　　* ready〔ˈrɛdɪ〕*adj.* 準備好的　　starve〔stɑrv〕*v.* 飢餓
　　　would like to V. 想要~　　***take sb. out*** 帶某人外出

6. (**A**) I dream of running my own business.

　　　我夢到我經營自己的公司。

　　(A) Does that mean you want to own a business?

　　　　<u>那表示你想要有自己的公司嗎？</u>

　　(B) Business is business. 公事公辦。

　　(C) Why do you run fast? 你為何跑得那麼快？

　　* dream〔drim〕*v.* 夢見＜*of*＞　　run〔rʌn〕*v.* 經營
　　　own〔on〕*adj.* 自己的　　*v.* 擁有
　　　business〔ˈbɪznɪs〕*n.* 公司；事業
　　　Business is business. 公事公辦。

7. (**B**) How much homework did you get today?

你今天有多少家庭作業？

(A) Yes, I have done my homework.

是的，我已經做完功課。

(B) Not too much. 沒有很多。

(C) Yes, there's a lot. 是的，有很多。

* homework〔'hom,wɜk〕*n.* 家庭作業；功課　　***a lot*** 很多

8. (**A**) How often do you take public transportation?

你多久搭一次大眾運輸工具？

(A) Every day. I don't drive, so I have to take the bus.

每天。我不開車，所以我必須搭公車。

(B) Of course! I enjoy it. 當然！我很享受。

(C) The public transportation is safe. 大眾運輸工具很安全。

* ***How often ~?*** 多久～一次？　　take〔tek〕*v.* 搭乘

public〔'pʌblɪk〕*adj.* 大眾的

transportation〔,trænspɚ'teʃən〕*n.* 運輸工具

drive〔draɪv〕*v.* 開車　　***Of course.*** 當然。

enjoy〔ɪn'dʒɔɪ〕*v.* 享受；喜歡　　safe〔sef〕*adj.* 安全的

9. (**B**) Would you like to watch a video at my place tonight?

你今晚想要來我家看影片嗎？

(A) Oh, sorry, I'm free tonight. 喔，抱歉，我今晚有空。

(B) Oh, sorry, I'm not free tonight.

喔，抱歉，我今晚沒空。

(C) Oh, thanks, I'm playing a video game.

喔，謝謝，我正在打電動。

* ***would like to V.*** 想要～　　video〔'vɪdɪ,o〕*n.* 影片　*adj.* 電視的

place〔ples〕*n.* 地點；家　　free〔fri〕*adj.* 有空的

video game 電視遊戲；電玩

10. (**B**) I'm not feeling too well. 我覺得不太舒服。

    (A) Sure. I feel better.

        當然。我感覺更好了。

    (B) Oh? What's the matter with you? <u>喔？你怎麼了？</u>

    (C) Thanks. I am fine. 謝謝。我很好。

    * *feel well* 感覺舒服；身體好   sure〔ʃur〕*adv.* 當然
    What's the matter with~? ~怎麼了？

第三部分：言談理解（第 11-20 題，共 10 題）

11. (**C**) M : What do you do exactly?

    男：妳究竟是做什麼的？

    W : I create paintings and drawings.

    女：我畫水彩和素描。

    Question : What does the woman mean?

        女士是什麼意思？

    (A) She is a doctor. 她是位醫生。

    (B) She is a dentist. 她是位牙醫。

    (C) She is an artist. <u>她是位畫家。</u>

    * exactly〔ɪgˋzæktlɪ〕*adv.* 精確地   *what exactly* 究竟是什麼
    create〔krɪˋet〕*v.* 創造   painting〔ˋpentɪŋ〕*n.* 畫；水彩畫
    drawing〔ˋdrɔ‧ɪŋ〕*n.* 圖畫；素描   mean〔min〕*v.* 意思是
    doctor〔ˋdɑktɚ〕*n.* 醫生   dentist〔ˋdɛntɪst〕*n.* 牙醫
    artist〔ˋɑrtɪst〕*n.* 藝術家；畫家

12. (**B**) W : Mark, don't get any closer to the oven.

    女：馬克，不要再靠近烤箱一步。

    M : I know, Mom. I won't.

    男：我知道，媽。我不會。

W : Find the recipe book for me on the table.

女：幫我找桌上的食譜。

M : OK.　Here you are.

男：好的。拿去吧。

Question : What is Mom trying to do?

媽媽正在嘗試做什麼？

(A) She is trying to get close to the kitchen.

她正試著接近廚房。

(B) She is trying to cook a new dish.

她正試著煮一道新菜。

(C) She is trying to write a book.

她正試著要寫一本書。

* ***get close to*** 接近　　oven〔′ʌvən〕*n.* 烤箱

recipe〔′rɛsəpɪ〕*n.* 烹飪法　　***recipe book*** 食譜

Here you are. 你要的東西在這裡；拿去吧。

dish〔dɪʃ〕*n.* 一道菜

13. (**A**) W : Tom, stop making faces at me.

女：湯姆，停止對我做鬼臉。

M : Jane, I just want you to be happy.

男：珍，我只是想要妳快樂。

W : Oh, thanks.　Do I look down?

女：喔，謝謝。我看起來很沮喪嗎？

M : Yes.　Cheer up!　Don't worry about the test.

男：是的，高興點！不要擔心考試。

Question : How does Jane look? 珍看起來如何？

(A) She looks sad. 她看起來很難過。

(B) She looks funny. 她看起來很好笑。

(C) She looks happy. 她看起來很快樂。

* ***stop V-ing*** 停止做～   ***make faces*** 做鬼臉
  look〔lʊk〕v. 看起來   down〔daʊn〕adj. 情緒低落的；沮喪的
  cheer up 振作精神；高興起來
  worry〔ˈwɝɪ〕v. 擔心 < *about* >

14. (**B**) M : Do you want to go bird-watching?

男：妳想要去賞鳥嗎？

W : No. It looks like rain.

女：不。看起來要下雨了。

M : How about seeing a movie?

男：看電影如何？

W : That sounds great.

女：那聽起來很棒。

Question : Where are they going? 他們要去哪裡？

(A) They are going to wear raincoats. 他們要去穿雨衣。

(B) They are going to a theater. 他們要去電影院。

(C) They are going to buy birds. 他們要去買鳥。

* ***go bird-watching*** 去賞鳥   ***look like*** 看起來像；很可能出現
  How about～? ～如何？   ***see a movie*** 看電影
  sound〔saʊnd〕v. 聽起來   raincoat〔ˈrenˌkot〕n. 雨衣
  theater〔ˈθiətɚ〕n. 電影院

15. (**C**) M : Here comes the shuttle bus.

男：接駁公車來了。

W : I don't have any change.

女：我沒有任何零錢。

M : That's all right. It's free.

男：沒關係。這是免費的。

W : Really?

女：眞的嗎？

Question : What are they going to do?

他們要做什麼？

(A) They are going to take a taxi. 他們要搭計程車。

(B) They are going to get small change ready.

他們他們要準備好零錢。

(C) They are going to take a bus. 他們要搭公車。

* *Here comes* ～. ～來了。

shuttle〔'ʃʌtl〕 *adj.* 定期往返的

shuttle bus 接駁公車　　change〔tʃendʒ〕 *n.* 零錢

That's all right. 沒關係。

free〔fri〕 *adj.* 免費的　　taxi〔'tæksɪ〕 *n.* 計程車

get…ready 準備好…　　*small change* 小面額硬幣；零錢

16. (**C**)　M : What did you do?

男：妳剛剛做了什麼？

W : I made a hospital appointment for my son.

女：我幫我兒子預約醫院看診。

M : What happened?

男：發生什麼事了？

W : He has a fever, and I want him to see a doctor.

女：他發燒，我要他去看醫生。

Question : What did the woman do? 女士做了什麼？

(A) She went to see a movie.

她去看電影。

(B) She took her son to see a doctor.

她帶她兒子去看醫生。

(C) She made an appointment for her son.

<u>她幫她兒子預約看診。</u>

* hospital〔ˊhɑspɪtl〕*n.* 醫院

appointment〔əˊpɔɪntmənt〕*n.* 約會；約診

make an appointment 預約

happen〔ˊhæpən〕*v.* 發生　　fever〔ˊfivɚ〕*n.* 發燒

see a doctor 看醫生　　***see a movie*** 看電影

17. (**C**) M：Excuse me, are you open on weekends?

男：對不起，你們週末有營業嗎？

W：Yes, but we close earlier.

女：有的，但是我們提早打烊。

M：What are the hours?

男：營業時間是幾點？

W：9 to 3.

女：九點到三點。

Question：What are the business hours of the store on
weekdays?

店家平日的營業時間是幾點？

(A) 9:00 a.m. to 3:00 p.m. 早上九點到下午三點。

(B) 9:00 a.m. to 1:00 p.m. 早上九點到下午一點。

(C) 9:00 a.m. to 5:00 p.m. <u>早上九點到下午五點。</u>

* open〔ˊopən〕*adj.* 營業的　　weekend〔ˊwikˋɛnd〕*n.* 週末

close〔kloz〕*v.* 關門；打烊

hours〔aʊrz〕*n. pl.* 營業時間【在此等於 business hours】

store〔stor〕*n.* 商店　　weekday〔ˊwikˋde〕*n.* 平日

a.m. 上午（＝ *ante meridiem*）　***p.m.*** 下午（＝ *post meridiem*）

18. (**B**) W : May I help you?

女：需要我的幫忙嗎？

M : Yes, I'm looking for some dairy products.

男：是的，我在找些乳製品。

W : Dairy products are in that case.

女：乳製品在那個箱子。

M : Thanks.

男：謝謝。

Question : Where are the speakers? 說話者在哪裡？

(A) In a bank. 在銀行。

(B) In a supermarket. 在超市。

(C) In a shopping mall. 在購物中心。

* help〔hɛlp〕*v.* 幫助　　***look for*** 尋找

dairy〔'dɛrɪ〕*adj.* 牛奶的；乳製的　　product〔'prɑdəkt〕*n.* 產品

case〔kes〕*n.* 盒子；箱子　　bank〔bæŋk〕*n.* 銀行

supermarket〔'supɚ,mɑrkɪt〕*n.* 超級市場

shopping mall 購物中心

19. (**C**) W : How was your final exam?

女：你期末考考得如何？

M : I did a terrific job. How about you?

男：我考得很好。妳呢？

W : I didn't study hard. It was terrible.

女：我沒有用功唸書。考得很糟糕。

M : Well, you should review before the test.

男：嗯，妳考前應該複習的。

Question : Who did better in the exam?

誰考試考得比較好？

(A) They both did. 兩人都考得好。

(B) The woman did. 女士考得好。

(C) The man did. <u>男士考得好。</u>

* ***final exam*** 期末考　　terrific〔tə'rɪfɪk〕*adj.* 驚人的；很棒的
do a terrific job 做得考；考得好　　***How about~?*** ~如何？
study hard 用功讀書　　well〔wɛl〕*interj.* （講話停頓）嗯
review〔rɪ'vju〕*v.* 複習　　***do better*** 考得比較好
exam〔ɪg'zæm〕*n.* 考試（= *examination*）

20. (**A**) W：Put the knife down before you hurt someone.

女：在你弄傷別人之前把刀子放下。

M：Mom, I need to cut a hole in the box.

男：媽，我需要在盒子上割一個洞。

W：Why didn't you ask me to help you?

女：你為何不叫我幫你呢？

M：Because you were busy with your housework.

男：因為妳忙著做家事。

Question：What was the woman doing?

女士當時正在做什麼？

(A) She was doing the housework. <u>她當時在做家事。</u>

(B) She was cutting a hole. 她當時正在割一個洞。

(C) She was putting the knife down.

她當時正在把刀子放下。

* knife〔naɪf〕*n.* 刀子　　hurt〔hɝt〕*v.* 使受傷
cut〔kʌt〕*v.* 割；切　　hole〔hol〕*n.* 洞
box〔bɑks〕*n.* 盒子　　ask〔æsk〕*v.* 要求
help〔hɛlp〕*v.* 幫助　　***be busy with*** 忙於
housework〔'haʊs,wɝk〕*n.* 家事

TEST 11

第一部分：辨識句意（第1-3題，共3題）

作答說明：第1-3題每題有三張圖片，請依據所聽到的內容，選出符合描述的圖片，每題播放兩次。

示例題：你會看到

(A)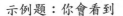

(B)

(C)

然後你會聽到……（播音）。依據所播放的內容，正確答案應該選 A，請將答案卡該題「Ⓐ」的地方塗黑、塗滿，即：● Ⓑ Ⓒ

1. (A)　　　　　　(B)　　　　　　(C)

2. (A)　　　　　　　(B)　　　　　　　(C)

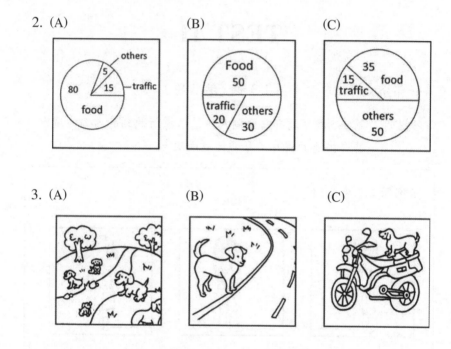

3. (A)　　　　　　　(B)　　　　　　　(C)

第二部分：基本問答（第 4-10 題，共 7 題）

作答說明： 第 4-10 題每題均有三個選項，請依據所聽到的內容，選出一個最適合的回應，每題播放兩次。

示例題：你會看到

(A) She is talking to the teacher.

(B) She is a student in my class.

(C) She is wearing a beautiful dress.

然後你會聽到……（播音）。依據所播放的內容，正確答案應該選 B，請將答案卡該題「Ⓑ」的地方塗黑、塗滿，即：Ⓐ ● Ⓒ

4. (A) Long time no see.
   (B) Nice to meet you.
       I'm in apartment 25.
   (C) I'd like to meet my
       friend.

5. (A) Maybe fifty kilograms.
   (B) Why don't you ask
       your parents?
   (C) I guess next year I will
       be much taller.

6. (A) Really? I think the
       best way is to work
       out in a health club.
   (B) Really? This one is a
       perfect fit.
   (C) I can give you a ride.

7. (A) Me either.
   (B) Really? How is that?
   (C) Me too.

8. (A) Happy birthday.
   (B) That's too bad.
   (C) Good for you.

9. (A) She does have a
       sweet tooth.
   (B) Poor Sandy.
   (C) She needs a dentist.

10. (A) In my opinion, the
        novel is boring.
    (B) To me, it's a terrible
        meal.
    (C) To me, the story is
        confusing.

第三部分：言談理解（第 11-20 題，共 10 題）

作答說明：第 11-20 題每題均有三個選項，請依據所聽到的內容，
　　　　　選出一個最適合的答案，每題播放兩次。

示例題：你會看到

(A) 9:50.　　(B) 10:00.　　(C) 10:10.

然後你會聽到……（播音）。依據所播放的內容，正確答案應該
選 B，請將答案卡該題「Ⓑ」的地方塗黑、塗滿，即：Ⓐ ● Ⓒ

---

11. (A) About a trip to China.
    (B) About a powerful shaking.
    (C) About a further message in China.

12. (A) She is always in trouble.
    (B) She will give a helping hand.
    (C) She can't be more helpful.

13. (A) It is new.
    (B) It is old.
    (C) The traffic is tied up.

14. (A) In a hospital.
    (B) In a hotel.
    (C) In a website.

15. (A) There's enough food for her.
    (B) There's plenty room for all.
    (C) There's no other room for her.

16. (A) We cannot be sure.
    (B) By bus.
    (C) They will not go.

17. (A) Playing a video game.
    (B) Running fast.
    (C) Playing hide-and-seek.

18. (A) He is not ready for it.
    (B) He thinks the test will be very easy.
    (C) He never studies hard.

19. (A) He doesn't like to play video games.
    (B) He always sends a message by e-mail.
    (C) He likes to text his friends.

20. (A) He is out partying every night.
    (B) He doesn't like to make friends.
    (C) Belonging to a student club is the best way to make friends.

TEST 11 詳解

第一部分：辨識句意（第1-3題，共3題）

1. (**C**) (A)   (B)   (C)

My car is parked in front of the house.

我的車停在房子前面。

* park〔park〕*v.* 停（車）   ***in front of*** 在…的前面

2. (**A**) (A)   (B)   (C)

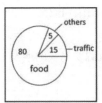 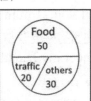

Poor families spend about 80 percent of their salary on food.

貧窮的家庭花百分之八十的薪水買食物。

* poor〔pur〕*adj.* 貧窮的
family〔'fæməlɪ〕*n.* 家庭
spend〔spɛnd〕*v.* 花（時間、金錢）
percent〔pə'sɛnt〕*n.* 百分之…
salary〔'sælərɪ〕*n.* 薪水

3. (**B**) (A)　　　　　　　(B)　　　　　　　(C)

The dog is trying to cross the street. 狗想要橫越街道。

* try〔traɪ〕 v. 嘗試　　cross〔krɔs〕 v. 橫越
　street〔strit〕 n. 街道

第二部分：基本問答（第 4-10 題，共 7 題）

4. (**B**) Welcome, neighbor! My name is Cody. I live in
　　apartment 20.

　　歡迎，好鄰居！我的名字是科迪。我住在 20 號公寓。

　　(A) Long time no see. 好久不見。

　　(B) Nice to meet you. I'm in apartment 25.
　　　　很高興認識你。我住在 25 號公寓。

　　(C) I'd like to meet my friend. 我想要見我的朋友。

　　* neighbor〔'nebɚ〕 n. 鄰居
　　　apartment〔ə'partmənt〕 n. 公寓
　　　Long time no see. 好久不見。
　　　meet〔mit〕 v. 認識；和…見面
　　　Nice to meet you. 很高興認識你。　　　*would like to V.* 想要～

5. (**A**) How much do you weigh? 你多重？

　　(A) Maybe fifty kilograms. 可能是五十公斤。

　　(B) Why don't you ask your parents? 你何不問你的父母？

　　(C) I guess next year I will be much taller.
　　　　我想明年我會長高很多。

* weigh〔we〕*v.* 重~　　maybe〔'mebɪ〕*adv.* 或許；可能
kilogram〔'kɪləˌgræm〕*n.* 公斤　　parents〔'pɛrənts〕*n. pl.* 父母
guess〔gɛs〕*v.* 猜想
much〔mʌtʃ〕*adv.* (強調比較級)~得多

6. (**A**) I think the best way to keep fit is to ride a bicycle.

　我覺得騎腳踏車是保持健康最好的方法。

　(A) Really? I think the best way is to work out in a health club. 真的嗎？我覺得最好的方式是去健身俱樂部運動。

　(B) Really? This one is a perfect fit.
　　　真的嗎？這一件很合身。

　(C) I can give you a ride. 我可以載你一程。

　* keep〔kip〕*v.* 保持
fit〔fɪt〕*adj.* 健康的　*n.* 合身；合身的衣服
ride〔raɪd〕*v.* 騎　*n.* 便車　bicycle〔'baɪˌsɪkḷ〕*n.* 腳踏車
work out 運動　**health club** 健身俱樂部
perfect〔'pɝfɪkt〕*adj.* 完美的；完全的
give *sb.* **a ride** 讓某人搭便車

7. (**C**) I really need to get more exercise. 我真的需要多運動。

　(A) Me either. 我也不。

　(B) Really? How is that? 真的嗎？那個怎麼樣？

　(C) Me too. 我也是。

　* exercise〔'ɛksɚˌsaɪz〕*n.* 運動　either〔'iðɚ〕*adv.* 也 (不)

8. (**B**) I didn't study for my exam, so I blew it.

　我考試沒讀書，所以我搞砸了。

　(A) Happy birthday. 生日快樂。

　(B) That's too bad. 真可惜。

　(C) Good for you. 你真棒。

* study〔'stʌdɪ〕v. 讀書
　　exam〔ɪg'zæm〕n. 考試（= examination）
　　blew〔blu〕v. 搞砸【blow 的過去式】
　　That's too bad. 真可惜。
　　Good for you. 你真棒。

9. (**A**) Wow. Sandy ate five cakes. 哇！珊蒂吃了五個蛋糕。

　　(A) She does have a sweet tooth.
　　　　她的確喜歡吃甜食。

　　(B) Poor Sandy. 可憐的珊蒂。

　　(C) She needs a dentist. 她需要一位牙醫。

　　* wow〔waʊ〕interj.（表示驚訝、喜悅等）哇
　　cake〔kek〕n. 蛋糕　　***do + V.*** 真的～；的確～
　　have a sweet tooth 喜歡吃甜食
　　dentist〔'dɛntɪst〕n. 牙醫

10. (**C**) What do you think of the movie?
　　你覺得電影如何？

　　(A) In my opinion, the novel is boring.
　　　　在我看來，小說很無聊。

　　(B) To me, it's a terrible meal.
　　　　對我來說，這是個很糟糕的一餐。

　　(C) To me, the story is confusing.
　　　　對我來說，故事情節令人困惑。

　　* ***What do you think of…?*** 你覺得…如何？
　　in one's opinion 依據某人的看法：在某人看來
　　novel〔'nɑvḷ〕n. 小說　　boring〔'bɔrɪŋ〕adj. 無聊的
　　terrible〔'tɛrəbḷ〕adj. 糟糕的　　meal〔mil〕n. 一餐
　　story〔'storɪ〕n. 故事；情節
　　confusing〔kən'fjuzɪŋ〕adj. 令人困惑的

第三部分：言談理解（第 11-20 題，共 10 題）

11. (**B**) M : Oh, my gosh.　Watch this.　A big earthquake.

　　　　男：喔，我的天啊。你看這個。一場大地震。

　　　　W : When did it happen?　Are the locals ok?

　　　　女：什麼時候發生的？當地的人都還好嗎？

　　　　M : It happened around ten o'clock this evening in China.
　　　　　　The news hasn't given any further information about
　　　　　　it.

　　　　男：大約是晚上十點發生在中國。這新聞還沒有提供任何更進一
　　　　　　步關於地震的消息。

　　　　Question : What were they talking about?

　　　　　　　　　　他們在談論什麼？

　　　　(A) About a trip to China.　關於去中國的旅行。

　　　　(B) About a powerful shaking.　關於一場強烈的地震。

　　　　(C) About a further message in China.

　　　　　　關於中國更進一步的消息。

　　　　* **My gosh**. 我的天啊。　　earthquake〔'ɝθ͵kwek〕*n.* 地震
　　　　　local〔'lokl〕*n.* 當地人　　around〔ə'raʊnd〕*prep.* 大約
　　　　　China〔'tʃaɪnə〕*n.* 中國　　news〔njuz〕*n.* 新聞
　　　　　further〔'fɝðɚ〕*adj.* 進一步的
　　　　　information〔͵ɪnfɚ'meʃən〕*n.* 資訊；情報　　trip〔trɪp〕*n.* 旅行
　　　　　powerful〔'paʊɚfəl〕*adj.* 強大的
　　　　　shaking〔'ʃekɪŋ〕*n.* 搖動；震動
　　　　　message〔'mɛsɪdʒ〕*n.* 訊息；消息

12. (**B**) M : Wow, I'm really in trouble.

　　　　男：哇，我真的遇到麻煩了。

　　　　W : What's wrong with you?

　　　　女：你怎麼了？

M : I have a lot of problems at school.

男：我在學校遇到很多問題。

W : Well, if you need a hand, I'm here for you.

女：嗯，如果你需要幫忙，我隨時準備好幫助你。

Question : What does the woman mean?

女士是什麼意思？

(A) She is always in trouble.

她總是遇到麻煩。

(B) She will give a helping hand.

她會幫忙。

(C) She can't be more helpful.

她非常有幫助。

* wow〔wau〕*interj.* （表示驚訝、喜悅等）哇
  be in trouble 遇到麻煩　　***What's wrong with~?*** ～怎麼了？
  problem〔'prɑbləm〕*n.* 問題　　***need a hand*** 需要幫忙
  be here for 目的是為了；準備好（ = *be ready for* ）
  mean〔min〕*v.* 意思是
  give a helping hand 幫忙；助一臂之力
  helpful〔'hɛlpfəl〕*adj.* 有幫助的
  can't be + 形容詞比較級　無法再…；非常…

13. (**B**) W : How pretty! Is that a new tie?

女：好漂亮喔！那是新的領帶嗎？

M : You've never see me wear it before?

男：妳以前從來沒看過我戴嗎？

W : Never.

女：從未看過。

M : It's been on my top shelf for a long time.

男：這放在我架子上層很久了。

Question : What do we know about the tie?

關於領帶我們知道什麼？

(A) It is new. 它是新的。

(B) It is old. 它是舊的。

(C) The traffic is tied up. 交通很擁擠。

* pretty〔'prɪtɪ〕*adj.* 漂亮的　　tie〔taɪ〕*n.* 領帶

wear〔wɛr〕*v.* 穿；戴　　top〔tɑp〕*adj.* 最上面的

shelf〔ʃɛlf〕*n.* 架子　　traffic〔'træfɪk〕*n.* 交通

tied up （交通）擁擠的

14. (**B**) W : Hello. I'd like to check in, please. My name's Mia
Lee.

女：哈囉。麻煩你，我想要登記住宿。我的名字是李米亞。

M : Yes. I have your reservation here, Ms. Lee. May I
have your I.D.?

男：好的。我這裡看到妳的預訂，李小姐。我可以看一下你的身
份證嗎？

W : Here you are. By the way, is there wireless Internet
in the room?

女：拿去吧。順便一提，房間裡有無線網路嗎？

M : Sure.

男：當然。

Question : Where could the woman be? 女士可能在哪裡？

(A) In a hospital. 在醫院。

(B) In a hotel. 在旅館。

(C) In a website. 在網站上。

* *would like to V.* 想要～　　*check in* 登記住宿

reservation〔ˌrɛzə'veʃən〕*n.* 預訂

I.D. 身份證（= *identity*）

Here you are. 你要的東西在這裡；拿去吧。

by the way 順便一提　　wireless（ˈwaɪrlɪs）*adj.* 無線的

Internet（ˈɪntɚˌnɛt）*n.* 網際網路　　room（rum）*n.* 房間

hospital（ˈhɑspɪtl）*n.* 醫院　　hotel（hoˈtɛl）*n.* 飯店；旅館

website（ˈwɛbˌsaɪt）*n.* 網站

15. (**C**)　W : Hello. This is Mary Smith in room 503. The room
has not been cleaned.

女：哈囉。我是 503 房的瑪麗‧史密斯。房間還沒有打掃。

M : Ok. Someone will be there to clean it shortly. Is there
anything else?

男：好的。很快會有人去打掃房間。還有其他的事情嗎？

W : Actually, I'd prefer to change rooms. There are
some little bugs on the floor.

女：事實上，我比較想要換房間。地板上有一些小蟲。

M : I'm sorry. But there are no other rooms available.

男：很抱歉。但是現在沒有其他的空房。

Question : What does the man mean?

男士是什麼意思？

(A) There's enough food for her. 有足夠的食物給她。

(B) There's plenty room for all.

空間夠大可以容納所有人。

(C) There's no other room for her.

沒有其他的房間可以給她。

* *This is* ~. 我是～。【用於講電話】　　clean（klin）*v.* 打掃；清理

shortly（ˈʃɔrtlɪ）*adv.* 不久；很快地

actually（ˈæktʃʊəlɪ）*adv.* 事實上

prefer（prɪˈfɝ）*v.* 比較喜歡；偏好

change〔tʃendʒ〕*v.* 改變;重換　　bug〔bʌg〕*n.* 蟲
floor〔flor〕*n.* 地板　　available〔ə'veləbḷ〕*adj.* 可獲得的
mean〔min〕*v.* 意思是　　plenty〔'plɛntɪ〕*adj.* 充分的;足夠的
room〔rum〕*n.* 空間

16. (**A**)　W : Should we take a bus to CKS Airport or should we drive?

女: 我們應該搭巴士去桃園國際機場,還是我們應該開車?

M : I think we should take a bus.

男: 我想我們應該搭巴士。

W : Really? I want to drive you there.

女: 真的嗎?我想要開車載你去。

M : Have you got your driver's license with you?

男: 妳有帶駕照嗎?

W : Oh, I'm not sure.

女: 喔,我不確定。

Question : How will they go to the airport?

他們會如何去機場?

(A)　We cannot be sure. <u>我們無法確定。</u>

(B)　By bus. 搭巴士。

(C)　They will not go. 他們不會去。

* bus〔bʌs〕*n.* 公車;巴士　　airport〔'ɛr,port〕*n.* 機場
  CKS Airport 台灣桃園國際機場【原名為 Chiang Kai-Shek
  International Airport (蔣中正國際機場),於 2006 年改為目前的名稱】
  drive〔draɪv〕*v.* 開車;開車載 (某人)

17. (**A**)　W : Let's see who can win the game.

女: 我們來看看誰會贏得這場遊戲。

M : OK. I'm ready when you are.

男: 好的。妳準備好的話,我也可以開始了。

W : Hey! Wait a second. I wasn't ready for that.

女：嘿！等一下。我還沒準備好。

M : Do you want to restart the game?

男：那妳要重新開始遊戲嗎？

Question : What are these people doing?

這些人正在做什麼？

(A) Playing a video game. 打電動。

(B) Running fast. 跑得很快。

(C) Playing hide-and-seek. 玩捉迷藏。

* *Let's ~* . 我們一起～吧。　　win〔wɪn〕*v.* 贏
  game〔gem〕*n.* 比賽；遊戲
  ready〔ˈrɛdɪ〕*adj.* 準備好的 *< for >*
  Wait a second. 等一下。　　restart〔riˈstɑrt〕*v.* 重新開始
  video game 電視遊戲；電玩
  run〔rʌn〕*v.* 跑　　hide-and-seek *n.* 捉迷藏

18. (**A**) W : What do you know about the monthly exam?

女：關於月考你知道些什麼嗎？

M : All I know is that it will be harder than before.

男：我知道的是，會比以前還困難。

W : Oh, no! I haven't studied at all.

女：喔，不！我完全沒讀書。

M : Neither have I. Maybe we can study together and learn more.

男：我也沒有。或許我們可以一起讀，會學得更多。

Question : What does the man say about the test?

關於考試，男士說了什麼？

(A) He is not ready for it. 他還沒準備好。

(B) He thinks the test will be very easy.

他覺得考試會很簡單。

(C) He never studies hard. 他從不用功讀書。

* monthly（'mʌnθlɪ）*adj.* 每月的
  exam（ɪg'zæm）*n.* 考試（= *examination*）
  hard（hɑrd）*adj.* 困難的　*adv.* 努力地　***than before*** 比以前
  not…at all 一點也不…；完全沒有…
  maybe（'mebɪ）*adv.* 或許；可能
  learn（lɜn）*v.* 學習　ready（'rɛdɪ）*adj.* 準備好的 < *for* >

19. (**C**) W：What are you doing?

女：你在做什麼？

M：I'm just sending an e-mail to my dad.

男：我只是在寄電子郵件給我爸爸。

W：Do you always use your phone to send e-mails?

女：你總是用手機寄電子郵件嗎？

M：Oh, no. All of my friends text nowadays.

男：喔，不是。我所有的朋友現在都傳簡訊。

Question：What does the man mean?

男士是什麼意思？

(A) He doesn't like to play video games.

他不喜歡打電動。

(B) He always sends a message by e-mail.

他總是用電子郵件傳送訊息。

(C) He likes to text his friends. 他喜歡傳簡訊給朋友。

* send（sɛnd）*v.* 送；寄　e-mail（'i,mel）*n.* 電子郵件
  use（juz）*v.* 使用　phone（fon）*n.* 電話；手機（= *cellphone*）
  text（tɛkst）*v.* 傳簡訊　nowadays（'nauə,dez）*adv.* 現在
  mean（min）*v.* 意思是　message（'mɛsɪdʒ）*n.* 訊息

20. (**C**) W : You have a lot of friends, Vince. How do you do it?

女：你交了很多朋友，文斯。你怎麼做到的？

M : Make friends?

男：交朋友嗎？

W : Yeah. I know you go to parties. Would you suggest that?

女：是的。我知道你會去派對。你建議那樣做嗎？

M : No. Actually I'd join some student club.

男：不。事實上我會加入學某個學生社團。

Question : What does the man mean?

男士是什麼意思？

(A) He is out partying every night.

他每晚外出參加派對。

(B) He doesn't like to make friends.

他不喜歡交朋友。

(C) Belonging to a student club is the best way to make friends. 成為學生社團的一員是交朋友最好的方式。

* ***a lot of*** 很多　　***make friends*** 交朋友

yeah〔jæ〕*adv.* 是的（= *yes*）

party〔'pɑrtɪ〕*n.* 派對　*v.* 參加派對

suggest〔səg'dʒɛst〕*v.* 建議

actually〔'æktʃuəlɪ〕*adv.* 事實上

join〔dʒɔɪn〕*v.* 加入　　some〔sʌm〕*adj.* 某個

club〔klʌb〕*n.* 社團　　***belong to*** 屬於；是…的成員

TEST 12

第一部分：辨識句意（第1-3題，共3題）

作答説明：第1-3題每題有三張圖片，請依據所聽到的內容，選出符合描述的圖片，每題播放兩次。

示例題：你會看到

(A) 　　(B) 　　(C)

然後你會聽到……（播音）。依據所播放的內容，正確答案應該選 A，請將答案卡該題「Ⓐ」的地方塗黑、塗滿，即：● Ⓑ Ⓒ

1. (A) 　　(B) 　　(C)

2. (A)  (B)  (C)

3. (A)  (B)  (C)

第二部分：基本問答（第 4-10 題，共 7 題）

作答說明： 第 4-10 題每題均有三個選項，請依據所聽到的內容，選出一個最適合的回應，每題播放兩次。

示例題：你會看到

(A) She is talking to the teacher.

(B) She is a student in my class.

(C) She is wearing a beautiful dress.

然後你會聽到……（播音）。依據所播放的內容，正確答案應該選 B，請將答案卡該題「Ⓑ」的地方塗黑、塗滿，即：Ⓐ ● Ⓒ

4. (A) I have no idea who will come to see me.
   (B) Yes. I should meet him in a public place.
   (C) Yes, I have made some friends through the Net.

5. (A) Leaving me to face the music.
   (B) Facebook doesn't really interest me.
   (C) It's a wonderful book.

6. (A) He knows nothing about me.
   (B) I heard of him before.
   (C) We have a lot in common.

7. (A) I buy only clothes that are on sale.
   (B) That's a good idea.
   (C) I stop taking buses.

8. (A) I prefer to use a computer.
   (B) I am good at cooking.
   (C) Excellent. I taught myself web design.

9. (A) April 15, 1912.
   (B) Under the sea.
   (C) Wow! It's a huge ship.

10. (A) Yeah, It's my favorite meal.
    (B) Yeah, my sister, Eva.
    (C) Yeah, I have a big family.

第三部分：言談理解（第 11-20 題，共 10 題）

作答說明： 第 11-20 題每題均有三個選項，請依據所聽到的內容，
選出一個最適合的答案，每題播放兩次。

示例題：你會看到

(A) 9:50.　　(B) 10:00.　　(C) 10:10.

然後你會聽到……（播音）。依據所播放的內容，正確答案應該
選 B，請將答案卡該題「Ⓑ」的地方塗黑、塗滿，即：Ⓐ ● Ⓒ

11. (A) There's a car coming.
    (B) His watch is fast.
    (C) Be careful.

12. (A) It was easy.
    (B) It was hard.
    (C) It was funny.

13. (A) He can't go to the library tomorrow.
    (B) He can go to the library tomorrow.
    (C) He has no idea how to go to the library.

14. (A) She went somewhere fun.
    (B) She went there by herself.
    (C) She went there with her dad and mom.

15. (A) The man's dinner.
    (B) The woman's dinner.
    (C) How to cook.

16. (A) Cook dinner.
    (B) Go to the doctor.
    (C) Take a shower.

17. (A) The woman's class is behind schedule.
    (B) Every class began on schedule.
    (C) The teacher made a mistake about the class schedule.

18. (A) She's worried about her bills.
    (B) She's worried about her fireplace.
    (C) She is a real worry for her family.

19. (A) Trying to change a booking.
    (B) Asking for information about flights.
    (C) Checking in for a fight.

20. (A) The man's nickname.
    (B) The woman's nickname.
    (C) A nickname is a real name.

TEST 12 詳解

第一部分：辨識句意（第1-3題，共3題）

1. (**A**) (A)　　　　　(B)　　　　　(C)

Judy is watering the plants. 茱蒂正在給植物澆水。

　* water〔'wɔtɚ〕 *v.* 給…澆水　　plant〔plænt〕 *n.* 植物

2. (**B**) (A)　　　　　(B)　　　　　(C)

We're ready to take off. Fasten your seatbelts.

我們準備起飛。繫好你的安全帶。

　* ready〔'rɛdɪ〕 *adj.* 準備好的　　***take off*** 起飛
　 fasten〔'fæsn̩〕 *v.* 繫上　　seatbelt〔'sit,bɛlt〕 *n.* 安全帶

3. (**C**) (A)　　　　　(B)　　　　　(C)

I need a backpack for my trip this summer.

這個夏天我去旅行需要一個背包。

* backpack〔'bæk͵pæk〕*n.* 背包　　trip〔trɪp〕*n.* 旅行
　summer〔'sʌmɚ〕*n.* 夏天

第二部分：基本問答（第 4-10 題，共 7 題）

4.(**B**) Do you know how to protect yourself when meeting an
　　 Internet friend? 你知道見網友時要如何保護自己嗎？

　(A) I have no idea who will come to see me.
　　　我不知道誰會來看我。

　(B) Yes. I should meet him in a public place.
　　　知道。我應該在公共場所跟他見面。

　(C) Yes, I have made some friends through the Net.
　　　知道，我已經透過網路交了一些朋友。

　* protect〔prə'tɛkt〕*v.* 保護　　meet〔mit〕*v.* 和…見面
　　 Internet friend 網友　　***have no idea*** 不知道
　　 public〔'pʌblɪk〕*adj.* 大眾的；公共的　　***make friends*** 交朋友
　　 through〔θru〕*prep.* 透過　　***the Net*** 網路（= *the Internet*）

5.(**B**) You should add me as Facebook friend.
　　　你應該把加我爲臉書的朋友。

　(A) Leaving me to face the music. 讓我去承擔後果。

　(B) Facebook doesn't really interest me.
　　　我對臉書不是很有興趣。

　(C) It's a wonderful book. 這是一本很棒的書。

　* add〔æd〕*v.* 加　　***Facebook*** 臉書【社交軟體】
　　 leave〔liv〕*v.* 任由；讓　　***face the music*** 承擔後果
　　 interest〔'ɪntrɪst〕*v.* 使感興趣
　　 wonderful〔'wʌndɚfəl〕*adj.* 很棒的

6. (**C**) Why did you and Alex become good friends?
你和愛力克斯為何會成為好朋友？
(A) He knows nothing about me. 他對我毫無所知。
(B) I heard of him before. 我之前聽說過他。
(C) We have a lot in common. 我們有很多共同點。

* ***hear of*** 聽說　　***have…in common*** 有…共同點
a lot 很多

7. (**B**) Something we can do is eat at home more often.
我們可以做的事，就是更常在家裡吃飯。
(A) I buy only clothes that are on sale.
我可以只買特價的衣服。
(B) That's a good idea. 那是個好主意。
(C) I stop taking buses. 我停止搭公車。

* buy 〔 baɪ 〕 *v.* 買　　clothes 〔 kloz 〕 *n. pl.* 衣服
on sale 特價的　　***stop + V-ing*** 停止做～
take buses 搭公車

8. (**C**) How are your computer skills? 你的電腦技能如何？
(A) I prefer to use a computer. 我比較喜歡用電腦。
(B) I am good at cooking. 我擅長煮飯。
(C) Excellent. I taught myself web design.
很棒。我自學網頁設計。

* computer 〔 kəm'pjutɚ 〕 *n.* 電腦　　skill 〔 skɪl 〕 *n.* 技能；技巧
prefer 〔 prɪ'fɝ 〕 *v.* 比較喜歡；偏好
use 〔 juz 〕 *v.* 使用　　***be good at*** 擅長
excellent 〔'ɛkslənt 〕 *adj.* 極好的
taught 〔 tɔt 〕 *v.* 教【teach 的過去式】
design 〔 dɪ'saɪn 〕 *n.* 設計　　***web design*** 網頁設計

9. (**A**) When did the Titanic sink? I just need the year.
鐵達尼號是何時沈沒？我需要知道是哪一年。

    (A) April 15, 1912. <u>1912 年 4 月 15 日。</u>

    (B) Under the sea. 在海裡。

    (C) Wow! It's a huge ship. 哇！它是一艘巨大的船。

    * titanic〔taɪˈtænɪk〕*adj.* 巨大的　***the Titanic*** 鐵達尼號
      sink〔sɪŋk〕*v.* 下沈；沉沒
      wow〔waʊ〕*interj.*（表示驚嘆、喜悅等）哇
      huge〔hjudʒ〕*adj.* 巨大的　　ship〔ʃɪp〕*n.* 船

10. (**B**) Are you waiting for someone? 你在等人嗎？

    (A) Yeah, it's my favorite meal.
        是的，這是我最喜愛的一餐。

    (B) Yeah, my sister, Eva. <u>是的，我妹妹，伊娃。</u>

    (C) Yeah, I have a big family. 是的，我有一個大家庭。

    * ***wait for*** 等待　　yeah〔jæ〕*interj.* 是的（= *yes*）
      favorite〔ˈfevərɪt〕*adj.* 最喜愛的
      meal〔mil〕*n.* 一餐　　family〔ˈfæməlɪ〕*n.* 家庭

第三部分：言談理解（第 11-20 題，共 10 題）

11. (**C**) W : Hey, watch out!
        女：嘿，小心！

    M : Thanks. That motorcycle almost hit me!
        男：謝謝。那台摩托車差點撞到我！

    Question : What does she want the man to do?
              女士要男士做什麼？

    (A) There's a car coming. 有車子來了。

    (B) His watch is fast. 他的錶走比較快。

    (C) Be careful. <u>要小心。</u>

* hey〔he〕*interj.* 嘿　　***watch out*** 注意；小心
　motorcycle〔'motɚ͵saɪkl̩〕*n.* 摩托車
　almost〔'ɔl͵most〕*adv.* 幾乎；差一點
　hit〔hit〕*v.* 撞【三態為：hit-hit-hit】
　watch〔watʃ〕*n.* 手錶　　careful〔'kɛrfəl〕*adj.* 小心的

12. (**B**) M：How did the test go yesterday?
　　　　　男：昨天的考試進行得如何？
　　　　　W：It was a little bit hard.
　　　　　女：有一點難。
　　　　　M：Do you think you passed it?
　　　　　男：妳覺得妳會通過嗎？
　　　　　W：Yes, and about 80% of my classmates got grade C or
　　　　　　　above.
　　　　　女：會，而且我的同學裡大約百分之八十的人拿到 C 或是更
　　　　　　　高的成績。
　　　　　Question：What did the woman think of the test?
　　　　　　　　　　女士覺得考試如何？
　　　　　(A) It was easy. 很簡單。
　　　　　(B) It was hard. <u>很困難。</u>
　　　　　(C) It was funny. 很好笑。

　　　* test〔tɛst〕*n.* 考試　　go〔go〕*v.* 進行
　　　a little bit 有一點　　hard〔hard〕*adj.* 困難的
　　　pass〔pæs〕*v.* 通過　　classmate〔'klæs͵met〕*n.* 同班同學
　　　grade〔gred〕*n.* 成績　　above〔ə'bʌv〕*adv.* 在…以上
　　　think of 認為　　funny〔'fʌnɪ〕*adj.* 好笑的

13. (**B**) M：Hi.　How's everything?
　　　　　男：嗨。一切還好嗎？

W : Great. Listen, would you like to go to the library later?

女：很棒。聽我說，你待會想要去圖書館嗎？

M : I'm sorry. I can't.

男：很抱歉。我不行。

W : Really? Why not?

女：眞的嗎？爲什麼不？

M : I have to go to work. Do you want to go tomorrow? I'm off then.

男：我必須去工作。妳明天想去嗎？我明天休假。

Question : What does the man mean? 男士是什麼意思？

(A) He can't go the library tomorrow.

他明天不能去圖書館。

(B) He can go to the library tomorrow.

他明天可以去圖書館。

(C) He has no idea how to go to the library.

他不知道怎麼去圖書館。

* *would like to V.* 想要~　　library〔'laɪˌbrɛrɪ〕*n.* 圖書館
later〔'letɚ〕*adv.* 待會　　*have to V.* 必須~
go to work 去工作　　off〔ɔf〕*adj.* 休息的
mean〔min〕*v.* 意思是　　*have no idea* 不知道

14. (**C**)　M : Where did you go on your last trip?

男：妳上次去哪裡旅行？

W : I went to Hong Kong.

女：我去香港。

M : Wow! Did you go alone?

男：哇！妳自己去嗎？

W：No, I traveled with my parents.

女：不，我跟我父母去。

Question：What does the woman mean?

女士是什麼意思？

(A) She went somewhere fun. 她去了一個有趣的地方。

(B) She went there by herself. 她獨自去。

(C) She went there with her dad and mom.

　　 她和她爸爸媽媽一起去。

* last〔læst〕*adj.* 上次的　　trip〔trɪp〕*n.* 旅行
　Hong Kong〔'haŋ'kaŋ〕*n.* 香港
　wow〔waʊ〕*interj.*（表示驚嘆、喜悅等）哇
　alone〔ə'lon〕*adv.* 單獨地　　travel〔'trævl̩〕*v.* 旅行；去
　parents〔'pɛrənts〕*n. pl.* 父母　　mean〔min〕*v.* 意思是
　fun〔fʌn〕*adj.* 有趣的　　*by oneself* 獨自地

15. (**B**) M：Good evening. May I take your order now?

男：晚安。我現在可以幫您點餐嗎？

W：Yes. Tell me, what's today's special?

女：好的。告訴我，今天的特餐是什麼？

M：Well, it's roast beef and steamed rice.

男：嗯，是烤牛肉和蒸飯。

W：Oh, what a pity! I can't eat beef.

女：喔，眞可惜！我不能吃牛肉。

Question：What are they talking about?

他們在談論什麼？

(A) The man's dinner. 男士的晚餐。

(B) The woman's dinner. 女士的晚餐。

(C) How to cook. 如何煮飯。

* ***take** one's **order*** 幫某人點餐　　special〔'spɛʃəl〕 *n.* 特餐
roast〔rost〕*adj.* 烤的　　beef〔bif〕*n.* 牛肉
steam〔stim〕*v.* 蒸　***steamed rice*** 蒸飯
pity〔'pɪtɪ〕*n.* 可惜的事
cook〔kʊk〕*v.* 烹飪；做飯

16. (**C**)　W：What happened to your finger?

女：你的手指怎麼了？

M：It got burned while I was cooking dinner yesterday.

男：我昨天煮晚餐的時候燙傷了。

W：Did you see the doctor?

女：你看醫生了嗎？

M：Of course.　She told me not to take a shower for at least three days.

男：當然。她告訴我至少三天不能淋浴。

Question：What couldn't the man do yesterday?

男士昨天不能做什麼？

(A) Cook dinner.　煮晚餐。

(B) Go to the doctor.　去看醫生。

(C) Take a shower.　<u>淋浴。</u>

* *sth.* ***happen to*** *sb.* 某事發生在某人身上
finger〔'fɪŋgɚ〕*n.* 手指　　burn〔bɝn〕*v.* 燒；燙
get burned 被燙傷　　***of course*** 當然　　***take a shower*** 淋浴
at least 至少　　***go to the doctor*** 去看醫生（= *see the doctor* ）

17. (**C**)　M：Good morning, class.　Today we'll talk about the chapter "Food & Health."

男：早安，各位同學。今天我們要講的是「食物與健康」這個章節。

W : But Mr. Smith, you already taught us that and gave us some homework.

女：但是史密斯先生，你已經教過我們這一章了，也指派我們一些家庭作業了。

M : Oh, the whole class has learned this already?

男：喔，全班的同學都已經學過了嗎？

W : Yes, it must be the other class that's behind, not us...

女：是的，一定是另一個班進度落後了，不是我們…

Question : What does the woman mean?

　　　　女士是什麼意思？

(A) The woman's class is behind schedule.

女士的班級進度落後。

(B) Every class began on schedule.

每一堂課都準時開始。

(C) The teacher made a mistake about the class schedule.

老師弄錯了班級進度。

* class〔klæs〕*n.* 全班同學；班級；課程
  chapter〔'tʃæptɚ〕*n.* 章節　　health〔hɛlθ〕*n.* 健康
  already〔ɔl'rɛdɪ〕*adv.* 已經
  homework〔'hom,wɝk〕*n.* 家庭作業；功課
  whole〔hol〕*adj.* 全部的　　learn〔lɝn〕*v.* 學習
  must〔mʌst〕*aux.* 一定
  behind〔bɪ'haɪnd〕*adv.* 落後
  mean〔min〕*v.* 意思是
  schedule〔'skɛdʒul〕*n.* 預定表；時間表
  behind schedule 進度落後
  began〔bɪ'gæn〕*v.* 開始【begin 的過去式】
  on schedule 按照進度；準時
  make a mistake 犯錯

18. (**A**) M : You look sad. What is wrong?

男：妳看起來很難過。怎麼了？

W : I got fired from my job yesterday and I must pay the rent today.

女：我昨天被解雇，而且我今天必須付房租。

M : Wow! That's terrible. I'm sorry.

男：哇！好糟糕。我很抱歉。

W : Don't worry. I will find another job.

女：別擔心。我會找另一個工作。

Question : Why does the woman look sad?

女士爲何看起來很難過？

(A) She's worried about her bills.

她擔心她的帳單。

(B) She's worried about her fireplace.

她擔心她的壁爐。

(C) She is a real worry for her family.

對她的家人來說，她眞是令人擔心。

* look〔luk〕*v.* 看起來

sad〔sæd〕*adj.* 難過的

What's wrong? 怎麼了？

fire〔faɪr〕*v.* 解雇

job〔dʒɑb〕*n.* 工作   pay〔pe〕*v.* 支付

rent〔rɛnt〕*n.* 房租

terrible〔'tɛrəbl̩〕*adj.* 糟糕的

worry〔'wɝɪ〕*v.* 擔心   *n.* 令人擔心的事或人

be worried about 擔心

bill〔bɪl〕*n.* 帳單

fireplace〔'faɪr͵ples〕*n.* 壁爐

19. (**B**) M : Are there any seats on Sunday's flight?

男：週日的班機還有座位嗎？

W : No, I'm afraid our Sunday flight is fully booked.

女：沒有，恐怕週日的班機已經客滿。

M : Oh. How about on Friday?

男：喔。那週五呢？

W : Yes, there are still some seats left on Friday's flight.

女：有的，週五的班機還有剩下一些座位。

Question : What is the man doing?

男士在做什麼？

(A) Trying to change a booking.

想要更改預訂。

(B) Asking for information about flights.

詢問班機的資訊。

(C) Checking in for a flight.

辦理登機手續。

* seat〔sit〕*n.* 座位

flight〔flaɪt〕*n.* 班機

I'm afraid 恐怕

fully〔'fʊlɪ〕*adv.* 完全地

book〔bʊk〕*v.* 預訂

How about~? ～如何？

left〔lɛft〕*adj.* 剩下的

try〔traɪ〕*v.* 嘗試

change〔tʃendʒ〕*v.* 更改

booking〔'bʊkɪŋ〕*n.* 預訂

ask for 要求；請求

information〔ˌɪnfə'meʃən〕*n.* 資訊

check in 報到；辦理登機手續

20. (**B**) M : Did you use to have a cute nickname as a child?

男：妳小時候有可愛的綽號嗎？

W : Yes. How interesting it was!

女：有。這很有趣！

M : How did you get it?

男：妳怎麼會有綽號的？

W : My little brother couldn't say my name clearly, and after that, everyone started using that as my nickname.

女：我弟弟無法清楚地說出我的名字，之後，每個人都開始用那個當作我的綽號。

Question : What are they talking about?

他們在談論什麼？

(A) The man's nickname.

男士的綽號。

(B) The woman's nickname.

<u>女士的綽號。</u>

(C) A nickname is a real name.

綽號是眞名。

* **used to V**. 以前～
cute〔kjut〕*adj.* 可愛的
nickname〔'nɪkˌnem〕*n.* 綽號
interesting〔'ɪntrɪstɪŋ〕*adj.* 有趣的
say〔se〕*v.* 說
clearly〔'klɪrlɪ〕*adv.* 清楚地

TEST 13

第一部分：辨識句意（第1-3題，共3題）

作答說明：　第1-3題每題有三張圖片，請依據所聽到的內容，選出
　　　　　　符合描述的圖片，每題播放兩次。

示例題：你會看到

(A) 　　(B) 　　(C)

然後你會聽到……（播音）。依據所播放的內容，正確答案應該
選A，請將答案卡該題「Ⓐ」的地方塗黑、塗滿，即：● Ⓑ Ⓒ

1. (A) 　　(B) 　　(C)

2. (A)　　　　　　(B)　　　　　　(C)

3. (A)　　　　　　(B)　　　　　　(C)

第二部分：基本問答（第 4-10 題，共 7 題）

作答說明：第 4-10 題每題均有三個選項，請依據所聽到的內容，選出一個最適合的回應，每題播放兩次。

示例題：你會看到

(A) She is talking to the teacher.

(B) She is a student in my class.

(C) She is wearing a beautiful dress.

然後你會聽到……（播音）。依據所播放的內容，正確答案應該選 B，請將答案卡該題「Ⓑ」的地方塗黑、塗滿，即：Ⓐ ● Ⓒ

---

4. (A) Then we can go
   skiing together.
   (B) I wonder when the
   rain will stop.
   (C) Why not play Frisbee
   with your dog?

5. (A) I don't have enough
   money for that.
   (B) Sorry, but I can't
   remember where I
   hid the money.
   (C) Sorry, Mom. I'll
   learn to control my
   spending.

6. (A) It's a street dog.
   (B) I have two pets.
   (C) Yes. It's so pitiful.

7. (A) It's 0956222333.
   (B) It's No. 56, Sec. 1,
   Keelong Rd.
   (C) It's May 1st.

8. (A) A Coke, please.
   (B) Sure.
   (C) I'm not thirsty.

9. (A) It sure is! The dessert's
   really delicious.
   (B) I know. It's ok.
   (C) Beautiful day, isn't it?

10. (A) Because he enjoys it.
    (B) Because he kept
    watching TV all day.
    (C) Because he has no
    money.

第三部分：言談理解（第 11-20 題，共 10 題）

作答説明： 第 11-20 題每題均有三個選項，請依據所聽到的內容，
選出一個最適合的答案，每題播放兩次。

示例題：你會看到

(A) 9:50.　　(B) 10:00.　　(C) 10:10.

然後你會聽到⋯⋯（播音）。依據所播放的內容，正確答案應該
選 B，請將答案卡該題「Ⓑ」的地方塗黑、塗滿，即：Ⓐ ● Ⓒ

11. (A) Sports.
    (B) Health.
    (C) Music.

12. (A) A baby.
    (B) A cat.
    (C) A dog.

13. (A) A Hello Kitty cup.
    (B) Some boys' socks.
    (C) A pair of sunglasses.

14. (A) It was written by Billy Westin.
    (B) Billy was in an accident.
    (C) Billy didn't get his memory back in the end.

15. (A) At the police station.
    (B) In the restroom.
    (C) In the classroom.

16. (A) Forty dollars.
    (B) Fifty dollars.
    (C) Ten dollars.

17. (A) She doesn't think people should drive carefully when in rain.
    (B) She hates it when the man is late.
    (C) She can understand the reason why the man was late.

18. (A) He can't wear the necktie he likes.
    (B) He doesn't have a blue necktie.
    (C) He didn't wash the necktie he wanted to wear.

19. (A) Her cat attacked her.
    (B) She fell to the ground.
    (C) She jumped out of a tree.

20. (A) Dumplings.
    (B) A cake.
    (C) A sandwich.

TEST 13 詳解

第一部分:辨識句意 (第 1-3 題,共 3 題)

1. (**C**) (A)   (B)   (C)

My right arm hurts a lot. 我的右手臂很痛。

* right〔raɪt〕*adj.* 右邊的   arm〔ɑrm〕*n.* 手臂
 hurt〔hɜt〕*v.* 痛   ***a lot*** 很多;非常

2. (**A**) (A)   (B)   (C)

You cannot drink or eat on the MRT.

你不可以在捷運上飲食。

* drink〔drɪŋk〕*v.* 喝   ***MRT*** 捷運 (= *Mass Rapid Transit*)

3. (**A**) (A)   (B)   (C)

Peter usually helps his father wash the car on Sundays.

彼得週日通常會幫他父親洗車。

* usually〔ˈjuʒʊəlɪ〕*adv.* 通常　　help〔hɛlp〕*v.* 幫助
　wash〔waʃ〕*v.* 洗　　car〔kɑr〕*n.* 汽車

第二部分：基本問答（第 4-10 題，共 7 題）

4.（ **B** ）It has been raining for a week!

雨已經下一週了！

(A) Then we can go skiing together.

那麼我們可以一起去滑雪。

(B) I wonder when the rain will stop.

<u>我想知道雨何時會停。</u>

(C) Why not play Frisbee with your dog?

何不和你的狗玩飛盤？

* rain〔ren〕*v.* 下雨　　***go skiing*** 去滑雪
　wonder〔ˈwʌndɚ〕*v.* 想知道
　Why not + V.? 你何不～？（= *Why don't you V.?*）
　Frisbee〔ˈfrɪzbi〕*n.* 飛盤

5.（ **C** ）David, you spent too much last month!

大衛，你上個月花太多錢了！

(A) I don't have enough money for that.

我沒有足夠的錢買那個。

(B) Sorry, but I can't remember where I hid the money.

抱歉，但是我不記得我把錢藏在哪裡。

(C) Sorry, Mom. I'll learn to control my spending.

<u>抱歉，媽。我會學著控制花費。</u>

* spend〔spɛnd〕*v.* 花（錢、時間）
　hid〔hɪd〕*v.* 藏【hide 的過去式】　　learn〔lɝn〕*v.* 學習
　control〔kənˈtrol〕*v.* 控制

6. (**C**) Do you see the cat in the cage? 你有看到籠子裡的貓嗎？

    (A) It's a street dog. 是隻流浪狗。

    (B) I have two pets. 我有兩隻寵物。

    (C) Yes. It's so pitiful. <u>有。牠好可憐。</u>

    * cage〔kedʒ〕*n.* 籠子
    street dog 流浪狗（= *stray dog*）   pet〔pɛt〕*n.* 寵物
    so〔so〕*adv.* 非常   pitiful〔'pɪtɪfəl〕*adj.* 可憐的

7. (**B**) Can you tell me your address? I want to mail something to you. 你可以告訴我你的地址嗎？我想要寄東西給你。

    (A) It's 0956222333. 是 0956222333。

    (B) It's No. 56, Sec. 1, Keelong Rd. <u>基隆路一段 56 號。</u>

    (C) It's May 1st. 五月一日。

    * address〔'ædrɛs〕*n.* 地址   mail〔mel〕*v.* 郵寄
    No. 號碼（= *Number*）   ***Rd.*** 路（= *Road*）
    Sec. 段（= *Section*）

8. (**B**) Can we get something to eat? 我們可以買些東西吃嗎？

    (A) A Coke, please. 請給我一杯可口可樂。

    (B) Sure. <u>當然。</u>

    (C) I'm not thirsty. 我不渴。

    * get〔gɛt〕*v.* 買   Coke〔kok〕*n.* 可口可樂（= *Coca-Cola*）
    thirsty〔'θɝstɪ〕*adj.* 口渴的

9. (**A**) This is a great welcome party. 這是個很棒的歡迎會。

    (A) It sure is! The dessert's really delicious.
        <u>的確是！甜點真的很好吃。</u>

    (B) I know. It's ok. 我知道。沒關係。

    (C) Beautiful day, isn't it? 美好的一天，不是嗎？

> * great〔 gret 〕*adj.* 很棒的　　***welcome party*** 歡迎會
> sure〔 ʃur 〕*adv.* 的確　　dessert〔 dɪˈzɜt 〕*n.* 甜點
> delicious〔 dɪˈlɪʃəs 〕*adj.* 好吃的
> ***It's ok.*** 沒關係。(= *That's ok.*)
> beautiful〔ˈbjutəfəl 〕*adj.* 美麗的；美好的

10. (**B**) Why didn't Andy do the housework?
    為何安迪不做家事？

    (A) Because he enjoys it. 因為他喜歡。

    (B) Because he kept watching TV all day.
    　　 <u>因為他整天一直看電視。</u>

    (C) Because he has no money. 因為他沒有錢。

    > * housework〔ˈhaʊsˌwɜk 〕*n.* 家事
    > enjoy〔 ɪnˈdʒɔɪ 〕*v.* 享受；喜歡　　***keep V-ing*** 持續~；一直~

第三部分：言談理解（第 11-20 題，共 10 題）

11. (**C**) W：I can play the flute.
    女：我會吹長笛。

    M：And I can play the drums.
    男：而我會打鼓。

    W：Good. Maybe we can practice together next time.
    女：很好。或許我們下次可以一起練習。

    Question：What do they know about? 他們懂什麼？

    (A) Sports. 運動。

    (B) Health. 健康。

    (C) Music. <u>音樂。</u>

    > * play〔 ple 〕*v.* 演奏　　flute〔 flut 〕*n.* 長笛
    > drum〔 drʌm 〕*n.* 鼓　　maybe〔ˈmebɪ 〕*adv.* 或許；可能
    > practice〔ˈpræktɪs 〕*v.* 練習　　***next time*** 下一次
    > sport〔 sport 〕*n.* 運動　　health〔 hɛlθ 〕*n.* 健康
    > music〔ˈmjuzɪk 〕*n.* 音樂

12. (**B**)　W : Can you help take care of Jessie for a week?　I'll be
　　　　　　 in Shanghai on business.

　　　女：你可以幫我照顧潔西一週嗎？我要去上海出差。

　　　M : No problem.　What should I do then?

　　　男：沒問題。那我應該怎麼做？

　　　W : You don't have to walk her or play with her.　She is
　　　　　 not a dog.　Just feed her twice a day and fill the bowl
　　　　　 with water for her.　By the way, don't give her fish.
　　　　　 She doesn't eat fish, not like any other cats do.

　　　女：你不需要帶牠散步或是跟牠完。牠不是狗。只要一天餵牠兩
　　　　　次，然後幫牠把碗裝滿水。順帶一提，不要給牠魚。牠不吃
　　　　　魚，不像其他的貓。

　　　Question : What is Jessie?　傑西是什麼？

　　　(A) A baby.　一個嬰兒。

　　　(B) A cat.　一隻貓。

　　　(C) A dog.　一隻狗。

　　　* **take care of** 照顧　　Shanghai〔'ʃæŋ'haɪ〕*n.* 上海
　　　　on business 出差　　**No problem.** 沒問題。
　　　　then〔ðɛn〕*adv.* 那麼
　　　　walk〔wɔk〕*v.* 溜（狗）；帶…去散步　　feed〔fid〕*v.* 餵
　　　　fill A **with** B　用 B 裝滿 A　　bowl〔bol〕*n.* 碗
　　　　by the way 順便一提

13. (**C**)　W : Dad, where is my Hello Kitty cup?

　　　女：爸，我的凱蒂貓杯子在哪裡？

　　　M : Isn't it on the top shelf in the living room?

　　　男：不是在客廳上面的架子上嗎？

　　　W : No, I only see your watch, Mom's sunglasses, and
　　　　　 Jack's cap there.

　　　女：不，我只有看到你的手錶、媽的太陽眼鏡，和傑克的帽子。

Question : What is on the shelf?

架子上有什麼？

(A) A Hello Kitty cup. 凱蒂貓杯子。

(B) Some boys' socks. 一些男用的短襪。

(C) A pair of sunglasses. 一副太陽眼鏡。

* **Hello Kitty** 凱蒂貓   cup〔kʌp〕n. 杯子
  shelf〔ʃɛlf〕n. 架子   **living room** 客廳
  watch〔watʃ〕n. 手錶
  sunglasses〔'sʌn,glæsɪz〕n. pl. 太陽眼鏡
  cap〔kæp〕n.（無邊的）帽子   socks〔saks〕n. pl. 短襪
  a pair of 一副；一對

14. (**B**) M : What are you reading?

男： 妳在讀什麼？

W : Joe Westin's new book.

女： 喬‧威斯汀的新書。

M : What's it about?

男： 書的內容是關於什麼？

W : A man named Billy was hit by a truck and lost his memory. He tries to get his memory back, but things are not as easy as he thinks.

女： 一位名叫比利的男子被卡車撞到，並失去記憶。他嘗試要恢復他的記憶，但是事情並不如他想像得容易。

M : Does he make it?

男： 他有成功嗎？

W : I don't know. I haven't finished it.

女： 我不知道。我還沒看完。

Question : What do we know about the book?

關於這本書我們知道什麼？

(A) It was written by Billy Westin.

這是由比利・威斯汀所寫。

(B) Billy was in an accident.

<u>比利發生一場車禍。</u>

(C) Billy didn't get his memory back in the end.

比利最後沒有恢復記憶。

* read〔rid〕*v.* 讀　　***named*** 名叫～
  hit〔hɪt〕*v.* 撞【三態爲：hit-hit-hit】　　　truck〔trʌk〕*n.* 卡車
  lost〔lɔst〕*v.* 失去【lose 的過去式】
  memory〔'mɛmərɪ〕*n.* 記憶　　try〔traɪ〕*v.* 嘗試
  get back 取回；恢復　　***make it*** 成功；辦到
  finish〔'fɪnɪʃ〕*v.* 完成；做完
  accident〔'æksədent〕*n.* 意外；車禍
  in the end 最後

15. (**C**) M：You stole my cellphone!

男：妳偷了我的手機！

W：No, I didn't. Watch your mouth.

女：不，我沒有。說話要小心。

M：Yes, you did. I left it on the desk before going to the restroom. I saw you standing next to my desk. Now I'm back in the classroom and my cellphone is gone.

男：有，妳偷的。我在去廁所前，把手機放在書桌上。我看到妳站在我書桌的旁邊。現在我回到教室了，而我的手機不見了。

W：I didn't do any such a thing. Let's go to the teacher's office to ask Ms. Lin for help.

女：我沒有做這樣的事。我們一起去老師的辦公室請林老師幫忙。

Question：Where are the two people now?

這兩個人現在在哪裡？

(A) At the police station. 在警察局。

(B) In the restroom. 在廁所。

(C) In the classroom. 在教室。

* stole〔stol〕v. 偷【steal 的過去式】

cellphone〔'sɛl,fon〕n. 手機 (= *cell phone*)

watch〔watʃ〕v. 小心;注意

watch** one's **mouth 說話當心

left〔lɛft〕v. 遺留【leave 的過去式】

desk〔dɛsk〕n. 書桌　　restroom〔'rɛst,rum〕n. 廁所

nex to 在…的旁邊　　classroom〔'klæs,rum〕n. 教室

gone〔gɔn〕adj. 遺失的;不見的　　***Let's + V.*** 我們一起~吧。

office〔'ɔfɪs〕n. 辦公室　　***ask** sb. **for help*** 向某人求助

police station 警察局

16. (**A**) W : John, how much money do you have now?

女:約翰,你現在有多少錢?

M : I have twenty dollars in my pocket. Why?

男:我口袋裡有二十元。為什麼這麼問?

W : The skirt is fifty dollars and I don't have enough
money for it. So lend me ten dollars, will you?

女:裙子要五十元,而我不夠錢買。所以,借我十元,好嗎?

Question : How much does the woman have?

女士有多少錢?

(A) Forty dollars. 四十元。

(B) Fifty dollars. 五十元。

(C) Ten dollars. 十元。

* pocket〔'pakɪt〕n. 口袋　　skirt〔skɝt〕n. 裙子

enough〔ɪ'nʌf〕adj. 足夠的　　lend〔lɛnd〕v. 借 (出)

17. (**C**) W : Hey, what took you so long?

女：嘿，什麼耽擱你這麼久？

M : Sorry, I was caught in a traffic jam.

男：抱歉，我遇到塞車。

W : Was that because of the heavy rain?

女：是因為大雨嗎？

M : Probably. People usually drive more carefully and slowly when it rains.

男：可能吧。人們通常下雨時開車會更小心，而且也更慢。

W : Right. You just can't be too careful when driving, especially in rain.

女：沒錯。你開車時要非常小心，特別是在雨中。

Question : What does the woman mean?

女士是什麼意思？

(A) She doesn't think people should drive carefully when in rain. 她不認為人們在下雨時應該小心開車。

(B) She hates it when the man is late.
她討厭男士遲到。

(C) She can understand the reason why the man was late.
她可以了解為何男士遲到。

* took〔tuk〕*v.* 花（時間）【take 的過去式】
 be caught in 遇到　　***a traffic jam*** 塞車
 because of 因為　　***heavy rain*** 大雨
 probably〔'prɑbəblɪ〕*adv.* 可能
 usually〔'juʒuəlɪ〕*adv.* 通常　　drive〔draɪv〕*v.* 開車
 carefully〔'kɛrfəlɪ〕*adv.* 小心地　　slowly〔'slolɪ〕*adv.* 緩慢地
 can't be too + *adj.* 再…也不為過；要非常…
 especially〔ə'spɛʃəlɪ〕*adv.* 特別地；尤其
 mean〔min〕*v.* 意思是　　hate〔het〕*v.* 討厭

late〔 let 〕*adj.* 晚的；遲到的
hate it when S. + V. 討厭某事發生【it 是虛受詞代替後面的 when 子句】
understand〔ˌʌndəˈstænd〕*v.* 了解
reason〔ˈrizn̩〕*n.* 理由

18. (**A**) M : Mom, where is my necktie? I can't go to the party without it.

男：媽？我的領帶在哪裡？我去派對不能沒有它。

W : I believe it is in the washing machine right now. Honey, can't you wear another one? The blue one in the drawer is nice too.

女：我相信領帶現在還在洗衣機裡。親愛的，你不能戴另一條嗎？抽屜裡面藍色那條也很好呀。

M : No, blue doesn't look good on me.

男：不，我戴藍色的不好看。

Question : What problem does the man have at the moment? 男士現在有什麼問題？

(A) He can't wear the necktie he likes.
他無法戴他喜歡的領帶。

(B) He doesn't have a blue necktie.
他沒有藍色的領帶。

(C) He didn't wash the necktie he wanted to wear.
他沒有洗他想要戴的領帶。

* necktie〔ˈnɛkˌtaɪ〕*n.* 領帶（= *tie*）　party〔ˈpɑrtɪ〕*n.* 派對
believe〔bəˈliv〕*v.* 相信　***washing machine*** 洗衣機
right now 現在　honey〔ˈhʌnɪ〕*n.*（暱稱）親愛的
wear〔wɛr〕*v.* 穿；戴　drawer〔ˈdrɔɚ〕*n.* 抽屜
***look good on** sb.* 適合某人
problem〔ˈprɑbləm〕*n.* 問題　***at the moment*** 此刻；現在

19. (**B**) W : I broke my arm.

女： 我摔斷了手臂。

M : How? What happened?

男： 怎麼會？發生什麼事？

W : I climbed up a tree to catch my cat, Dudu, but it jumped away. Then I fell out of the tree.

女： 我爬樹要去抓我的貓，嘟嘟，但牠跳走了。然後我就從樹上摔下來。

M : Did you get Dudu?

男： 妳有抓到嘟嘟嗎？

W : No, it jumped to another tree.

女： 沒有，牠跳到另一棵樹。

Question : How did the girl's arm get hurt?

女孩的手臂是如何受傷的？

(A) Her cat attacked her.

她的貓攻擊她。

(B) She fell to the ground.

她摔到地上。

(C) She jumped out of a tree.

她從樹上跳下來。

* broke〔brok〕*v.* 摔斷【break 的過去式】
  arm〔ɑrm〕*n.* 手臂
  happen〔'hæpən〕*v.* 發生
  climb〔klaɪm〕*v.* 爬
  catch〔kætʃ〕*v.* 抓
  jump〔dʒʌmp〕*v.* 跳
  fall〔fɔl〕*v.* 掉落   *get hurt* 受傷
  attack〔ə'tæk〕*v.* 攻擊
  ground〔graʊnd〕*n.* 地面

20. (**B**)　W : Here are milk, flour, eggs and sugar.　Now, add some
　　　　　　　water to the flour.

女：這裡有牛奶、麵粉、蛋，和糖。現在，加點水到麵粉裡。

M : Okay.　And next?

男：好的。接下來呢？

W : Then put three eggs and two cups of milk into it.

女：然後放三顆蛋和兩杯牛奶進去。

M : Done.

男：好了。

W : Now you're ready to put it in the oven and start
　　baking it.

女：現在你可以準備把它放進烤箱開始烤了。

Question：What is the woman teaching the man to make?

　　　　女士在教男士做什麼？

(A) Dumplings.　水餃。

(B) A cake.　<u>蛋糕。</u>

(C) A sandwich.　三明治。

* milk〔mɪlk〕*n.* 牛奶　　flour〔flaʊr〕*n.* 麵粉
  egg〔ɛg〕*n.* 蛋　　sugar〔'ʃʊgɚ〕*n.* 糖
  add〔æd〕*v.* 加　　next〔nɛkst〕*adv.* 接下來
  cup〔kʌp〕*n.* 一杯的量
  done〔dʌn〕*adj.* 完成的
  ready〔'rɛdɪ〕*adj.* 準備好的
  oven〔'ʌvən〕*n.* 烤箱　　bake〔bek〕*v.* 烤
  dumpling〔'dʌmplɪŋ〕*n.* 水餃
  cake〔kek〕*n.* 蛋糕
  sandwich〔'sændwɪtʃ〕*n.* 三明治

TEST 14

第一部分：辨識句意（第 1-3 題，共 3 題）

作答說明： 第 1-3 題每題有三張圖片，請依據所聽到的內容，選出
符合描述的圖片，每題播放兩次。

示例題：你會看到

(A) 　(B) 　(C)

然後你會聽到……（播音）。依據所播放的內容，正確答案應該
選 A，請將答案卡該題「Ⓐ」的地方塗黑、塗滿，即：● Ⓑ Ⓒ

---

1. (A) 　(B) 　(C)

2. (A)   (B)   (C)

  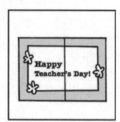

3. (A)   (B)   (C)

第二部分：基本問答（第 4-10 題，共 7 題）

作答說明： 第 4-10 題每題均有三個選項，請依據所聽到的內容，選出一個最適合的回應，每題播放兩次。

> 示例題：你會看到
>
> (A) She is talking to the teacher.
> (B) She is a student in my class.
> (C) She is wearing a beautiful dress.
>
> 然後你會聽到……（播音）。依據所播放的內容，正確答案應該選 B，請將答案卡該題「Ⓑ」的地方塗黑、塗滿，即：Ⓐ ● Ⓒ

4. (A) Yes, the shopping mall is around the corner.
   (B) Yes, my mom works in a flower shop.
   (C) Sorry, I am new in the city too.

5. (A) I want to be an astronaut too.
   (B) That is also mine.
   (C) How about your dream?

6. (A) I don't have any hats.
   (B) I don't like the color blue.
   (C) It didn't look good on me.

7. (A) You borrowed the book from Tom, not me.
   (B) Oops. I'm sorry. I can't lend you the book.
   (C) Can I give it back to you next Friday, please?

8. (A) One fifty p.m.
   (B) It's two fifty now.
   (C) It is fifty minutes.

9. (A) He didn't mean it.
   (B) He's fine.
   (C) He's doing homework.

10. (A) I had a great childhood.
    (B) I need to exercise more and more.
    (C) I used to play basketball.

第三部分：言談理解（第 11-20 題，共 10 題）

作答說明： 第 11-20 題每題均有三個選項，請依據所聽到的內容，選出一個最適合的答案，每題播放兩次。

示例題：你會看到

(A) 9:50.　　(B) 10:00.　　(C) 10:10.

然後你會聽到……（播音）。依據所播放的內容，正確答案應該選 B，請將答案卡該題「Ⓑ」的地方塗黑、塗滿，即：Ⓐ ● Ⓒ

11. (A) Grace.
    (B) Cathy.
    (C) Lilian.

12. (A) In a market.
    (B) In a hospital.
    (C) At an airport.

13. (A) A mail deliverer.
    (B) A shopkeeper.
    (C) A taxi driver

14. (A) Nobody.
    (B) The woman.
    (C) The woman's husband.

15. (A) Their plans for a
        holiday.
    (B) The fireworks near
        Taipei 101.
    (C) How important friends
        and family are.

16. (A) At a gym.
    (B) At a sports shop.
    (C) On the school team.

17. (A) Her son got bad
        grades in math.
    (B) Her son did
        something wrong at
        school.
    (C) She can't teach her
        son math.

18. (A) She is going to leave
        soon.
    (B) She will not go if she
        finds the glasses.
    (C) She will leave when
        she finds her glasses.

19. (A) The gas station.
    (B) The movie theater.
    (C) Their home.

20. (A) A trip to America.
    (B) How to learn a
        language well.
    (C) How difficult a
        language is.

TEST 14 詳解

第一部分：辨識句意（第 1-3 題，共 3 題）

1. (**B**) (A)   (B)   (C)

Anna sang the song terribly. 安娜歌唱得很糟糕。

* sang〔sæŋ〕*v.* 唱歌【sing 的過去式】
   song〔sɔŋ〕*n.* 歌   terribly〔'tɛrəblɪ〕*adv.* 糟糕地

2. (**C**) (A)   (B)   (C)

The students made a card for their teacher.

學生做了一張卡片給他們的老師。

* card〔kɑrd〕*n.* 卡片

3. (**A**) (A)   (B)   (C)

Look! The man on TV is doing magic tricks.
你看！電視上的男子正在表演魔術。

* magic (ˈmædʒɪk) *adj.* 魔術的
  trick (trɪk) *n.* 把戲；戲法　　***do tricks*** 變戲法

第二部分：基本問答（第 4-10 題，共 7 題）

4. (**C**) Excuse me. Is there a flower shop near here?
   對不起。這附近有花店嗎？

　　(A) Yes, the shopping mall is around the corner.
　　　　有，購物中心就在轉角。

　　(B) Yes, my mom works in a flower shop.
　　　　有，我媽媽在花店工作。

　　(C) Sorry, I am new in the city too.
　　　　抱歉，我也是剛來到這城市。

　　* ***Excuse me.*** 對不起。【用於引起注意】
　　flower shop 花店　　***shopping mall*** 購物中心
　　around the corner 在轉角處
　　work (wɜk) *v.* 工作　　new (nju) *adj.* 新來的

5. (**B**) My dream is to travel around the world.
   我的夢想是環遊世界。

　　(A) I want to be an astronaut too.
　　　　我也想要當太空人。

　　(B) That is also mine. 那也是我的夢想。

　　(C) How about your dream? 你的夢想呢？

　　* dream (drim) *n.* 夢想　　travel (ˈtrævl̩) *v.* 旅行
　　around the world 全世界
　　astronaut (ˈæstrə‚nɔt) *n.* 太空人
　　How about ~? ～如何？

6. (**C**) Why didn't you buy the red cap?

你為什麼沒有買那頂紅色的帽子?

(A) I don't have any hats. 我沒有任何帽子。

(B) I don't like the color blue. 我不喜歡藍色。

(C) It didn't look good on me. 那不適合我。

* buy〔baɪ〕*v.* 買　　cap〔kæp〕*n.* (無邊的) 帽子

look good on *sb.* 適合某人

7. (**C**) Please give me the book I lent you last week.

請給我我上週借給你的那本書。

(A) You borrowed the book from Tom, not me.

你是跟湯姆借,不是我。

(B) Oops. I'm sorry. I can't lend you the book.

唉呀。對不起。我無法借那本書給你。

(C) Can I give it back to you next Friday, please?

我下週五再還給你好嗎?

* book〔bʊk〕*n.* 書　　lent〔lɛnt〕*v.* 借 (出)【lend 的過去式】

borrow〔'baro〕*v.* 借 (入)

oops〔ʊps〕*interj.* (表示驚訝、驚慌等) 唉呀

give back 歸還　　please〔pliz〕*adv.* 請;好嗎

8. (**A**) What time is the English class? 英文課是幾點幾分?

(A) One fifty p.m. 下午一點五十分。

(B) It's two fifty now. 現在是兩點五十分。

(C) It is fifty minutes. 五十分鐘。

* class〔klæs〕*n.* 課程　　***p.m.*** 下午 (= *post meridiem*)

minute〔'mɪnɪt〕*n.* 分鐘

9. (**B**) How's your brother doing? 你弟弟好嗎？

    (A) He didn't mean it. 他不是故意的。

    (B) He's fine. <u>他很好。</u>

    (C) He's doing homework. 他正在做功課。

    * do〔do〕*v.*（生活）過得　　mean〔min〕*v.* 有意；故意
    homework〔'hom,wɜk〕*n.* 家庭作業

10. (**C**) What kind of things did you do as a kid?
    你小時候都做些什麼事情？

    (A) I had a great childhood. 我有一個很棒的童年。

    (B) I need to exercise more and more. 我越來越需要運動。

    (C) I used to play basketball. <u>我以前常打籃球。</u>

    * kind〔kaɪnd〕*n.* 種類　　kid〔kɪd〕*n.* 小孩　　*as a kid* 小時候
    childhood〔'tʃaɪld,hʊd〕*n.* 童年　　exercise〔'ɛksə,saɪz〕*v.* 運動
    used to V. 以前常常~　　*play basketball* 打籃球

第三部分：言談理解（第 11-20 題，共 10 題）

11. (**C**) M : Grace is bicycle-riding. Cathy is roller-skating.
           Lilian is surfing the Net.

    男：格蕾絲在騎腳踏車。凱茜在溜冰。莉莉安在瀏覽網路。

    W : They are so busy.

    女：他們好忙。

    Question : Who is not exercising? 誰沒在運動？

    (A) Grace. 格蕾絲。　　　　(B) Cathy. 凱茜。

    (C) Lilian. <u>莉莉安。</u>

    * bicycle-ride〔'baɪ,sɪkl̩,raɪd〕*v.* 騎腳踏車
    roller-skate〔'rolə,sket〕*v.* 溜冰　　surf〔sɜf〕*v.* 瀏覽
    the Net 網路（= *the Internet*）　　busy〔'bɪzɪ〕*adj.* 忙碌的
    exercise〔'ɛksə,saɪz〕*v.* 運動

12. (**B**) W : Good afternoon, sir.

女：先生，午安。

M : Good afternoon. I have an appointment with Dr. Fitch at three p.m.

男：午安。我和費奇醫生有預約下午三點看診。

W : Let me check. Are you Mr. Huang?

女：讓我查一下。您是黃先生嗎？

M : Yes, I am.

男：是的，我是。

W : Please wait over there. I will call your name as soon as the doctor is ready.

女：請在那裡稍等一下。醫生準備好時，我會叫您的名字。

Question : Where are they? 他們在哪裡？

(A) In a market. 在市場。

(B) In a hospital. 在醫院。

(C) At an airport. 在機場。

* appointment〔ə'pɔɪntmənt〕*n.* 預約；約診
  Dr. 醫生（ = *Doctor* ）
  p.m. 下午（ = *post meridiem* ）
  check〔tʃɛk〕*v.* 查看   wait〔wet〕*v.* 等待
  over there 在那裡   ***as soon as*** 一…就～
  ready〔'rɛdɪ〕*adj.* 準備好的   market〔'mɑrkɪt〕*n.* 市場
  hospital〔'hɑspɪtl̩〕*n.* 醫院   airport〔'ɛr,port〕*n.* 機場

13. (**A**) M : This is for you. Please sign your name at the bottom.

男：這是給妳的。請在底下簽名。

W : Okay, it's done. How heavy the package is! It must be from my parents.

女：好的，簽好了。這包裹真重！一定是我爸媽寄來的。

Question : What is the man? 男士的職業是什麼？

(A) A mail deliverer. 郵差。

(B) A shopkeeper. 商店老闆。

(C) A taxi driver. 計程車司機。

* sign〔saɪn〕v. 簽（名）　　bottom〔'batəm〕n. 底部
done〔dʌn〕adj. 完成的　　heavy〔'hɛvɪ〕adj. 重的
package〔'pækɪdʒ〕n. 包裹　　must〔mʌst〕aux. 一定
parents〔'pɛrənts〕n. pl. 父母　　mail〔mel〕n. 信件
deliverer〔dɪ'lɪvərɚ〕n. 遞送者　　***mail deliverer*** 郵差
shopkeeper〔'ʃap,kipɚ〕n. 商店老闆
taxi〔'tæksɪ〕n. 計程車　　driver〔'draɪvɚ〕n. 司機

14. (**C**)　W : I was locked outside last night.

女：我昨晚被鎖在外面。

M : What? Why couldn't you enter the house?

男：什麼？妳為什麼無法進家門？

W : I forgot to bring the key.

女：我忘了帶鑰匙。

M : Why not ring the doorbell?

男：妳何不按電鈴？

W : I did! But my husband was deep in sleep. He didn't hear the ringing at all.

女：我按了！但是我老公睡得很熟。他完全沒聽到電鈴聲。

Question : Who was in the woman's house last night?

誰昨晚在女士的家裡？

(A) Nobody. 沒人。

(B) The woman. 女士。

(C) The woman's husband. 女士的老公。

* lock〔lak〕v. 鎖
outside〔'aʊt'saɪd〕adv. 在外面　　enter〔'ɛntɚ〕v. 進入

forgot〔fəˋgɑt〕*v.* 忘記【forget 的過去式】

key〔ki〕*n.* 鑰匙　　***Why not~?*** 你何不~?

ring〔rɪŋ〕*v.* 響(鈴);按(鈴)　　doorbell〔ˋdor͵bɛl〕*n.* 門鈴

husband〔ˋhʌzbənd〕*n.* 丈夫;老公　　***deep in sleep*** 熟睡

not~at all 一點也不~;完全沒有~

15. (**A**) M : What will you do on New Year's Eve?

　　　男: 妳除夕夜要做什麼?

　　　W : I will go to Taipei 101 with my friend. There will be a fireworks show. How about you?

　　　女: 我會和朋友去台北 101。那裡會有煙火秀。你呢?

　　　M : I will have a big dinner with my family. My grandparents are coming back from America.

　　　男: 我會和我的家人吃頓大餐。我祖父母要從美國回來。

　　　Question : What are they talking about? 他們在談論什麼?

　　　(A) Their plans for a holiday. 他們假日的計畫。

　　　(B) The fireworks near Taipei 101.

　　　　　台北 101 附近的煙火。

　　　(C) How important friends and family are.

　　　　　朋友和家人有多重要。

　　　* ***New Year's Eve*** 除夕夜　　fireworks〔ˋfaɪə͵wɝks〕*n. pl.* 煙火

　　　show〔ʃo〕*n.* 表演　　big〔bɪg〕*adj.* 豐盛的

　　　family〔ˋfæməlɪ〕*n.* 家人

　　　grandparents〔ˋgrænd͵pɛrənts〕*n. pl.* (外) 祖父母

　　　talk about 談論　　plan〔plæn〕*n.* 計畫

　　　holiday〔ˋhɑlə͵de〕*n.* 假日　　important〔ɪmˋpɔrtn̩t〕*adj.* 重要的

16. (**B**) M : Do you have children's gloves and bats?

　　　男: 妳們有兒童的手套和球棒嗎?

　　　W : Yes. You can find them on the second floor, in the Children's Department. How old is your boy?

女：有。你可以在二樓兒童部找到。你的兒子多大？

M : In fact, they are for my daughter. She is eleven and she will join the school team this spring.

男：事實上，是給我的女兒的。她十一歲，而且他今年春天加入校隊。

Question : Where are they? 他們在哪裡？

(A) At a gym. 在體育館。

(B) At a sports shop. <u>在運動用品店。</u>

(C) On the school team. 在校隊。

* glove〔glʌv〕*n.* 手套　　bat〔bæt〕*n.* 球棒
floor〔flor〕*n.* 樓層　　children〔'tʃɪldrən〕*n. pl.* 兒童
department〔dɪ'pɑrtmənt〕*n.* 部門　　boy〔bɔɪ〕*n.* 男孩；兒子
in fact 事實上　　daughter〔'dɔtɚ〕*n.* 女兒
join〔dʒɔɪn〕*v.* 加入　　*school team* 校隊
gym〔dʒɪm〕*n.* 體育館　　*sports shop* 運動用品店

17. (**B**) M : You looked angry. What's the matter?

男：妳看起來很生氣。怎麼了？

W : I had a talk with my son's teacher this morning. My son was caught cheating on the math quiz again!

女：我今天早上和我兒子的老師談話。我兒子又被抓到數學小考作弊！

M : He shouldn't have done that.

男：他當時不該那麼做。

Question : Why is the woman so angry?

爲何女士如此生氣？

(A) Her son got bad grades in math. 她的兒子數學考不好。

(B) Her son did something wrong at school.
<u>她的兒子在學校做錯事。</u>

(C) She can't teach her son math. 她無法敎她兒子數學。

```
* look〔lʊk〕v. 看起來    angry〔'æŋgrɪ〕adj. 生氣的
  What's the matter? 怎麼了?    have a talk with 與…談話
  be caught + V-ing 被抓到~
  math〔mæθ〕n. 數學 ( = mathematics )    quiz〔kwɪz〕n. 小考
  shouldn't have + p.p. 當時不該~    grade〔gred〕n. 成績
```

18. (**C**) M : It's late. Why are you still in the library?

男: 很晚了。妳怎麼會還在圖書館?

W : I can't find my glasses. I am sure they are somewhere in the library. I won't leave until I find them.

女: 我找不到我的眼鏡。我確定一定是在圖書館的某個地方。我找到他們才會離開。

Question : What does the girl mean? 女孩是什麼意思?

(A) She is going to leave soon. 她要很快就要離開。

(B) She will not go if she finds the glasses. 如果她找到眼鏡,就不會離開。

(C) She will leave when she finds her glasses. 當她找到眼鏡,就會離開。

```
* late〔let〕adj. 晚的    library〔'laɪ,brɛrɪ〕n. 圖書館
  glasses〔'glæsɪz〕n. pl. 眼鏡    leave〔liv〕v. 離開
  not…until~ 直到~才…    mean〔min〕v. 意思是
```

19. (**A**) M : Hurry up! The movie begins at 5:30. We only have twenty minutes to drive to the theater.

男: 快一點!電影五點三十分開始。我們只有二十分鐘開車到電影院。

W : But I am afraid that we don't have enough gas to drive there.

女: 但恐怕我們沒有足夠的油開到那裡。

M : Don't worry. There is a gas station on the way to the theater. We can go there first.

男：別擔心。到電影院的路上有一間加油站。我們可以先去那裡。

Question : Where will they go next? 他們接下來會去哪裡？

(A) The gas station. 加油站。

(B) The movie theater. 電影院。

(C) Their home. 他們的家。

* ***hurry up*** 趕快　　movie〔'muvɪ〕*n.* 電影
minute〔'mɪnɪt〕*n.* 分鐘　　drive〔draɪv〕*v.* 開車
theater〔'θiətə〕*n.* 電影院　　***I am afraid*** 恐怕
enough〔ɪ'nʌf〕*adj.* 足夠的　　gas〔gæs〕*n.* 汽油
worry〔'wɜɪ〕*v.* 擔心　　***gas station*** 加油站
on the way to 到…的路上　　next〔nɛkst〕*adv.* 接下來

20. (**B**)　W : You speak English so well. How do you do it?

女：你英文說得真好。你怎麼做到的？

M : Use any chance to practice it. Also, I take a trip to America once a year. There, I can practice speaking English more.

男：利用任何可以練習英文的機會。另外，我每年去美國旅行一次。在那裡，我可以更常練習說英文。

Question : What are they talking about? 他們在談論什麼？

(A) A trip to America. 去美國的旅行。

(B) How to learn a language well. 如何學好語言。

(C) How difficult a language is. 語言有多困難。

* speak〔spik〕*v.* 說（語言）　　well〔wɛl〕*adv.* 良好地
use〔juz〕*v.* 使用；利用　　chance〔tʃæns〕*n.* 機會
practice〔'præktɪs〕*v.* 練習　　also〔'ɔlso〕*adv.* 而且；另外
trip〔trɪp〕*n.* 旅行　　once〔wʌns〕*adv.* 一次
learn〔lɜn〕*v.* 學習　　language〔'læŋgwɪdʒ〕*n.* 語言
difficult〔'dɪfə,kʌlt〕*adj.* 困難的

TEST 15

第一部分：辨識句意（第1-3題，共3題）

作答說明：第1-3題每題有三張圖片，請依據所聽到的內容，選出
符合描述的圖片，每題播放兩次。

示例題：你會看到

(A) 　　(B) 　　(C)

然後你會聽到……（播音）。依據所播放的內容，正確答案應該
選 A，請將答案卡該題「Ⓐ」的地方塗黑、塗滿，即：● Ⓑ Ⓒ

---

1. (A) 　　(B) 　　(C)

2. (A)　　　　　(B)　　　　　(C)

3. (A)　　　　　(B)　　　　　(C)

第二部分：基本問答（第 4-10 題，共 7 題）

作答說明： 第 4-10 題每題均有三個選項，請依據所聽到的內容，選出一個最適合的回應，每題播放兩次。

示例題：你會看到

(A) She is talking to the teacher.

(B) She is a student in my class.

(C) She is wearing a beautiful dress.

然後你會聽到……（播音）。依據所播放的內容，正確答案應該選 B，請將答案卡該題「Ⓑ」的地方塗黑、塗滿，即：Ⓐ ● Ⓒ

4. (A) Um, I plan to take the recycling out.
   (B) Um, I'll try to be quick.
   (C) Um, it sounds fun.

5. (A) They are expensive.
   (B) They were sent here yesterday.
   (C) They are hers.

6. (A) That would be nice.
   (B) This is Allen speaking.
   (C) No one answered the phone.

7. (A) Have you seen any in the room?
   (B) Didn't you look for it?
   (C) Isn't it beside the lamp?

8. (A) Why? I thought you liked teaching.
   (B) Being a secretary is difficult.
   (C) What a good idea!

9. (A) Not really. It tastes like mud.
   (B) Wow. It sounds amazing!
   (C) Thanks. It's my pleasure.

10. (A) I hope not. I'm going camping.
    (B) Why? Do you have any plans?
    (C) I'll make your wish come true.

第三部分：言談理解（第 11-20 題，共 10 題）

作答說明： 第 11-20 題每題均有三個選項，請依據所聽到的內容，選出一個最適合的答案，每題播放兩次。

示例題：你會看到

(A) 9:50.　　(B) 10:00.　　(C) 10:10.

然後你會聽到……（播音）。依據所播放的內容，正確答案應該選 B，請將答案卡該題「Ⓑ」的地方塗黑、塗滿，即：Ⓐ ● Ⓒ

11. (A) At nine ten.
    (B) At nine twenty.
    (C) At nine thirty.

12. (A) The woman bought
       many shoes.
    (B) The man agreed
       with the woman.
    (C) The shoes are going
       to be sold.

13. (A) In the museum.
    (B) On the beach.
    (C) At the zoo.

14. (A) By bus.
    (B) By taxi.
    (C) By running.

15. (A) Linda has gone on
       a trip.
    (B) Kevin won't return
       the hair dryer this
       week.
    (C) Linda asks Kevin to
       lend her something.

16. (A) It erased the man's data
       suddenly.
    (B) The data was collected
       from many countries.
    (C) The data was from
       garbage e-mails.

17. (A) A watch.
    (B) A pair of jeans.
    (C) It is not said.

18. (A) She didn't have enough
       sleep.
    (B) She spent little time
       studying.
    (C) She couldn't
       concentrate at night.

19. (A) A magic show.
    (B) A business meeting.
    (C) A costume party.

20. (A) The girl got the ticket
       from her cousin.
    (B) David's seat number is
       B46.
    (C) David is going to a
       concert.

TEST 15 詳解

第一部分：辨識句意（第 1-3 題，共 3 題）

1. (**A**) (A)　　　　　(B)　　　　　(C)

The girl thinks the TV program is very boring.

女孩覺得電視節目很無聊。

* think〔θɪŋk〕 *v.* 覺得；認爲
program〔'progræm〕 *n.* 節目　　boring〔'borɪŋ〕 *adj.* 無聊的

2. (**B**) (A)　　　　　(B)　　　　　(C)

Everyone has to prepare some snacks for the party.

每個人都必須爲派對準備一些點心。

* prepare〔prɪ'pɛr〕 *v.* 準備　　snack〔snæk〕 *n.* 點心
party〔'partɪ〕 *n.* 派對

3. (**A**) (A)　　　　　(B)　　　　　(C)

Jack copied his classmate's answers during test.

傑克在考試時抄襲同學的答案。

* copy〔'kɑpɪ〕v. 抄寫；抄襲
  classmate〔'klæs,met〕n. 同班同學
  answer〔'ænsɚ〕n. 答案

第二部分：基本問答（第 4-10 題，共 7 題）

4. (**A**) Do you have any plans later?

你待會有任何計畫嗎？

　(A) Um, I plan to take the recycling out.

　　　嗯，我打算要把回收的垃圾丟掉。

　(B) Um, I'll try to be quick. 嗯，我會試著快一點。

　(C) Um, it sounds fun. 嗯，這聽起來很有趣。

* plan〔plæn〕n. 計畫　v. 打算
  um〔ʌm〕interj.（表示遲疑）嗯
  take~out 把～拿出去　recycling〔,ri'saɪklɪŋ〕n. 回收的物品
  try〔traɪ〕v. 嘗試　sound〔saʊnd〕v. 聽起來
  fun〔fʌn〕adj. 有趣的

5. (**C**) Whose packages are they? 這些是誰的包裹？

　(A) They are expensive. 它們很貴。

　(B) They were sent here yesterday.

　　　它們是昨天送過來的。

　(C) They are hers. 是她的。

* package〔'pækɪdʒ〕n. 包裹
  expensive〔ɪk'spɛnsɪv〕adj. 昂貴的
  sent〔sɛnt〕v. 送【send 的過去式和過去分詞】

6. (**B**) May I speak to Allen? 我可以跟艾倫說話嗎？

(A) That would be nice. 那會很好。

(B) This is Allen speaking. <u>我是艾倫。</u>

(C) No one answered the phone. 沒人接電話。

* speak〔spik〕v. 說話
  This is ~ speaking. 我是~。【用於講電話】
  answer〔'ænsɚ〕v. 接 (電話)

7. (**C**) Mom, I can't find my math textbook.
   媽，我找不到我的數學課本。

   (A) Have you seen any in the room?
       你有在房間看到嗎？

   (B) Didn't you look for it? 你沒有找它嗎？

   (C) Isn't it beside the lamp?
       <u>它不是在檯燈旁邊嗎？</u>

   * math〔mæθ〕n. 數學 (= *mathematics*)
     textbook〔'tɛkst,bʊk〕n. 課本　***look for*** 尋找
     beside〔bɪ'saɪd〕*prep.* 在…旁邊
     lamp〔læmp〕n. 檯燈

8. (**A**) I am so tired of teaching English.
   我厭倦了教英文。

   (A) Why? I thought you liked teaching.
       <u>為什麼？我以為你喜歡教書。</u>

   (B) Being a secretary is difficult.
       當秘書很困難。

   (C) What a good idea! 好主意！

   * ***be tired of*** 厭倦　　secretary〔'sɛkrə,tɛrɪ〕n. 秘書
     difficult〔'dɪfə,kʌlt〕*adj.* 困難的
     What a good idea! 好主意！

9. (**A**) Tommy, do you like the spaghetti?

湯米，你喜歡義大利麵嗎？

(A) Not really. It tastes like mud.

不完全是。它嚐起來像泥巴。

(B) Wow. It sounds amazing!

哇。這聽起來好驚人！

(C) Thanks. It's my pleasure.

謝謝。這是我的榮幸。

* spaghetti〔spə'gɛtɪ〕*n.* 義大利麵

Not really. 不完全是。

taste〔test〕*v.* 嚐起來　　mud〔mʌd〕*n.* 泥巴

wow〔waʊ〕*interj.* （表示驚訝、喜悅等）哇

sound〔saʊnd〕*v.* 聽起來

amazing〔ə'mezɪŋ〕*adj.* 驚人的

pleasure〔'plɛʒɚ〕*n.* 榮幸

10. (**B**) I hope it'll be sunny tomorrow.

我希望明天是晴天。

(A) I hope not. I'm going camping.

我希望不是。我要去露營。

(B) Why? Do you have plans?

為什麼？你有計畫嗎？

(C) I'll make your wish come true.

我會讓你的願望成真。

* hope〔hop〕*v.* 希望　　sunny〔'sʌnɪ〕*adj.* 晴的

camp〔kæmp〕*v.* 露營　　plan〔plæn〕*n.* 計畫

make〔mek〕*v.* 使　　wish〔wɪʃ〕*n.* 願望

come true 成真；實現

第三部分：言談理解（第 11-20 題，共 10 題）

11. (**C**) M : Hurry up. We are going to be late for Miss Wang's class.

男：快點。王老師的課我們要遲到了。

W : Don't worry. It's only twenty after nine. We still have ten more minutes.

女：別擔心。才九點二十分。我們還有十分鐘。

Question : What time will the class begin?

何時開始上課？

(A) At nine ten. 九點十分。

(B) At nine twenty. 九點二十分。

(C) At nine thirty. 九點三十分。

* ***hurry up*** 趕快　　late〔let〕*adj.* 遲到的
class〔klæs〕*n.* 課程　　worry〔'wɜɪ〕*v.* 擔心
minute〔'mɪnɪt〕*n.* 分鐘　　begin〔bɪ'gɪn〕*v.* 開始

12. (**A**) M : What's in the bag?

男：袋子裡面有什麼？

W : The shoes I want to throw away.

女：我想要丟掉的鞋子。

M : What? So many? That's a waste of money! Why don't you sell them?

男：什麼？這麼多？那眞是浪費錢！你何不賣掉它們？

W : No one will buy used shoes.

女：沒有人會買穿過的鞋子。

Question : Which is true?

何者爲眞？

(A) The woman bought many shoes.

　　女士買了很多鞋。

(B) The man agreed with the woman.

　　男士同意女士的說法。

(C) The shoes are going to be sold.

　　鞋子要被賣掉。

* bag〔bæg〕*n.* 包包　　shoes〔ʃuz〕*n. pl.* 鞋子
  throw away 丟掉　　waste〔west〕*n.* 浪費
  sell〔sɛl〕*v.* 賣【三態為：sell-sold-sold】
  used〔juzt〕*adj.* 用過的；舊的；二手的
  bought〔bɔt〕*v.* 買【buy 的過去式】　　***agree with*** 同意

13. (**C**) M : Oh, no. It's raining. I won't be able to see the
　　　　　　animals.

　　　男：喔，不。下雨了。我無法看到動物了。

　　　W : Don't worry. It's not raining hard. Most animals
　　　　　will enjoy the rain. They won't hide away.

　　　女：別擔心。不是下很大。大部分的動物都喜歡雨。牠們不會躲
　　　　　起來。

　　Question : Where are they? 他們在哪裡？

　　(A) In the museum. 在博物館。

　　(B) On the beach. 在海邊。

　　(C) At the zoo. 在動物園。

* rain〔ren〕*v.* 下雨　　*n.* 雨　　***be able to V.*** 能夠
  animal〔'ænəml̩〕*n.* 動物　　hard〔hɑrd〕*adv.* 猛烈地
  enjoy〔ɪn'dʒɔɪ〕*v.* 享受；喜歡
  hide away 躲起來
  museum〔mju'ziəm〕*n.* 博物館
  beach〔bitʃ〕*n.* 海灘　　zoo〔zu〕*n.* 動物園

14. (**A**) W : Hey, you are late!

女：嘿，你遲到了！

M : Sorry. I tried to take the bus here as usual, but the bus was too full for me to get on.

男：抱歉。我想要跟平常一樣搭公車，但是公車太滿了，我上不去。

W : So you took a taxi here?

女：所以你就搭計程車來這裡？

M : No, I couldn't find any taxis along the way, so I waited for the next bus. It took me another half hour.

男：不，沿路上我找不到任何計程車，所以我等下一班公車。這又花了我半小時。

Question : How did the man go to meet the woman?

男士如何去和女士會面？

(A) By bus. 搭公車。

(B) By taxi. 搭計程車。

(C) By running. 跑步。

* late〔let〕*adj.* 遲到的　　try〔traɪ〕*v.* 嘗試
take〔tek〕*v.* 搭乘；花（時間）
bus〔bʌs〕*n.* 公車
as usual 如往常　　*too…to~* 太…以致於不~
full〔fʊl〕*adj.* 滿的
get on 上（公車、火車等）
taxi〔'tæksɪ〕*n.* 計程車　　*along the way* 沿路上
wait for 等待　　*by* + 交通工具　搭~

15. (**B**) W : This is Linda. I am not home right now. Please leave a message after the BEEP.

女：我是琳達。我現在不在家。請在嗶一聲後留言。

M : Linda, this is Kevin. Remember the hair dryer I borrowed from you last week? I may need to use it for another week because I'll take a trip with it. Thanks.

男：琳達，我是凱文。記得我上週跟妳借的吹風機嗎？我可能需要再用一個禮拜，因為我旅行要帶著它。謝謝。

Question : What is the message about?

留言是關於什麼？

(A) Linda has gone on a trip. 琳達已經去旅行了。

(B) Kevin won't return the hair dryer this week.

凱文這週無法歸還吹風機。

(C) Linda asks Kevin to lend her something.

琳達要求凱文借她東西。

* *This is~speaking.* 我是~。【用於講電話】

right now 現在　　leave〔liv〕v. 留下

message〔'mɛsɪdʒ〕n. 訊息；留言

leave a message 留言　　beep〔bip〕n. 嗶嗶聲

remember〔rɪ'mɛmbɚ〕v. 記得　　*hair dryer* 吹風機

need〔nid〕v. 需要　　borrow〔'bɔro〕v. 借（入）

use〔juz〕v. 使用　　*take a trip* 去旅行

go on a trip 去旅行　　return〔rɪ'tɝn〕v. 歸還

ask〔æsk〕v. 要求　　lend〔lɛnd〕v. 借（出）

16. (**A**) M : I can't stand this old computer!

男：我無法忍受我的舊電腦！

W : Why? What's it done to you this time?

女：為什麼？它這次對你做了什麼？

M : Well, it deleted all my important data suddenly for no reason.

男：嗯，它突然間無緣無故就刪除了我所有重要的資料。

W : Really? So next time you must remember to save all your files first.

女：眞的嗎？所以下一次你一定要記得先存檔。

Question : What happened to the man's computer?

男士的電腦發生什麼事？

(A) It erased the man's data suddenly.

它突然間刪除了男士的資料。

(B) The data was collected from many countries.

資料是從很多國家收集來的。

(C) The data was from garbage e-mails.

資料是來自垃圾郵件。

* stand〔stænd〕v. 忍受　　computer〔kəmˊpjutɚ〕n. 電腦
this time 這一次　　well〔wɛl〕interj.（說話停頓）嗯
delete〔dɪˊlit〕v. 刪除　　important〔ɪmˊpɔrtṇt〕adj. 重要的
data〔ˊdetə〕n. pl. 資料【單數爲 datum〔ˊdetəm〕】
suddenly〔ˊsʌdṇlɪ〕adv. 突然地　　**for no reason** 無緣無故
next time 下次　　save〔sev〕v. 儲存
file〔faɪl〕n. 檔案　　**happen to** 發生於
erase〔ɪˊres〕v. 刪除　　collect〔kəˊlɛkt〕v. 收集
garbage e-mail 垃圾郵件

17. (**A**)　W : What do you want for your birthday, Joe?

女：你生日禮物想要什麼，喬？

M : I want a new pair of jeans.

男：我要一條牛仔褲。

W : Didn't you get one for your last birthday?

女：你去年生日不是得到一件嗎？

M : No, I didn't. Carol did. I got a watch last year.

男：不，我沒有。凱蘿有。我去年拿到一支手錶。

Question : What was the man's birthday present last
year? 男士去年的生日禮物是什麼？

(A) A watch. 一支手錶。

(B) A pair of jeans. 一條牛仔褲。

(C) It is not said. 沒有說。

* **a pair of** 一雙；一對；一條（長褲）
  jeans〔dʒinz〕 *n. pl.* 牛仔褲   watch〔wɑtʃ〕 *n.* 手錶
  present〔'prɛznt〕 *n.* 禮物

18. (**A**) W : Mr. Lee, I failed the exam again! But I prepared
for it for a long time.

女：李老師，我考試又不及格了！但是我準備了很久。

M : Tell me how you prepared for the exam.

男：告訴我妳如何準備考試。

W : I studied hard all last week. I reviewed and
reviewed until midnight every night.

女：我上週整週都很用功。我每天晚上都複習到半夜。

M : That's not a good study habit. You shouldn't have
stayed up so late.

男：那不是一個好的讀書習慣。妳當時不該熬夜到這麼晚。

Question : What problem does the girl have?
女孩有什麼問題？

(A) She didn't have enough sleep.
她沒有足夠的睡眠。

(B) She spent little time studying.
她沒花什麼時間唸書。

(C) She couldn't concentrate at night.
她晚上無法專心。

* fail〔fel〕*v.* 考（試）不及格
  exam〔ɪg'zæm〕*n.* 考試（= *examination*）
  prepare〔prɪ'pɛr〕*v.* 準備 < *for* >　　***study hard*** 用功讀書
  review〔rɪ'vju〕*v.* 複習　　midnight〔'mɪd,naɪt〕*n.* 半夜
  habit〔'hæbɪt〕*n.* 習慣　　***study habit*** 讀書習慣
  shouldn't have + p.p. 當時不該～　　***stay up*** 熬夜
  late〔let〕*adv.* 晚地　　problem〔'prɑbləm〕*n.* 問題
  enough〔ɪ'nʌf〕*adj.* 足夠的　　spend〔spɛnd〕*v.* 花費
  concentrate〔'kɑnsn̩,tret〕*v.* 專心

19. (**C**) W : You look just like Superman.

女：你看起來很像超人。

M : Thanks. And you are dressed like an old witch.

男：謝謝。而妳穿得像一個老巫婆。

W : Let's go inside and see what the others dressed
themselves as.

女：我們一起進去看看別人打扮成什麼樣子。

Question : Where are they going?

他們要去哪裡？

(A) A magic show. 魔術表演。

(B) A business meeting. 商務會議。

(C) A costume party. 化妝舞會。

* look〔lʊk〕*v.* 看起來　　Superman〔'supɚ,mæn〕*n.* 超人
  be dressed like 穿得像　　witch〔wɪtʃ〕*n.* 巫婆
  Let's + V. 我們一起～吧　　inside〔'ɪn'saɪd〕*adv.* 往裡面
  dress oneself as 打扮成　　magic〔'mædʒɪk〕*n.* 魔術
  show〔ʃo〕*n.* 秀；表演　　meeting〔'mitɪŋ〕*n.* 開會；會議
  business meeting 商務會議
  costume〔'kɑstjum〕*n.* 服裝
  costume party 化妝舞會（= *masquerade*〔,mæskə'red〕）

20. (**C**)　W：Hi, David.　Are you also here for the concert?

　　　　女：嗨，大衛。你也來這看演唱會嗎？

　　　　M：Yes.　I got the ticket from my cousin.　She is too busy
　　　　　　to come.

　　　　男：是的。我從我堂妹那拿到了門票。她太忙無法來。

　　　　W：Where is your seat?

　　　　女：你的座位在哪裡？

　　　　M：B45.

　　　　男：B45。

　　　　W：Great!　I'm in B46.　You are next to me.

　　　　女：太棒了！我在 B46。你在我旁邊。

　　　　Question：Which is true?　何者為真？

　　　(A)　The girl got the ticket from her cousin.

　　　　　女孩從她的堂妹那拿到了門票。

　　　(B)　David's seat number is B46.

　　　　　大衛的座位號碼是 B46。

　　　(C)　David is going to a concert.

　　　　　大衛正要去演唱會。

　　* concert〔'kɑnsɚt〕*n.* 演唱會　　ticket〔'tɪkɪt〕*n.* 門票
　　cousin〔'kʌzn̩〕*n.* 堂（表）兄弟（姊妹）
　　too…to~ 太…以致於不~　　busy〔'bɪzɪ〕*adj.* 忙碌的
　　seat〔sit〕*n.* 座位　　great〔gret〕*adj.* 很棒的
　　next to 在…旁邊　　number〔'nʌmbɚ〕*n.* 號碼

TEST 16

第一部分：辨識句意（第1-3題，共3題）

作答說明： 第1-3題每題有三張圖片，請依據所聽到的內容，選出符合描述的圖片，每題播放兩次。

示例題：你會看到

(A)
(B)
(C)

然後你會聽到……（播音）。依據所播放的內容，正確答案應該選 A，請將答案卡該題「Ⓐ」的地方塗黑、塗滿，即：● Ⓑ Ⓒ

1. (A)
(B)
(C)

2. (A)   (B)   (C)

3. (A)   (B)   (C)

第二部分：基本問答（第 4-10 題，共 7 題）

作答說明： 第 4-10 題每題均有三個選項，請依據所聽到的內容，選出一個最適合的回應，每題播放兩次。

示例題：你會看到

(A) She is talking to the teacher.

(B) She is a student in my class.

(C) She is wearing a beautiful dress.

然後你會聽到……（播音）。依據所播放的內容，正確答案應該選 B，請將答案卡該題「Ⓑ」的地方塗黑、塗滿，即：Ⓐ ● Ⓒ

4. (A) The train leaves at 6 o'clock.
 (B) Walk along this street two blocks.
 (C) You can find the store in the station.

5. (A) They are looking at a picture.
 (B) They look happy.
 (C) The teacher is writing something on the board.

6. (A) It cost me NT$2,000.
 (B) I don't go to school on holidays.
 (C) I stayed at home all day.

7. (A) The red one over there.
 (B) I want the cheaper one.
 (C) This is my bicycle.

8. (A) Last summer.
 (B) About three weeks.
 (C) By plane.

9. (A) It was in City Park.
 (B) It was very interesting and exciting.
 (C) It was between the Elephants and Tigers.

10. (A) It was in a senior high school.
 (B) The reading was a little difficult.
 (C) It was at 10:30 a.m.

第三部分：言談理解（第 11-20 題，共 10 題）

作答說明：第 11-20 題每題均有三個選項，請依據所聽到的內容，
　　　　　選出一個最適合的答案，每題播放兩次。

示例題：你會看到

(A) 9:50.　　(B) 10:00.　　(C) 10:10.

然後你會聽到……（播音）。依據所播放的內容，正確答案應該
選 B，請將答案卡該題「Ⓑ」的地方塗黑、塗滿，即：Ⓐ ● Ⓒ

11. (A) To see a movie.
    (B) To exercise.
    (C) To take a trip.

12. (A) A post office.
    (B) A police station.
    (C) A stationery store.

13. (A) He'll go very soon.
    (B) He doesn't want to go now.
    (C) He has been there twice.

14. (A) He didn't meet her.
    (B) He didn't call her earlier.
    (C) He didn't have a cellphone.

15. (A) She will have a new math teacher.
    (B) She will have a math test tomorrow.
    (C) She cannot keep her mind on her studies.

16. (A) A teacher.
    (B) A police officer.
    (C) A doctor.

17. (A) How they spent their vacations.
    (B) Where they went shopping.
    (C) When the ball game began.

18. (A) She spent nothing for the things this dog needed.
    (B) She spent only a little money buying this dog.
    (C) She spent little money on this dog.

19. (A) The man's girlfriend.
    (B) The woman's husband.
    (C) Their father.

20. (A) On July 11.
    (B) On July 9.
    (C) She hasn't decided yet.

TEST 16 詳解

第一部分：辨識句意（第 1-3 題，共 3 題）

1. (**B**) (A) 　(B) 　(C)

This is a butterfly. 這是一隻蝴蝶。

* butterfly〔'bʌtə͵flaɪ〕*n.* 蝴蝶

2. (**A**) (A) 　(B) 　(C)

Merry Christmas! 聖誕快樂！

* merry〔'mɛrɪ〕*adj.* 歡樂的；快樂的
  Christmas〔'krɪsməs〕*n.* 聖誕節

3. (**A**) (A) 　(B) 　(C)

Would you like to try some bubble tea?

你要喝看看泡沫奶茶嗎？

* try〔traɪ〕*v.* 嘗試　　bubble〔ˈbʌbḷ〕*n.* 泡泡；泡沫
bubble tea 泡沫奶茶

第二部分：基本問答（第 4-10 題，共 7 題）

4. (**A**) Excuse me, when does the train leave?

對不起，火車什麼時候開？

(A) The train leaves at 6 o'clock. 火車六點開。

(B) Walk along this street two blocks.

沿著這條街走兩個街區。

(C) You can find the store in the station.

你可以在車站找到這家商店。

* ***Excuse me.*** 對不起。【用於引起注意】
train〔tren〕*n.* 火車　　leave〔liv〕*v.* 離開
walk〔wɔk〕*v.* 行走；步行　　along〔əˈlɔŋ〕*prep.* 沿著
street〔strit〕*n.* 街道　　block〔blɑk〕*n.* 街區
store〔stor〕*n.* 商店　　station〔ˈsteʃən〕*n.* 車站

5. (**B**) How do the students look? 這些學生看起來如何？

(A) They are looking at a picture. 他們正在看一幅畫。

(B) They look happy. 他們看起來很快樂。

(C) The teacher is writing something on the board.

老師正在黑板上寫東西。

* look〔lʊk〕*v.* 看起來　　***look at*** 看；注視
picture〔ˈpɪktʃɚ〕*n.* 圖畫　　happy〔ˈhæpɪ〕*adj.* 快樂的
board〔bord〕*n.* 木板；黑板（= *blackboard*）

6. (**A**) How much did it cost you to buy this dress?

買這件洋裝花了妳多少錢？

(A) It cost me NT$2,000. 它花了我台幣 2,000 元。

(B) I don't go to school on holidays. 我假日不去學校。

(C) I stayed at home all day. 我整天都待在家。

* cost〔kɔst〕*v.* 花（某人）（錢）
  buy〔baɪ〕*v.* 買　　dress〔drɛs〕*n.* 洋裝
  NT$ 新台幣（*= New Taiwan Dollar*）
  holiday〔'hɑlə,de〕*n.* 假日　　stay〔ste〕*v.* 停留

7. (**B**) Which computer do you want, the cheaper one or the lighter one?
你想要哪一台電腦，比較便宜的，還是比較輕的？

(A) The red one over there. 那裡那台紅色的。

(B) I want the cheaper one. 我要比較便宜的那台。

(C) This is my bicycle. 這是我的腳踏車。

* computer〔kəm'pjutɚ〕*n.* 電腦
  cheap〔tʃip〕*adj.* 便宜的　　light〔laɪt〕*adj.* 輕的
  over there 在那裡　　bicycle〔'baɪ,sɪkl̩〕*n.* 腳踏車

8. (**A**) When did you spend your vacation there?
你什麼時候去那裡度假的？

(A) Last summer. 去年夏天。

(B) About three weeks. 大約三個星期。

(C) By plane. 搭飛機。

* spend〔spɛnd〕*v.* 度過　　vacation〔ve'keʃən〕*n.* 假期
  summer〔'sʌmɚ〕*n.* 夏天　　week〔wik〕*n.* 週；星期
  by + 交通工具　搭～　　plane〔plen〕*n.* 飛機

9. (**A**) Where was my dog when you found it?
你在哪裡找到我的狗？

(A) It was in City Park. 在市立公園。

(B) It was very interesting and exciting.
它非常有趣而且刺激。

(C) It was between the Elephants and Tigers.
牠在象隊和虎隊中間。

* city〔'sıtı〕*n.* 都市   park〔pɑrk〕*n.* 公園
interesting〔'ıntrıstıŋ〕*adj.* 有趣的
exciting〔ık'saıtıŋ〕*adj.* 刺激的
elephant〔'ɛləfənt〕*n.* 大象   tiger〔'taɪgɚ〕*n.* 老虎

10. (**B**) How do you feel about the English examination last
Saturday? 上禮拜六的英文考試你覺得如何？

(A) It was in a senior high school. 它在高中。

(B) The reading was a little difficult.
<u>閱讀部分有一點難。</u>

(C) It was at 10:30 a.m. 它在早上十點半。

* examination〔ıg,zæmə'neʃən〕*n.* 考試 (= *exam*)
senior high school 高中
reading〔'ridıŋ〕*n.* 閱讀   *a little* 有點
difficult〔'dıfə,kʌlt〕*adj.* 困難的
a.m. 上午 (= *ante meridiem*)

第三部分：言談理解（第 11-20 題，共 10 題）

11. (**B**) M：Hurry up. We only have twenty minutes.
男：快點。我們只有二十分鐘。

W：Then we have to take a taxi to the gym.
女：那麼我們得搭計程車去健身房。

Question：What are they going to do?
他們接下來要做什麼？

(A) To see a movie. 去看電影。

(B) To exercise. 去運動。

(C) To take a trip. 去旅行。

* ***hurry up*** 趕快　　minute〔'mɪnɪt〕*n.* 分鐘
  take〔tek〕*v.* 搭乘　　taxi〔'tæksɪ〕*n.* 計程車
  gym〔dʒɪm〕*n.* 體育館；健身房　　***see a movie*** 看電影
  exercise〔'ɛksə‚saɪz〕*v.* 運動
  trip〔trɪp〕*n.* 旅行　　***take a trip*** 去旅行

12. (**C**) Would you go with me to Gama? I need to get some
    markers. 你要跟我一起去 Gama 嗎？我必須去買一些麥克筆。

    Question : What's Gama? Gama 是什麼？

    (A) A post office. 郵局。

    (B) A police station. 警察局。

    (C) A stationery store. 文具店。

    * get〔gɛt〕*v.* 買　　marker〔'markə〕*n.* 麥克筆；奇異筆
      post office 郵局　　***police station*** 警察局
      stationery〔'steʃən‚ɛrɪ〕*n.* 文具

13. (**B**) W : Are you ready to go?

    女：你準備要走了嗎？

    M : Sorry. I still need more time to finish it.

    男：對不起。我還需要更多時間才能完成。

    Question : What does the man mean?

    　　　　男士是什麼意思？

    (A) He'll go very soon. 他很快就會走。

    (B) He doesn't want to go now. 他不想現在走。

    (C) He has been there twice. 他去過那裡兩次。

    * ready〔'rɛdɪ〕*adj.* 準備好的　　finish〔'fɪnɪʃ〕*v.* 做完
      mean〔min〕*v.* 意思是　　twice〔twaɪs〕*adv.* 兩次

14. (**A**) W : Why didn't I see you last night? Although I came
     late, I still waited for you for thirty minutes.

   女：為什麼我昨天晚上沒看到你？我雖然遲到了，還是等你等了
     三十分鐘。

   M : I'm sorry. I remembered the wrong date. I thought it
     was tonight.

   男：很抱歉。我記錯日期了。我以為是今天晚上。

   Question : Why was the woman not happy with the man?
       為什麼女士對男士不太滿意？

   (A) He didn't meet her. <u>他沒有去她見面。</u>

   (B) He didn't call her earlier. 他沒有早點打電話給她。

   (C) He didn't have a cellphone. 他沒有手機。

   * late〔let〕*adv.* 晚地；遲到地 wait〔wet〕*v.* 等待 *< for >*
    minute〔'mɪnɪt〕*n.* 分鐘 wrong〔rɔŋ〕*adj.* 錯誤的
    date〔det〕*n.* 日期
    cellphone〔'sɛl,fon〕*n.* 手機 (= *cell phone*)

15. (**A**) W : We will have a new math teacher to take Ms.
     Johnson's place tomorrow. I feel nervous because
     math is always difficult for me.

   女：明天我們會有一位新的數學老師，來接替詹森老師的工作。
     我覺得很緊張，因為數學對我來說總是很難。

   M : Take it easy. If you do your best, everything will be
     fine.

   男：放輕鬆。只要你盡力，一切都會很順利。

   Question : What is the woman worried about?
       女士在擔心什麼？

   (A) She will have a new math teacher.
     <u>她將有位新的數學老師。</u>

(B) She will have a math test tomorrow.

她明天會有一個數學考試。

(C) She cannot keep her mind on her studies.

她無法專注在課業上。

* math〔mæθ〕*n.* 數學（= *mathematics*）
take one's place 代替某人　　nervous〔'nɝvəs〕*adj.* 緊張的
difficult〔'dɪfə,kʌlt〕*adj.* 困難的　　*take it easy* 放輕鬆
do one's best 盡力　　*be worried about* 擔心
test〔tɛst〕*n.* 考試　　*keep one's mind on* 專心於（= *focus on*）
studies〔'stʌdɪz〕*n. pl.* 學業

16. (**C**) M：Mary, you should take care of yourself well. You
don't look good. Did you take what I gave you in
my office last time?

男：瑪麗，妳應該好好照顧自己。妳看起來不太好。妳有吃我
上次在診所給妳的藥嗎？

W：Yes, I did. But I really have a lot of homework to do.
So I do not have time to take a rest.

女：是，我有。但我真的有很多的功課要做。所以我沒有時
間休息。

Question：What could the man be?

男士的職業可能是什麼？

(A) A teacher. 老師。

(B) A police officer. 警察。

(C) A doctor. 醫生。

* *take care of* 照顧　　take〔tek〕*v.* 吃（藥）
office〔'ɔfɪs〕*n.* 診所　　*last time* 上一次　　*a lot of* 很多的
homework〔'hom,wɝk〕*n.* 回家作業；功課　　*take a rest* 休息
police officer 警察　　doctor〔'dɑktɚ〕*n.* 醫生

17. (**B**) M : Where did you go last weekend?

男：妳上個週末去哪裡？

W : I went shopping in Sogo because everything is on
　　sale for Mother's Day. How about you?

女：我去 SOGO 購物，因為母親節所有東西都在特價。你呢？

M : I went shopping in Breeze with my girlfriend for her
　　birthday present.

男：我和我女朋友去微風買她的生日禮物。

Question : What are they talking about?

　　　　　　他們在談論什麼？

(A) How they spent their vacations.　他們如何度過假期。

(B) Where they went shopping.　他們去哪裡購物。

(C) When the ball game began.　球賽何時開始。

* weekend〔'wik'ɛnd〕n. 週末　　***go shopping***　去購物
on sale 特價中　　***Mother's Day*** 母親節
How about~?　～如何？　　breeze〔briz〕n. 微風
girlfriend〔'gɝl,frɛnd〕n. 女朋友　　present〔'prɛzṇt〕n. 禮物
spend〔spɛnd〕v. 度過　　vacation〔ve'keʃən〕n. 假期
ball game 球賽

18. (**C**) W : I would like you to meet Wawa. He's my new dog.

女：我想要你見娃娃。他是我新養的狗。

M : How much did he cost?

男：牠花了妳多少錢？

W : I found him on the street, so he was free. I just
　　had to pay for things like the food bowl and a dog
　　house.

女：我在街上找到牠的，所以是免費的。我只要支付像是狗碗和
　　狗屋之類的東西。

Question : How much did the woman spend for the dog?

女士花了多少錢買狗？

(A) She spent nothing for the things this dog needed.

她完全沒花錢買這隻狗需要的東西。

(B) She spent only a little money buying this dog.

她只花了一點錢買這隻狗。

(C) She spent little money on this dog.

她沒花什麼錢在這隻狗身上。

* meet〔mit〕*v.* 和…會面　　cost〔kɔst〕*v.* 花（錢）
steet〔strit〕*n.* 街道　　free〔fri〕*adj.* 免費的
have to V. 必須　　pay〔pe〕*v.* 支付 < *for* >
bowl〔bol〕*n.* 碗　　**dog house** 狗屋
a little 一點　　little〔ˈlɪtl̩〕*adj.* 很少的

19. (**C**) W : Michael, I like the watch. It's cool. I think Dad will like it.

女：麥可，我喜歡那支手錶。好酷喔。我覺得爸爸會喜歡。

M : But Jane, look at the price. It's much too high.

男：但是珍，妳看看價格。太貴了。

W : How about the shirt over there? It's fashionable. It will look good on Dad.

女：那那裡的那件襯衫如何？很時髦。很適合爸爸穿。

M : Ok. Ok. It's not too expensive.

男：好的。好的。這不會太貴。

Question : Who will they buy the present for?

他們要買禮物給誰？

(A) The man's girlfriend. 男士的女朋友。

(B) The woman's husband. 女士的老公。

(C) Their father. 他們的爸爸。

* watch〔 watʃ 〕*n.* 手錶　　cool〔 kul 〕*adj.* 很酷的
price〔 praɪs 〕*n.* 價格　　***much too*** 太；非常
How about ~ ? ～如何？　　shirt〔 ʃɜt 〕*n.* 襯衫
over there 在那裡
fashionable〔 'fæʃnəbḷ 〕*adj.* 流行的；時髦的
look good on *sb.* 適合某人
expensive〔 ɪk'spɛnsɪv 〕*adj.* 昂貴的
present〔 'prɛzn̩t 〕*n.* 禮物
girlfriend〔 'gɜl,frɛnd 〕*n.* 女朋友
husband〔 'hʌzbənd 〕*n.* 丈夫；老公

20.（ **B** ）　W：When will Betty come back from Kaohsiung?

女：貝蒂何時會從高雄回來？

M：She wanted to come back on July eleventh.　But she changed his mind and decided to come back two days earlier.

男：她原本要七月十一日回來。但是她改變心意，決定提早兩天回來。

Question：When will Betty come back?

貝蒂何時會回來？

(A) On July 11. 七月十一日。

(B) On July 9. 七月九日。

(C) She hasn't decided yet. 她還沒決定。

* ***change*** *one's* ***mind*** 改變心意
decide〔 dɪ'saɪd 〕*v.* 決定　　yet〔 jɛt 〕*adv.* 尚（未）
not…yet 尚未…；還沒…

TEST 17

第一部分：辨識句意（第 1-3 題，共 3 題）

作答說明： 第 1-3 題每題有三張圖片，請依據所聽到的內容，選出符合描述的圖片，每題播放兩次。

示例題：你會看到

(A)   (B)   (C)

然後你會聽到……（播音）。依據所播放的內容，正確答案應該選 A，請將答案卡該題「Ⓐ」的地方塗黑、塗滿，即：● Ⓑ Ⓒ

1. (A)   (B)   (C)

2. (A)　　　　(B)　　　　(C)

3. (A)　　　　(B)　　　　(C)

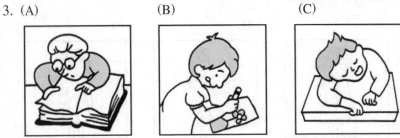

第二部分：基本問答（第 4-10 題，共 7 題）

作答說明： 第 4-10 題每題均有三個選項，請依據所聽到的內容，選出一個最適合的回應，每題播放兩次。

示例題：你會看到

(A) She is talking to the teacher.

(B) She is a student in my class.

(C) She is wearing a beautiful dress.

然後你會聽到……（播音）。依據所播放的內容，正確答案應該選 B，請將答案卡該題「Ⓑ」的地方塗黑、塗滿，即：Ⓐ ● Ⓒ

---

4. (A) It will probably rain in the city.
   (B) There are dark clouds over the mountain.
   (C) There are a lot of boats on the sea.

5. (A) No, there is still room for improvement.
   (B) Yes, it has a good view.
   (C) Yes, I am looking for a big one.

6. (A) Sorry, but I have never been there.
   (B) Of course. What do you need?
   (C) I need to do something tomorrow.

7. (A) It was easier than I thought.
   (B) That's OK. I already had one.
   (C) It was terrible! It rained every day.

8. (A) The number is 0-949-168-999.
   (B) No, I don't have one.
   (C) Yes, it's on the desk.

9. (A) No, I don't.
   (B) Yes, I'd like some tea.
   (C) It's nice to meet you.

10. (A) Water, please.
    (B) Neither, thanks. I'm full.
    (C) It's my honor.

第三部分：言談理解（第 11-20 題，共 10 題）

作答説明： 第 11-20 題每題均有三個選項，請依據所聽到的內容，選出一個最適合的答案，每題播放兩次。

示例題：你會看到

(A) 9:50.　　(B) 10:00.　　(C) 10:10.

然後你會聽到……（播音）。依據所播放的內容，正確答案應該選 B，請將答案卡該題「Ⓑ」的地方塗黑、塗滿，即：Ⓐ ● Ⓒ

11. (A) She designs her works
        naturally.
    (B) She looks natural.
    (C) She was a born designer.

12. (A) He needs to find out his
        feelings.
    (B) He needs to relax
        himself by helping
        people.
    (C) He needs to express his
        feelings in some way.

13. (A) Because she will come
        along with him.
    (B) Because she is getting
        better and better.
    (C) Because she gets along
        with him.

14. (A) No, he didn't.
    (B) Yes, he accepted it.
    (C) No, he doesn't know
        why.

15. (A) A cook.
    (B) A reporter.
    (C) A secretary.

16. (A) At a farm.
    (B) On a plane.
    (C) In Taipei.

17. (A) No, she doesn't
        know the cake is
        good to eat.
    (B) No, she doesn't like
        to eat this chocolate
        cake.
    (C) Yes, she agrees with
        what the boy said.

18. (A) He loves his art
        school.
    (B) He feels bad about
        art.
    (C) He studied art.

19. (A) The dentist will pull
        it out.
    (B) It hurts badly.
    (C) It will be killed by
        the dentist.

20. (A) Mary.
    (B) Jack.
    (C) Susan.

TEST 17 詳解

第一部分：辨識句意（第 1-3 題，共 3 題）

1. (**B**) (A)　　　　　　　(B)　　　　　　　(C)

Mike is doing sit-ups. 麥可正在做仰臥起坐。

* sit-up〔'sɪtˌʌp〕*n.* 仰臥起坐

2. (**A**) (A)　　　　　　　(B)　　　　　　　(C)

My parrot can talk. 我的鸚鵡會說話。

* parrot〔'pærət〕*n.* 鸚鵡

3. (**A**) (A)　　　　　　　(B)　　　　　　　(C)

Max is reading a book. 麥可斯正在讀書。

* read〔rid〕*v.* 讀

第二部分：基本問答（第 4-10 題，共 7 題）

4.（ **C** ） Can you see anything on the sea?
　　　你可以看到海上有任何東西嗎？

　　(A) It will probably rain in the city. 市區可能會下雨。

　　(B) There are dark clouds over the mountain. 山上有烏雲。

　　(C) There are a lot of boats on the sea. <u>有許多艘船在海上。</u>

　　* probably〔'prɑbəblɪ〕*adv.* 可能　　rain〔ren〕*v.* 下雨
　　city〔'sɪtɪ〕*n.* 城市　　***dark clouds*** 烏雲
　　over〔'ovɚ〕*prep.* 在…上面　　mountain〔'maʊntn̩〕*n.* 山
　　a lot of 很多　　boat〔bot〕*n.* 小船

5.（ **C** ） Is your apartment too small? 你的公寓太小了嗎？

　　(A) No, there is still room for improvement.
　　　　不，還有進步的空間。

　　(B) Yes, it has a good view. 是的，它的視野很好。

　　(C) Yes, I am looking for a big one.
　　　　<u>是的，我正在找一間大的公寓。</u>

　　* apartment〔ə'pɑrtmənt〕*n.* 公寓　　room〔rum〕*n.* 房間；空間
　　improvement〔ɪm'pruvmənt〕*n.* 改善；進步
　　room for improvement 進步的空間　　view〔vju〕*n.* 視野
　　look for 尋找

6.（ **B** ） Can you please do me a favor? 可以請你幫我一個忙嗎？

　　(A) Sorry, but I have never been there.
　　　　對不起，但我從來沒去過那裡。

　　(B) Of course. What do you need? <u>當然。你需要什麼？</u>

　　(C) I need to do something tomorrow.
　　　　我明天需要做一件事情。

　　* ***do*** *sb.* ***a favor*** 幫某人忙　　***Of course.*** 當然。

7. (**C**) Welcome back. How was your vacation?
歡迎回來。你的假期過得如何？

    (A) It was easier than I thought.
        它比我想像的簡單。

    (B) That's OK. I already had one.
        沒關係。我已經有一個了。

    (C) It was terrible! It rained every day.
        <u>很糟糕！每天都在下雨。</u>

    * vacation〔ve'keʃən〕*n.* 休假；假期
      That's OK. 沒關係。   already〔ɔl'rɛdɪ〕*adv.* 已經
      terrible〔'tɛrəbl〕*adj.* 可怕的；糟糕的   rain〔ren〕*v.* 下雨

8. (**A**) What number is your cellphone? 你手機號碼幾號？

    (A) The number is 0-949-168-999.
        <u>我的號碼是 0-949-168-999。</u>

    (B) No, I don't have one. 不，我沒有手機。

    (C) Yes, it's on the desk. 是的，它在書桌上。

    * number〔'nʌmbɚ〕*n.* 號碼   cellphone〔'sɛl,fon〕*n.* 手機
      desk〔dɛsk〕*n.* 書桌

9. (**B**) Would you like some tea? 你想要喝點茶嗎？

    (A) No, I don't. 不，我不想。

    (B) Yes, I'd like some tea. <u>好的，我想要喝點茶。</u>

    (C) It's nice to meet you. 很高興認識你。

    * ***would like*** 想要   tea〔ti〕*n.* 茶
      meet〔mit〕*v.* 認識；和…會面

10. (**B**) It's time for lunch. Which do you want, pork or chicken?
午餐時間到了。你想要吃什麼，豬肉還是雞肉？

(A) Water, please. 請給我水。

 (B) Neither, thanks. I'm full.

  都不需要，謝謝。我吃飽了。

 (C) It's my honor. 這是我的榮幸。

 * ***It's time for***… 該是…的時候了 pork〔pork〕*n.* 豬肉

  chicken〔'tʃɪkən〕*n.* 雞肉 neither〔'niðɚ〕*pron.* 兩者皆不

  full〔fʊl〕*adj.* 飽的

  honor〔'ɑnɚ〕*n.* 榮幸

第三部分：言談理解（第 11-20 題，共 10 題）

11. (**C**) M：You are good at designing. You are a natural.

   男：你很擅長設計。你是天生的好手。

   W：Thanks for saying so. I will do better with your compliment.

   女：謝謝你這麼說。有了你的稱讚，我會做得更好的。

   Question：What does the man think about this woman?

      男士覺得這位女士如何？

   (A) She designs her works naturally.

    她能自然地設計她的作品。

   (B) She looks natural. 她看起來不做作。

   (C) She is a born designer.

    她天生就是個設計師。

   * ***be good at*** 擅長 design〔dɪ'zaɪn〕*v.* 設計

    natural〔'nætʃərəl〕*n.* 天生具有特定才能的人 *adj.* 自然的；不做作的 compliment〔'kɑmpləmənt〕*n.* 稱讚

    naturally〔'nætʃərəlɪ〕*adv.* 自然地

    look〔lʊk〕*v.* 看起來

    born〔bɔrn〕*adj.* 天生的

    designer〔dɪ'zaɪnɚ〕*n.* 設計師

12. (**C**) W : You need to let your feelings out. Visiting a museum can help you do that.

女：你需要將你的情感抒發出來。參觀博物館能夠幫助你做到這一點。

M : Thanks for your tip about how to relax.

男：謝謝妳給我關於如何放鬆的建議。

Question : What does the man need to do?

這位男士需要做什麼？

(A) He needs to find out his feelings.

他需要發現他自己的感情。

(B) He needs to relax himself by helping people.

他需要藉由幫助別人來讓自己放鬆。

(C) He needs to express his feelings in some way.

他需要以某種方式來抒發他的情感。

* **let out** 釋放；抒發　　feelings ('filɪŋz) *n. pl.* 感情；感受
visit ('vɪsɪt) *v.* 參觀；拜訪；去
museum (mju'ziəm) *n.* 博物館
help *sb.* **(to)** *V.* 幫助某人～　　**thanks for**… 謝謝…
tip (tɪp) *n.* 建議　　relax (rɪ'læks) *v.* 放鬆
find out 找到；發現　　express (ɪk'sprɛs) *v.* 表達
some (sʌm) *adj.* 某個　　way (we) *n.* 方式

13. (**B**) W : Grace's English is really coming along.

女：葛蕾絲的英文真的有進步了。

M : Yes, I really want to know how she does it.

男：沒錯，我真想知道她是如何做到的。

Question : Why does the man want to know about Grace's English?

為什麼男士想要知道有關於葛蕾絲英文的事？

(A) Because she will come along with him.

因爲她會和他一起來。

(B) Because she is getting better and better.

因爲她變得越來越好。

(C) Because she gets along with him.

因爲她和他相處得很好。

* ***come along*** 進步　***along with*** 和…一起

get + 比較級 + ***and*** + 比較級　變得越來越…

get along 和睦相處

14. (**B**) W：Can you mop the floors on Mondays?

女：你星期一可以拖地嗎？

M：I don't see why not. That works for me.

男：當然沒問題。我可以在星期一拖地。

Question：Did the man agree to the woman's idea?

男士同意女士的想法嗎？

(A) No, he didn't. 不，他不同意。

(B) Yes, he accepted it. 是的，他接受。

(C) No, he doesn't know why. 不，他不知道爲什麼。

* mop〔map〕*v.*（用拖把）拖　　floor〔flor〕*n.* 地板

see〔si〕*v.* 了解；想像　　work〔wɜk〕*v.* 可以；行得通

sth. ***work for*** *sb.* 某人同意某事　　agree〔ə'gri〕*v.* 同意；贊成

agree to *sth.* 同意某事　　idea〔aɪ'diə〕*n.* 主意；想法

accept〔ək'sɛpt〕*v.* 接受

15. (**C**) M：Maureen, give me a cup of coffee and then copy

these letters.

男：莫琳，給我一杯咖啡，然後影印這些信件。

W：I am talking to a customer, so I will do it later.

女：我正在跟顧客談話，所以我待會再幫你做。

Question : What could the woman be?

女人的職業可能是什麼？

(A) A cook. 廚師。

(B) A reporter. 記者。

(C) A secretary. 秘書。

* coffee〔'kɔfɪ〕n. 咖啡   copy〔'kɑpɪ〕v. 影印
  customer〔'kʌstəmɚ〕n. 顧客
  later〔'letɚ〕adv. 待會   cook〔kʊk〕n. 廚師
  reporter〔rɪ'portɚ〕n. 記者   secretary〔'sɛkrə,tɛrɪ〕n. 秘書

16. (**A**) W : Hi, this is Stephanie. I'm having a great time at the farm camp now.

女：嗨，我是史蒂芬妮。我現在在農場露營區玩得很愉快。

M : Wow, I have never been there. Tell me more after you come back.

男：哇，我從來沒去過那裡。妳回來之後，要多告訴我一些有關農場營區的事。

W : OK. Please tell my mom I will fly back to Taipei next weekend.

女：好的。請告訴我媽我下週末就會搭飛機回台北了。

Question : Where is the woman on the phone?

講電話的女士現在在哪裡？

(A) At a farm. 在農場。

(B) On a plane. 在飛機上。

(C) In Taipei. 在台北。

* *This is* ~. 我是～。【用於講電話】
  have a great time 玩得愉快   farm〔fɑrm〕n. 農場
  camp〔kæmp〕n. 露營場地

wow〔waʊ〕*interj.*（表示驚嘆、喜悅等）哇
fly〔flaɪ〕*v.* 搭飛機　　weekend〔'wik'ɛnd〕*n.* 週末
on the phone 在講電話　　plane〔plen〕*n.* 飛機

17.（**C**）M：This chocolate cake is delicious. I have bought many
　　　　　　　as my friends' presents.

　　　　男：這個巧克力蛋糕很好吃。我買了很多，當作我朋友的禮物。

　　　　W：You bet! I have done the same.

　　　　女：的確！我也做過同樣的事。

　　　　Question：Do you know if the woman likes the cake?

　　　　　　　　　你知道女士喜歡這個蛋糕嗎？

　　　　(A) No, she doesn't know the cake is good to eat.

　　　　　　 不，她不知道這個蛋糕很好吃。

　　　　(B) No, she doesn't like to eat this chocolate cake.

　　　　　　 不，她不喜歡吃這個巧克力蛋糕。

　　　　(C) Yes, she agrees with what the boy said.

　　　　　　 是的，她同意男孩所說的。

　　　　* chocolate〔'tʃɔkəlɪt〕*n.* 巧克力
　　　　　cake〔kek〕*n.* 蛋糕
　　　　　delicious〔dɪ'lɪʃəs〕*adj.* 好吃的
　　　　　bought〔bɔt〕*v.* 買【buy 的過去式和過去分詞】
　　　　　present〔'prɛznt〕*n.* 禮物
　　　　　You bet. 的確；當然。
　　　　　the same 同一事物　　**agree with** 同意

18.（**C**）M：Nobody would believe I graduated from an art school.
　　　　　　　In fact, I am terrible at art.

　　　　男：沒有人會相信我是從美術學校畢業的。事實上，我很不擅長
　　　　　　美術。

W : I can't believe it, either.

女：我也無法相信。

Question : What doesn't the woman believe?

女士不相信什麼？

(A) He loves his art school.

他喜歡他的美術學校。

(B) He feels bad about art.

他對美術感到失望。

(C) He studied art.

<u>他研讀美術。</u>

* believe〔bə'liv〕*v.* 相信

graduate〔'grædʒu,et〕*v.* 畢業

art〔ɑrt〕*n.* 藝術；美術

art school 美術學校

in fact 事實上

terrible〔'tɛrəbl̩〕*adj.* 糟糕的

be terrible at 不擅長

either〔'iðɚ〕*adv.* 也（不）

feel bad about 對…感到失望

study〔'stʌdɪ〕*v.* 研讀；學習

19. (**B**) W : Why are you going to the dentist? Is there something wrong with your teeth?

女：你為什麼要去看牙醫？你的牙齒有什麼問題嗎？

M : My tooth is killing me. I have to make an appointment.

男：我的牙齒痛死我了。我必須要預約門診。

Question : What does the man's tooth feel like?

男士的牙齒令他覺得如何？

(A) The dentist will pull it out.
　　牙醫會把它拔掉。

(B) It hurts badly. 它劇烈疼痛。

(C) It will be killed by the dentist.
　　它會被牙醫殺死。

* dentist〔ˈdɛntɪst〕*n.* 牙醫
　something is wrong with… …有問題；…出毛病
　teeth〔tuθ〕*n. pl.* 牙齒【單數為 tooth】
　be killing *sb.* 讓某人疼痛難耐
　have to V. 必須~
　appointment〔əˈpɔɪntmənt〕*n.* 預約；約診
　feel〔fil〕*v.* 使人感覺
　pull out 拔出　　　hurt〔hɝt〕*v.* 疼痛
　badly〔ˈbædlɪ〕*adv.* 劇烈地；嚴重地
　kill〔kɪl〕*v.* 殺死

20. (**A**) Mary is reading. Jack is doing his homework. Susan is
　　washing the dishes. Everyone is busy.
　　瑪麗正在讀書。傑克正在做功課。蘇珊正在洗碗。每個人都很忙。

　　Question : Who is reading? 誰在讀書？

(A) Mary. 瑪麗。

(B) Jack. 傑克。

(C) Susan. 蘇珊。

* read〔rid〕*v.* 閱讀；讀書
　homework〔ˈhom͵wɝk〕*n.* 家庭作業；功課
　wash the dishes 洗碗
　busy〔ˈbɪzɪ〕*adj.* 忙碌的

TEST 18

第一部分：辨識句意（第1-3題，共3題）

作答說明： 第1-3題每題有三張圖片，請依據所聽到的內容，選出符合描述的圖片，每題播放兩次。

示例題：你會看到

(A) 　　(B) 　　(C)

然後你會聽到……（播音）。依據所播放的內容，正確答案應該選 A，請將答案卡該題「Ⓐ」的地方塗黑、塗滿，即：● Ⓑ Ⓒ

---

1. (A) 　　(B) 　　(C)

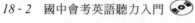

2. (A) (B) (C)

3. (A) (B) (C)

第二部分：基本問答（第 4-10 題，共 7 題）

作答説明： 第 4-10 題每題均有三個選項，請依據所聽到的內容，選出一個最適合的回應，每題播放兩次。

示例題：你會看到

(A) She is talking to the teacher.

(B) She is a student in my class.

(C) She is wearing a beautiful dress.

然後你會聽到……（播音）。依據所播放的內容，正確答案應該選 B，請將答案卡該題「Ⓑ」的地方塗黑、塗滿，即：Ⓐ ● Ⓒ

---

4. (A) It is at 6 o'clock.
   (B) It is 7 p.m.
   (C) No, I have no time.

5. (A) Yes, they often fight each other.
   (B) I thought they had married.
   (C) No, they love each other very much.

6. (A) It cost me NT$2,000.
   (B) I spend a little every day.
   (C) My daily life pays off.

7. (A) Sure.
   (B) You are flattering me.
   (C) It's nice of you.

8. (A) Two thousand kilograms.
   (B) About three miles.
   (C) Around one hundred centimeters.

9. (A) I want to wash my clothes.
   (B) We should watch the sun rising.
   (C) I would like to see something scary.

10. (A) The one who finds the most hidden balls.
    (B) The one who loses the most hidden eggs.
    (C) The one who pays the most money for it.

第三部分：言談理解（第 11-20 題，共 10 題）

作答說明：第 11-20 題每題均有三個選項，請依據所聽到的內容，
選出一個最適合的答案，每題播放兩次。

示例題：你會看到

(A) 9:50.   (B) 10:00.   (C) 10:10.

然後你會聽到⋯⋯（播音）。依據所播放的內容，正確答案應該
選 B，請將答案卡該題「Ⓑ」的地方塗黑、塗滿，即：Ⓐ ● Ⓒ

11. (A) To walk to school.
    (B) To drive a car by himself.
    (C) To run after the bus.

12. (A) A fish.
    (B) A lizard.
    (C) A bird.

13. (A) He'll go this way.
    (B) He will help her.
    (C) He congratulates the girl on her good job.

14. (A) Peter.
    (B) Paul.
    (C) Joey.

15. (A) Why the boy wants to know the girl.
    (B) Who the girl over there is.
    (C) Which boy Claire likes.

16. (A) All weekend.
    (B) On Saturday.
    (C) On Sunday.

17. (A) She got a lot of money luckily.
    (B) She will help other poor people.
    (C) She didn't know what to do with the money.

18. (A) The police towed his car away.
    (B) He couldn't find his car.
    (C) He lost his memory.

19. (A) She wants him to swim with her in the pool.
    (B) She wants him to ride in a car together with them.
    (C) She wants him to go for a car ride.

20. (A) He will go to a ball game in Europe.
    (B) He will do his best in his vacation.
    (C) He will have a good time in Europe.

TEST 18 詳解

第一部分：辨識句意（第1-3題，共3題）

1. (**B**) (A)   (B)   (C)

Mr. Smith is having dinner.

史密斯先生正在吃晚餐。

* have〔hæv〕*v.* 吃   dinner〔'dɪnɚ〕*n.* 晚餐

2. (**A**) (A)   (B)   (C)

Caution: men at work.

注意：施工中。

* caution〔'kɔʃən〕*n. v.* 小心；注意   ***at work*** 工作中

3. (**A**) (A)   (B)   (C)

The Lantern Festival is a fun holiday.

元宵節是一個很有趣的節日。

* lantern〔'læntən〕*n.* 燈籠　　festival〔'fɛstəvḷ〕*n.* 節日；節慶
Lantern Festival 元宵節　　fun〔fʌn〕*adj.* 有趣的
holiday〔'halə,de〕*n.* 節日

第二部分：基本問答（第 4-10 題，共 7 題）

4. (**B**) Excuse me, do you have the time?

　　　對不起，請問現在幾點？

(A) It is at 6 o'clock. 它在六點鐘。

(B) It is 7 p.m. <u>現在晚上七點。</u>

(C) No, I have no time. 不，我沒有時間。

* ***Excuse me.*** 對不起。【用於引起注意】
Do you have the time? 現在幾點？
【比較】***Do you have time?***（你有時間嗎？）
o'clock〔ə'klɑk〕*adv.* …點鐘
p.m. 下午（ = *post meridiem* ）

5. (**B**) Do you think Sally and Martin should get married?

　　　你認為莎莉跟馬汀應該結婚嗎？

(A) Yes, they often fight each other.

　　 是的，他們經常互相打架。

(B) I thought they had married.

　　 <u>我以為他們已經結婚了。</u>

(C) No, they love each other very much.

　　 不，他們都很愛對方。

* think〔θɪŋk〕*v.* 想；認為　　***get married*** 結婚
fight〔faɪt〕*v.* 和…打架　　***each other*** 互相；彼此
marry〔'mærɪ〕*v.* 結婚

6. (**B**) How much do you spend on your daily expenses?
   你花多少錢在你的日常開銷上？

   (A) It cost me NT$2,000. 它花了我台幣兩千元。

   (B) I spend a little every day. 我每天都花一點點。

   (C) My daily life pays off. 我的日常生活很成功。

   * spend〔spɛnd〕v. 花（錢、時間）
     daily〔'delɪ〕adj. 每天的；日常的
     expense〔ɪk'spɛns〕n. 花費；費用　cost〔kɔst〕v. 花（錢）
     NT$ 新台幣（= *New Taiwan Dollar*）
     pay off 有回報；成功；達到目的

7. (**A**) Thank you very much for helping me a lot, Julie.
   茱莉，謝謝妳幫了我很多忙。

   (A) Sure. 不必客氣。

   (B) You are flattering me. 你過獎了。

   (C) It's nice of you. 你人眞好。

   * **thank** *sb.* **for** *V-ing* 謝謝某人～
     help〔hɛlp〕v. 幫忙　**a lot** 很多
     sure〔ʃur〕adv. 不必客氣【用於回覆 Thank you.】
     flatter〔'flætɚ〕v. 奉承；討好
     You are flattering me. 你過獎了。

8. (**B**) How far will you run in this marathon race?
   這次的馬拉松比賽你會跑多遠？

   (A) Two thousand kilograms. 兩千公斤。

   (B) About three miles. 大約三英里。

   (C) Around one hundred centimeters.
   　　大約一百公分。

   * marathon〔'mærə,θɑn〕n. 馬拉松
     race〔res〕n. 賽跑　kilogram〔'kɪlə,græm〕n. 公斤

mile〔maɪl〕*n.* 英里【約 1.6 公里】
around〔ə'raʊnd〕*prep.* 大約
centimeter〔'sɛntə,mitɚ〕*n.* 公分

9. (**C**) What kind of movie should we watch?
　　　　我們應該看哪一種電影？

　　　(A) I want to wash my clothes.
　　　　　我要洗我的衣服。

　　　(B) We should watch the sun rising.
　　　　　我們應該要看太陽升起。

　　　(C) I would like to see something scary.
　　　　　<u>我想要看恐怖片。</u>

　　* kind〔kaɪnd〕*n.* 種類　　movie〔'muvɪ〕*n.* 電影
　　　wash〔wɑʃ〕*v.* 洗　　clothes〔kloz〕*n. pl.* 衣服
　　　rise〔raɪz〕*v.* 上升；升起　　**would like to V.** 想要～
　　　scary〔'skɛrɪ〕*adj.* 可怕的；恐怖的

10. (**A**) Who will win the last free ticket?
　　　　誰會贏得最後一張免費的票？

　　　(A) The one who finds the most hidden balls.
　　　　　<u>找到最多隱藏的球的人。</u>

　　　(B) The one who loses the most hidden eggs.
　　　　　弄丟最多隱藏的蛋的人。

　　　(C) The one who pays the most money for it.
　　　　　付最多錢的人。

　　* win〔wɪn〕*v.* 贏得　　last〔læst〕*adj.* 最後的
　　　free〔fri〕*adj.* 免費的　　ticket〔'tɪkɪt〕*n.* 票
　　　hidden〔'hɪdn̩〕*adj.* （被）隱藏的　　ball〔bɔl〕*n.* 球
　　　lose〔luz〕*v.* 失去；弄丟　　egg〔ɛg〕*n.* 蛋
　　　pay〔pe〕*v.* 支付 <*for*>

第三部分：言談理解（第 11-20 題，共 10 題）

11. (**A**) W：Wake up. You are late again. The school bus has gone. I have no time to drive you this time. You have to walk.

女：起床。你又遲到了。校車已經開走了。我這次沒有時間載你去。你必須走路去。

M：OK. OK.

男：好的。好的。

Question：What is the man going to do?

男士將會做什麼？

(A) To walk to school. 走路去上學。

(B) To drive a car by himself. 自己開車。

(C) To run after the bus. 去追公車。

* *wake up* 起床　　 late〔let〕*adj.* 遲到的
　school bus 校車　　 drive〔draɪv〕*v.* 開車載（某人）
　this time 這次　　 *have to V.* 必須~
　by oneself 獨自；靠自己　　 *run after* 追

12. (**C**) W：Have you ever seen a wawa?

女：你有看過加拿大的雪雁嗎？

M：No, but I think it flies fast and is beautiful.

男：沒有，但我想牠應該飛得很快，而且很漂亮。

Question：What's a wawa?

wawa 是什麼？

(A) A fish. 一種魚。

(B) A lizard. 一種蜥蜴。

(C) A bird. 一種鳥。

* ever〔'ɛvɚ〕 *adv.* 曾經
　wawa〔'wɑwɑ〕 *n.* (加拿大的) 雪雁 (= *wavey*)
　fly〔flaɪ〕 *v.* 飛　　beautiful〔'bjutəfəl〕 *adj.* 漂亮的
　lizard〔'lɪzɚd〕 *n.* 蜥蜴

13. (**C**) W : Sorry to bother you.　I need your help.
　　　女：抱歉打擾你。我需要你的幫助。
　　　M : What's up?
　　　男：怎麼了？
　　　W : I am going to enter an English speech contest next
　　　　　week.
　　　女：下星期我要去參加英語演講比賽。
　　　M : Way to go!　I am proud of you.
　　　男：做得好！我以妳為榮。
　　　Question : What does the man mean by saying "way to
　　　　　　　　go"?
　　　　　　　　男人說"way to go"是什麼意思？
　　　(A) He'll go this way. 他會走這邊。
　　　(B) He will help her. 他會幫助她。
　　　(C) He congratulates the girl on her good job.
　　　　　他向女孩恭喜她做得很好。

* bother〔'bɑðɚ〕 *v.* 困擾；打擾
　help〔hɛlp〕 *n.* 幫助　　***What's up?*** 怎麼了？
　enter〔'ɛntɚ〕 *v.* 報名參加
　speech〔spitʃ〕 *n.* 演講
　contest〔'kɑntɛst〕 *n.* 比賽
　Way to go. 做得好。　　***be proud of*** 以…為榮
　mean *sth.* ***by V-ing*** 做…的意思是
　congratulate〔kən'grætʃə,let〕 *v.* 恭喜 < *on* >
　good job 好的表現

14. (**C**) Peter is jumping rope. Paul is decorating a tree. Joey is
doing laundry. Everyone is doing their own thing.

彼得正在跳繩。保羅正在佈置樹。喬伊正在洗衣服。每個人都在
做自己的事。

Question：Who is doing the laundry?

誰正在洗衣服？

(A) Peter. 彼得。

(B) Paul. 保羅。

(C) Joey. 喬伊。

* ***jump rope*** 跳繩　　decorate〔'dɛkə‚ret〕*v.* 裝飾；佈置
laundry〔'lɔndrɪ〕*n.* 待洗的衣服
do (***the***) ***laundry*** 洗衣服（= *wash clothes*）
own〔on〕*adj.* 自己的

15. (**B**) M：Claire, do you see the girl over there? I want to
know her but I don't know what to do.

男：克萊兒，妳有看到在那裡的女孩嗎？我想要認識她，但我不
知道怎麼做。

W：It's easy. You just say hi and ask whether she needs
help. She is new at school.

女：這很簡單。你只要打招呼，並問她需是否需要幫忙。她是新
來的學生。

M：How do you know this?

男：妳是怎麼知道的？

W：Actually, she is my cousin.

女：事實上，她是我的表妹。

Question：What are they talking about?

他們正在談論什麼？

(A) Why the boy wants to know the girl.

為什麼男孩想要認識女孩。

(B) Who the girl over there is. 在那裡的女孩是誰。

(C) Which boy Claire likes. 克萊兒喜歡哪個男孩。

* **over there** 在那裡　　hi〔haɪ〕*interj.* 嗨（用於打招呼）

whether〔ˈhwɛðɚ〕*conj.* 是否　　help〔hɛlp〕*n.* 幫助

actually〔ˈæktʃʊəlɪ〕*adv.* 實際上

new〔nju〕*adj.* 新來的；不熟悉的 < *at* >

cousin〔ˈkʌzn̩〕*n.*（堂）表兄弟（姊妹）

16. (**B**)　W：Hi, John.　Did you have a good weekend?

女：嗨，約翰。你週末過得好嗎？

M：Yes, I did.　I flew around Taiwan on Saturday, and I saw lots of cool places when I was up in the air, especially Taipei 101.　Then I came back to Taipei at night.

男：是的，我過得很好。星期六的時候我繞著台灣的上空飛行，而當我在空中的時候，我看到了很多很酷的地方，特別是台北 101。然後我在晚上的時候回到台北。

W：Wow!　Flying around Taiwan sounds like a lot of fun.

女：哇！繞著台灣飛行聽起來好像很好玩。

Question：When did the man have a good time?

男士什麼時候過得很開心？

(A) All week. 整個星期。

(B) On Saturday. 在星期六。

(C) On Sunday. 在星期日。

* weekend〔ˈwikˈɛnd〕*n.* 週末　　fly〔flaɪ〕*v.* 飛行

around〔əˈraʊnd〕*prep.* 環繞　　**lots of** 許多

cool〔kul〕*adj.* 很酷的　　**the air** 天空；空中

up in the air 在空中

especially〔ə'spɛʃəlɪ〕*adv.* 尤其；特別是

sound〔saʊnd〕*v.* 聽起來

fun〔fʌn〕*n.* 樂趣　　*have a good time* 玩得愉快

17. (**A**) W：You know what? I won the lottery today. I am so happy that I can buy what I want with this money.

女：你知道嗎？我今天贏了樂透。我很高興，我可以用這筆錢買我想要的東西。

M：Congratulations! But don't forget to help people in need with it.

男：恭喜！但別忘了要用這筆錢來幫助窮困的人。

Question：Why was the woman excited?

爲什麼女士很興奮？

(A) She got a lot of money luckily. 她幸運地獲得了很多錢。

(B) She will help other poor people. 她會幫助其他的窮人。

(C) She didn't know what to do with the money.

她不知道該如何運用這筆錢。

* win〔wʌn〕*v.* 贏【win 的過去式和過去分詞】

lottery〔'latərɪ〕*n.* 彩券；樂透

congratulations〔kən,grætʃə'leʃənz〕*n. pl.* 恭喜

forget〔fə'gɛt〕*v.* 忘記　　*in need* 貧困的

excited〔ɪk'saɪtɪd〕*adj.* 興奮的

luckily〔'lʌkɪlɪ〕*adv.* 幸運地　　poor〔pʊr〕*adj.* 貧窮的

18. (**B**) W：What's wrong with you?

女：你怎麼了嗎？

M：I can't find my car. I do remember I parked my car here.

男：我找不到我的車。我真的記得我把我的車停在這裡。

W : Maybe you didn't park in the right place. And the police towed it away.

女：或許你沒有停在正確的位子。所以警察把它拖走了。

Question : Why was the man worried?

　　　　　為什麼男士很擔心？

(A) The police towed his car away.

　　警察把他的車拖走了。

(B) He couldn't find his car. <u>他找不到他的車。</u>

(C) He lost his memory. 他失去記憶了。

* **What's wrong with ~?** ～怎麼了？　　**do + V.** 真的～；的確～
  park (pɑrk) v. 停（車）　　　maybe ('mebɪ) adv. 或許；可能
  the police 警察　　tow (to) v. 拖
  worried ('wɜɪd) adj. 擔心的　　memory ('mɛmərɪ) n. 記憶

19. (**B**) M : Carpooling helps us pollute less and save money.

男：汽車共乘能幫助我們降低污染並節省金錢。

W : Yes. I carpool with my coworkers every day. You can ride with us.

女：對啊。我每天都和我的同事一起共乘汽車。你也可以和我們一起搭車。

Question : What does the woman want the man to do?

　　　　　女士要男士做什麼？

(A) She wants him to swim with her in the pool.

　　她要他和她一起在游泳池游泳。

(B) She wants him to ride in a car together with them.

　　<u>她要他和他們一起搭車。</u>

(C) She wants him to go for a car ride. 她要他開車去兜風。

* carpool〔'kɑr,pul〕v. 汽車共乘　　pollute〔pə'lut〕v. 污染
save〔sev〕v. 節省　　co-worker〔'ko,wɜkɚ〕n. 同事
ride〔raɪd〕v. 搭（車）　　swim〔swɪm〕v. 游泳
pool〔pul〕n. 游泳池（= *swimming pool*）
together with 和…一起
go for a + 交通工具 + ***ride*** 以某交通工具兜風

20. (**C**)　W：You must have a ball in Europe.　It will be the best
　　　　　　　 part of your vacation.

　　女：你在歐洲一定會玩得很愉快！它將會成爲你這次假期中最
　　　　美好的一部分。

　　M：Thanks for the trip plan you made for me.　If it is fun
　　　　this time, I will book another trip with you next year.

　　男：謝謝你幫我安排的行程規畫。如果這次玩得很開心，明年
　　　　我會和妳一起預訂另一趟旅行。

　　Question：What is the woman sure of about the man's
　　　　　　　 trip?

　　　　　　　 關於這位男士的旅行，女士很肯定什麼事？

　　(A) He will go to a ball game in Europe.
　　　　他在歐洲會去看一場球賽。

　　(B) He will do his best in his vacation.　他在假期中會盡力。

　　(C) He will have a good time in Europe.
　　　　他在歐洲會玩得很愉快。

　　* ***have a ball*** 玩得愉快　　Europe〔'jurəp〕n. 歐洲
　　vacation〔ve'keʃən〕n. 假期　　trip〔trɪp〕n. 旅行
　　plan〔plæn〕n. 計畫　　fun〔fʌn〕adj. 有趣的；好玩的
　　book〔buk〕v. 預訂　　***be sure of*** 確定；對…有把握
　　ball game 球賽　　***have a good time*** 玩得愉快
　　do one's ***best*** 盡力

國中會考英語聽力入門

主　　　編／李冠勳

發　行　所／學習出版有限公司　　☎ (02) 2704-5525

郵 撥 帳 號／05127272 學習出版社帳戶

登　記　證／局版台業 2179 號

印　刷　所／文聯彩色印刷有限公司

台 北 門 市／台北市許昌街 10 號 2 F　☎ (02) 2331-4060

台灣總經銷／紅螞蟻圖書有限公司　　☎ (02) 2795-3656

美國總經銷／Evergreen Book Store　☎ (818) 2813622

本公司網址　www.learnbook.com.tw

電 子 郵 件　learnbook@learnbook.com.tw

書＋MP3 一片售價：新台幣二百八十元正

MP3 一片約 280 分鐘，相當於 3 片半 CD

2015 年 11 月 1 日新修訂